Queen in Cornwall
A partial history of the world's greatest rock band

Rupert White

Front cover: Queen performing in Penzance in 1974. Back cover: Roger Taylor in Truro School uniform, 1965.

ISBN 978-1-4477-7647-5

Copyright © 2011 Rupert White
www.rupertwhite.co.uk

ANTENNA PUBLICATIONS
www.queenincornwall.blogspot.com

All rights reserved. No part of this book may be reproduced in any form or by any electronic or mechanical means, including information storage or retrieval systems, without permission from the publisher or author.

Every effort had been made to trace the copyright holders of the photographs in the book, but one or two were unreachable. We would be grateful if the photographers concerned would contact us.

Foreword

We were extremely pleased when Rupert White asked us to write the foreword to this book. Initially we demurred, feeling that he would be better served by a more illustrious personage: someone of stature in 'the business'. However, we allowed ourselves to be persuaded that between the two of us we did, in fact, have an involvement and continuity that was unique.

Over the years, of course, there have been many biographies and histories, official and otherwise, of Queen and its individual members. What distinguishes this book from those previous histories is the way that it documents the unique relationship between Roger Taylor and the county he grew up in, and the birth of what became one of the biggest bands in the world.

Since Rupert first contacted us in June 2010, saying that he was carrying out research on Queen and music in Cornwall in the 60's, we have watched in fascination as he slowly recreated that very special time in history. With his blog 'Queen in Cornwall' putting out the call, Rupert has traced and compiled a comprehensive list of individuals, music, and venues of that time. Following him through this period gave us the opportunity to take a journey that truly evokes the feeling of that special point in time: a moment when the elements of location, and individuals, and social structure combined to create a musical mix, the gestalt of which had an effect far greater than anyone could have expected.

Cornwall in the 60's was truly a magical place. It nurtured and supported more music and musicians than, given its remoteness, would seem possible. As teenagers though, its particular merits could frequently be obscured by the frustration of being, as we thought, seriously annexed from everything that was cool and happening!

However, in our own way, we did manage to 'raise a little hell'. We had an opportunity to experiment with limited risk: hitch-hiking to the beach, moonlight swims, midnight car rallies, and of course the music. Nothing was really that bad or dangerous - or so it seemed. To us the county performed the role of a benevolent parent that allows you to kick the walls and be 'bad' within a protected environment that was itself a microcosm of the big city.

Most of us were consumed with a burning desire to get out and up to that big city and no one was more determined than Roger. We all had our various aspirations, and had to put up with a lot of ribbing because of them. But, for some reason, when Roger would declare that he was going to be bigger than Keith Moon no one contradicted him. Perhaps we all knew!

After our first meeting in 1965 at a folk night at Little Canaan Farm, our lives and those of our respective bands were intertwined, socially, romantically and occasionally musically. This continued for several years until inevitably one by one we were pulled away by the necessity of making school, college and other life choices. Fortunately, however, this was not the end, and as with many friendships made at that time of one's life, several of these connections successfully made the transition and played a role in the next phase that ultimately became Queen.

This book unwinds the history of those days and reveals more than we could ever have imagined or remembered. Not only has it brought back memories and events long forgotten, but it has installed a renewed longing for the county and its people, and a pride in being Cornish. To say that our teenage years were fascinating is true. It seems incredible now that all of the events mentioned actually took place, and yet at the time we thought the answer was to be in London, not in 'the sticks'. How lucky we were…

Jillian Johnson-Sharp and Susan Johnstone   April 2011

Introduction

Out here on the street we'd gather and meet
And scuff up the sidewalk
With endlessly restless feet
Half of the time we'd broaden our minds
More in the pool hall
Than we did in the school hall
With the down town chewing gum bums
Watching the night life the lights and the fun
Never wanted to be the boy next door
Always thought I'd be something more
But it ain't easy for a small-town boy
It ain't easy at all
from 'Drowse' by Roger Taylor (Queen's 'A Day at the Races' (1976))

Cornwall is a rural county in the far South West of the UK. It is about 250 miles from London and, even in the 21st century, feels far removed from the urban rat-race. As a peninsula it has lots of beaches, and in the post-war period its economy - which has some farming but little or no industry - has become more and more reliant on tourism.

Cornwall's rurality, with its rugged coastline and moorlands and its isolated fishing hamlets, would make it seem an unlikely setting for Rock 'n' Roll to take root and flourish, yet the impact of Americana and pop culture on the post-war youth of Cornwall seems to have been at least as far-reaching as it was elsewhere in the UK.

From the late 50's to the early 70's, there was a network of church halls, rugby clubs, village halls, hotels and larger venues that were regularly commandeered to host 'beat dances'. During this period live music played by teenagers for teenagers was everywhere in Cornwall. These were, after all, the days when few families had TV's, let alone Youtube, Facebook and i-tunes. Young people were more suggestible, and had fewer distractions than they do now. As a result - particularly in Cornwall - they made their own entertainment.

Skiffle was a variety of simple do-it-yourself trad jazz or blues-grass played using cheap home-made instruments. In 1958 skiffle contests were held all over Cornwall, and there were two, in particular, in Truro's City Hall that proved extremely popular. From 1960 these contests evolved into the annual Rock and Rhythm Championship which took place at the beginning of every year.

Roger Taylor, as evoked by the dreamy nostalgia of the song 'Drowse', spent most of his childhood and teenage years in the small town of Truro. He was a musician that, with his group 'The Reaction', took part in the Championship on four successive years. He may or may not have been the most able competitor but, as the drummer with Queen, in the 1970's he certainly went on to become the most famous.

Amongst UK acts, for many years Queen have been second only to The Beatles in terms of worldwide record sales. They have also left their mark in other ways. For example, the concert that followed the death of Freddie Mercury in 1991 was watched worldwide by an estimated 1.2 billion people.

This book is not intended to be a biography of Roger Taylor, rather it is an attempt to describe the specific cultural and social context in which he emerged as a musician of international repute, playing as a member of a hugely popular and original British rock band.

The book also describes the unlikely relationship that Queen itself had with Cornwall and this same context. Cornwall, like other relatively remote rural areas, did not have much in the way of Higher Education

Colleges for most of the 20th century, and so for several generations there was an exodus of young people leaving the county after A-levels. Roger Taylor was one of them. Like many provincial lads before and after him he went to London to go to College, but in his case it was not merely for a degree, but also to seek fame and fortune as a rock star.

Queen and its precursor Smile ended up forming in West London, where Roger moved in 1968. Queen and Smile often played at Imperial College where their guitarist Brian May was studying for a PhD, but their success did not arrive overnight, and the musical skills and the stage performances for which they became so famous were perfected on the road. Their travels in the early years included the pubs and clubs of Cornwall where they had many friends, and where their first fan-base formed. Here the members of Queen were able to test themselves musically in a friendly and forgiving environment. And, in fact, as we shall see, Queen's first ever concert was near Roger Taylor's home in the quiet cathedral City of Truro.

Acknowledgements

The people who were interviewed or who gave new information for the book were (roughly in order of when I spoke to them and listed with the band or place they were most associated with):

Rik Evans (Reaction/Queen), Roger Brokenshire (Reaction), Pete Bawden (PJs), John Laity (Hurland Road), Rick Penrose (Reaction), Geoff Daniel (Reaction), Dave Penprase (Room at the Top), Paul Brown (Arthur Brown's Kingdom Come), Tim Staffell, (Smile), Jill Johnson (Jayfolk), Mike Grose (PJs, Queen), Richard Thompson (Smile), Jim Craven (Reaction), Karen Silverlock (Hall for Cornwall), Toni Carver, Roo Fairbairn, Dave Dowding (Beat Unlimited), Doug Puddifoot (Queen), Mike Dudley (Reaction), Graham Hankins (Reaction), Jack Pascoe, Clive Palmer (Incredible String Band, Famous Jug Band), John The Fish (Folk Cottage), Connie Bawden (PJs), Les Walker (Warm Dust), Tony Coxon (Marvelous Kid), Colin Brokenshire (Ginhouse) Sue Johnstone (Jayfolk/Queen), Linda Roach (PJs), David Hook (Graphite), Peter Gill-Carey (Reaction), Pete Baron (Reaction), Dorothy Gill-Carey, David Vinden (Cathedral School), Viv Hendra (Truro), Peter Boggia (Truro), Eric Langman (Redruth), Finton Lawley (Saints), Manny Cockle (Deadbeats), Pat Johnstone (Queen), Jenny Doble, Jim Jenkins (Queen), Pete Edmonds (Smile/Queen), Wendy Edmonds (Queen), Paul Treseder (Reaction), Nigel Chappell (PJs), Trevor Mannell (PJs), Malcolm Rushton (Good Times/Safron), Alan Mair (Kensington Market), Neil Battersby (Reaction), Gerry Gill (Bowie/Queen), Richard Halliwell (Truro), Bert Biscoe (Truro), John Snell (Reaction – including 'The Reaction Story'), Penny North (Jayfolk), Les Brown (Smile/Sinclair Gardens), Chris Chesney (Dummett) (Sour Milk Sea), Peter Kelsey (Sinclair Gardens), Vaughan Hankins (Truro), Keith Harding (Truro), Denise Craddock (Ferry Road), Pete Stanton (Al Scott and the Klan), Will Wright (Mr Lucifer), Josie James (Jayfolk), Ian Lynch (Smile/Queen), Wizz Jones....many had to put up with a lot of pestering, and I'm very grateful for their patience and generosity…

Special thanks to John Snell who wrote an extended essay on The Reaction called 'The Reaction Story' which is available on www.queenincornwall.blogspot.com, to Jillian Johnson-Sharp and Sue Johnstone who wrote the forward and to Denise Craddock who permitted access to her personal diaries.

Thanks also to fellow enthusiasts, writers and archivists: Richard Prest www.kernowbeat.co.uk, Mark Blake, Jim Jenkins, Jo Wood (Truro School), Greg Brooks, Martin Skala www.queenconcerts.com, Alex Wade, Lee Trewhela, Mark Hodgkinson and Jacky Smith (Queen Fan Club), and to the photographers who provided photographs (credited in the book) especially Christine Parnell (author of several books on Truro) and The West Briton newspaper.

Where reference has been made to other books this is marked in the text as follows: AIB (As It Began: Jim Jenkins and Jacky Gunn (nee Smith), RC (Record Collector Magazine), Mojo (Mojo), DMW (Daily Mail Weekend Magazine), TEY (The Early Years: Mark Hodgkinson), MS74 (cutting 74), TMY (The Magic Years (video)), EDP Eastern Daily Press. DD refers to dates etc recorded in Denise Craddock's diaries, and 'soapbox' to Brian May's website.

For more information on all the research as well as audio, unpublished images and info please go to www.queenincornwall.blogspot.com

The 1950s: Skiffle becomes Rock 'n' Roll

When he was less than a week old, future Queen drummer Roger Taylor was introduced to royalty. On 26th July 1949 he was one of the first children to have been born in the new maternity unit of the hospital in King's Lynn, Norfolk. It was opened only days later by the Queen who, that same day, spoke to his proud mother, Winifred.

At the time the family lived at 87, High Street, King's Lynn but soon after his birth they moved to one of a terrace of brick houses in nearby Beulah Street. The street, as Roger recalls, was a cul-de-sac that lead to a river: *'The road used to be very quiet. I remember going down to the end of the street and looking into the river. I used to see the odd pike or two. I was constantly warned not to fall in'.*EDP

Roger's father was called Michael: *My Dad worked for the potato marketing board based in Lynn. He used to go out to visit farmers and occasionally I'd go with him.*

Roger's maternal grandparents, Arthur and Annie Hickman, also lived in King's Lynn but Michael's side of the family had stronger links to Cornwall and as soon as his job permitted, in 1957, the family moved there.

At the age of 8 Roger enrolled at Bosvigo primary school in Truro. Alongside St Mary's, St Paul's and Fairmantle Street, Bosvigo was one of four primary schools in the town. The Bosvigo register indicates that Roger Taylor's home address was, initially, 7, Little Castle Street: a short road which now comprises nine or ten small shops around the corner from the school. For most of the time he was at Bosvigo, however, his family lived on Falmouth Road on the hill out of Truro, in a row of elegant Victorian houses then known as Vivian Terrace.

Viv Hendra, whose father was a local pharmacist, is an author and gallery-owner in Truro. He lived on the terrace at the same time, and is two years younger: *I lived in number four (now number seven) and Roger and his family were at the end of the row, further up the hill. There was a lane behind the houses that a group of us would play in, and we would be in and out of each other's gardens. There was a lot less traffic then and we could sit cross-legged on Barrack Lane and*

Vivian Terrace (2010)

play marbles or cycle on a circuit down Barrack Lane and back up Strangways Terrace. Sometimes we would venture further away, and cycle a mile or so out of Truro to the village of Calenick and beyond.

Opposite Vivian Terrace in a building that for many years was the Farley Hotel, lived a boy in Roger's class at Bosvigo called David Vinden who has since become a Professor of Music. The two were friends for two or three years, as David recalls: *My sister went to school with his sister Clare. We both enjoyed cycling together but Roger did not at that stage show the interest he was to develop in drumming, or in any music to be honest. He must have been a late developer.*

One of the older boys at Bosvigo, saxophonist John Snell, would later recruit Roger to play in his first semi-pro band, The Reaction. John: *I used to play recorder at Bosvigo: I think I was the only boy that did. Roger was a couple of years younger. I remember often seeing him walking to school down Infirmary Hill from Falmouth Road, but he always seemed to be in his own world at that time.*

The school had its own playing fields parallel to Chapel Hill that have since been built over. John: *At the lower side of the playgrounds were the toilets: very much an open air affair! These were on the boundary of Lake's Pottery, and when the pottery fired up the kilns, the playground could be very smoky if the wind was in the wrong direction. Bosvigo had large classes of 40 or 50 in size because the expansion in Truro primary schools lagged behind the post-war baby boom. It was quite a tough school and corporal punishment was applied freely, but it was brilliant at ensuring all its pupils achieved a good basic educational grounding.*

The Saints playing to an audience of children and young teenagers in Truro WI Hall:
L to R Max Treloar, Finton Lawley, John Northey, Leon Treloar and 'Ginger' Pascoe

Lemon Street was then the A39 - one of the main roads through Cornwall. *Living in Lemon Street, I was zoned for Fairmantle Street School but my parents were not happy with me having to cross Lemon Street to go to school.*

Roger, who did have to cross the main road, is known to have formed his first group 'The Bubbling-over Boys' whilst still at Bosvigo. It was a skiffle band complete with tea-chest bass, in which he played the ukulele. Jim Jenkins co-wrote the Queen official biography: *Roger put egg boxes around his garage to provide some soundproofing so they could rehearse there. The first time Roger did a gig was in a neighbour's garage and the second one he did was at a school dance. It probably all happened in the space of a few weeks.*

Skiffle was a simple style of music which had an instant impact and a lasting legacy. It can be traced back to 1956 when Lonnie Donegan's record 'Rock Island Line' was an unlikely hit on both sides of the Atlantic. In an early interview, Roger Taylor described listening to Donegan on Children's Favourites with Uncle Mac, a popular Saturday morning radioshow: *'I've been interested in music ever since. Lonnie Donegan, Bill Haley and Tommy Steel were my idols in those days. That was a good time to start getting into music. I supposed I've always been obsessed with it'*. MS74

In 1984 this formative experience would inspire Roger to write the song 'Radio Ga Ga', which was Queen's opening number at Live Aid the following year.

In the late 50's relatively few families in Cornwall had a television. The transmitters initially only covered the South East, and the signal elsewhere in the country was poor. Living in Truro Manny Cockle was an older, teenaged singer that was inspired by the TV show 'Six Five Special', first aired in 1957: *Television was starting to get a hold in Cornwall by then, but I reckon only about 3 in 10 families had sets. The quality was a joke though. It was a very weak B&W signal so pictures were mostly like a snow storm! I well remember having our aerial on a long pole in the garden which would turn slightly in high wind so we would lose reception completely...*

Despite limited media outlets, by 1957 the skiffle craze, which had spread like wildfire across the country, had firmly taken hold of Cornwall too. In the same way that it inspired Lennon and McCartney in Liverpool, so it inspired most of the boys that would form bands in Cornwall in the 60's to learn to play music together. Older lads amongst them, like Rick Penrose and Pete Bawden - with whom Roger Taylor was to work later - were in skiffle groups that performed widely at the time and took part in concerts and competitions.

The first skiffle group to make a name for itself in the Truro area was The Six Squares and at 16, Manny Cockle was its youngest member. Apart from his brothers he was almost certainly the only black musician in Cornwall at the time, his grandfather having been an African stowaway. Manny: *In 1957 we used to do the 'Bits and Pieces' concert party in the City Hall, ran by a man called George Davey. Anyone who could do a turn on the stage used to get roped in. And we used to also play at the Memorial Hall in Perranporth, as the 'Bits and Pieces' concert party. We would play all over the county because skiffle had become quite the thing. We also used to play in pubs like The Globe in River Street, and play, and in fact rehearse, in the back room of the Hope Inn at the bottom of Mitchell Hill.*

The Six Squares featured two guitars, two harmonicas, a tea-chest bass and a washboard. Initially none of the instruments were amplified, but Manny did have a microphone: *There was an electrician's called Cecil Gill in Pydar Street. We'd go in and hire a microphone off him, and he was a fussy old devil. He would make a great fuss about how we were to set it up, and sometimes he would come along and set it up for us. Then we got pick-ups for the harmonicas, because in all the din you couldn't hear them. So we got these little amps that distorted and the boys would be blowing away, and they couldn't really play in truth and it sounded hellish. Like cats being tortured! It was miserable! But people liked it. They would play so enthusiastically their lips would be sore so they'd always be rubbing salve into them!*

During 1958 Manny joined another Truro skiffle group called The Deadbeats. The group was made up of boys his own age from Truro Tech. It included his friend Pete Bawden, known as Bugsy Bawden, and later as 'P.J.'. In the 70's Pete helped organise some of Queen's earliest gigs. Manny: *We were invited to play in the Palace Cinema which was near the Britannia pub. All the kids would go there on a Saturday afternoon. It was like bedlam! Roger Lemin the guitarist used to play the guitar in the Palace and to try and get enough volume he hit the guitar so hard his fingers would be bleeding when we came off! In those days it got to be the fashion that as soon as you started playing, all the girls would start screaming: the auditorum would just explode. They'd scream because this is what they'd seen on the films coming from America...*

The Blue Aces of Truro featured future Reaction bassist, Rick Penrose on guitar.

There were lots of skiffle competitions in Cornwall in 1957 and 1958 and members of Roger Taylor's future group, The Reaction, either took part or watched from the audience. The Truro group 'The Saints' were winners of the first of the biggest of the contests that were held in the City Hall in July 1958. Finton Lawley played the tea-chest bass with them: *I made it at Agar Road out of a tea-chest and a broom handle. If you thump the string and pull the old broom-handle back you get different pitches out of it. The tea-chest is just an amplifier.*

The DIY aesthetic of skiffle was born of necessity, not choice, as electrified instruments were unavailable: *When we were first playing there were no electric guitars. Then places like Moon's on River Street that sold records suddenly saw a niche as things were changing, and started selling little pickups that you could screw onto the guitar and then you bought steel strings and went to a local radio shop and asked if they had any old amplifiers.*

Manny Cockle: *We discovered that you could get old radios and use them as amplifiers. The Deadbeats would have all these radios lined up on along the front of the stage. And they'd be feeding back and crackling and the leads always used to fail. A modern health and safety man would have had a baby!*

When we first started visiting the old village halls etc we discovered a variety of different sockets. Some places had round pin 15 or 5 amp sockets, some of which were defunct leaving us with no alternative other than to bodge something into a light socket. I made up a socket board with a multiplug on the end which was always jamming. Imagine a hall full of screaming kids and us with no power!! So we'd yank the bare wires out of the plug and poke them into the wall socket with matchsticks and get on with the show! Blowing the main fuse was a frequent event but it all added to the buzz of the evening, and the kids loved it!

Rick Penrose, who played in The Reaction, was also caught up in the skiffle boom. His group The Blue Aces (see picture) played in the second of the Truro City Hall contests in 1958. He was only 14 at the time: *It was very exciting for us being so young. We were probably thought of as rebels. The music then being played was Sinatra, Crosby, Vera Lynn, Doris Day and the big bands so you could say we were somewhat revolutionary! For the first time musicians were performing on stage in jeans and shirts instead of a dress suit and bow tie. With skiffle, music would change forever.*

The Deadbeats also played in the second of the contests. Manny: *At the contests you'd get 25 groups on the night. They'd have one set up* behind the main curtain then there'd be the next one set up behind another curtain. There was this Woody Guthrie song 'The Grand Coulee Dam' that was popular then. And the first group would play The Grand Coulee Dam, then the next group would push forward, with their cymbals crashing and banging. 'Now we have the so and so's, and they're *also* going to play the Grand Coulee Dam'...and once you'd heard the Grand Coulee Dam ten times you'd want to shoot yourself! And it would often over run. It would be 11 o'clock and there would still be 3 or 4 groups still to go! But the place was packed out with young teenagers aged maybe 13 or 14. Several hundred of them.

The Deadbeats came third and The West Briton write-up gave a clinical description of the performance: *The Deadbeats received 43 marks for quite colourful presentation, with good personality, though there was one odd shirt and the positioning was ragged. There was a good 'gimmick' in having the drums elevated'.*

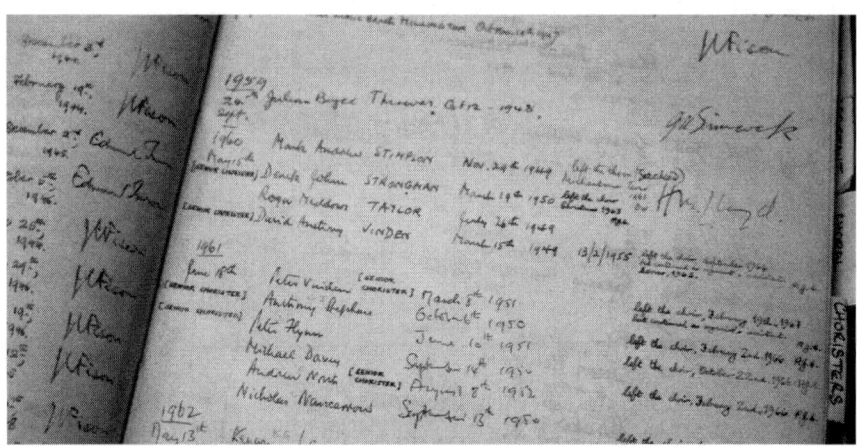

Register of choir members kept in the crypt of Truro Cathedral

Though also infected with the same skiffle bug, Roger Taylor's musical career took a step in a different direction when, aged ten, he passed voice trials to become a chorister at Truro Cathedral. For a ten-year old the commitment then, as now, was considerable, with services on a Sunday and practice and evensong most days of the week as well. But he wasn't alone: his friend David from Bosvigo became a chorister at exactly the same time. In return the Cathedral Dean and Chapter paid their fees to the Cathedral School: one of two boy's private schools in the Truro vicinity. The school archives have a record of Roger starting there in September 1959.

David Vinden: *We were in the same class at the Cathedral school (P1) if my memory is correct. He was actually quite a bright boy from what I can remember.* The senior school then was still very close to the Cathedral in the centre of Truro, and within walking distance from their houses, though it was to move up to Kenwyn in 1960.

The original Truro Cathedral School (now an office used by Social Services)

Rick Penrose attended the school: *I was older than Roger but the school was not big - not much more than 100 pupils - so we all knew each other. Most of us had tatty uniforms, but Roger's was immaculate. I remember him looking very small and very neat, with blond hair.*

The organist at the Cathedral was Guillaume Ormond. David: *Dicky - as Guillaume Ormond was known - was as eccentric as they come.*

Although respected for his ability he could be quite fierce, and it was not unheard of for him to drop hymn books from the organ loft onto the choristers below if they were talking too much. The boys also saw a lot of the assistant organist John Winter: nicknamed Charley. *John was a difficult but very talented musician. His moods were notorious. Overall, though, I look back on those days at the Cathedral with enormous affection as they were the beginnings of my music training and food for my musical spirit.*

One of the other, more senior, choristers in the choir was Richard 'Oscar' Carveth, who gave advice and support to Roger and later played with The Reaction, the band with which Roger made his name in Cornwall.

The experience of singing in the choir, though short-lived, would have given him a taste of serious, professional music-making at a young age. It also required Roger to follow cues from a conductor, much as he did later playing on stage with Freddie Mercury.

In the 50's there were many more cinemas in Cornwall than there are now, and in November 1956, 'Rock around the Clock', which was far from being a mainstream film, had been screened in a handful of the village cinemas like the Palace Cinema in Roskear and the Regal in St Agnes. Eric Langman saw it in Roskear: *Rock around the Clock' was on the news and in the papers. I saw it in Roskear. The teenagers in Cornwall knew what had happened in other places, and it got inundated with them. They were actually clapping along and dancing in the aisles.*

Graham Hankins of The Reaction saw it in Truro: *I remember the queues that formed to see Rock around the Clock in The Palace Cinema, because I queued with them. The cinema was in the old assembly rooms there and they quite often had skiffle groups playing in the interval.*

In Truro in the 50's places like The City Hall and the Drill Hall in Moresk were used to stage formal ballroom dances or 'Grand Dances' with band leaders such as Bob Batley, Bill Harding, and Frank Fuge each of whom would appear with 'his Orchestra'. The Seahawks, the

RAF band from Culdrose, were another favourite. Eric: *Most dances then were still for people over 20. It was the quick-quick-slows, pally glides, gay gordons, sambas and foxtrots: like 'Strictly Come Dancing' on TV now.*

The Deadbeats in the WI Hall, Truro circa 1959. L to R: Bob Mansbridge (drums) Harry Taylor (bass), Manny Cockle (guitar) Pete Bawden (guitar). The WI Hall was also the venue for ballroom dancing classes attended by Roger Taylor and other members of The Reaction. Ten years later Pete Bawden founded PJ's club, where Queen played.

But by 1959 teenagers had started to promote their own dances. One such event was a regular Saturday evening in the W.I. Hall: a space that is now used as a nightclub. Jack Pascoe was there: *I worked with Rex Webb in the Truro W.I. Hall round the corner from the Cathedral. We had club membership, but it still went wrong one night when Manny Cockle was singing and there was a big fight that got in the papers. Truro was a rough place in the late fifties.*

Manny Cockle: *Once we had amplifiers we were always looking for somewhere to rehearse, and we discovered that at the WI you could hire a room. I remember there was a caretaker there who was a randy old dog who would tell us dirty stories! At the time the Deadbeats had been invited to play in Tabbs Hotel in Redruth. There was a man in Truro called Rex Webb who was an entrepreneur. And he heard us in there and came in and said 'What are you doing in here then boys?' He caught on to the idea that we could run dances there. So he would have us playing and charge two bob on the door and all the kids would go in there on a Saturday night. His wife and he would go around handing out leaflets and putting up posters and on the night she'd stand on the door like a Rottweiler. She'd say 'you can't come in you look like trouble'. But there were always a lot of fights in there. You'd get older ones in there aged 18 or 19 who'd had a few pints. The police made complaints and it was eventually closed down.*

A photo of the group in about 1959 suggests that the Deadbeats were, by then, a clean-cut professional outfit, with winning smiles and matching guitars as well as shirts. Manny: *Not sure where the shirts came from. They were possibly sent down from Cecil Gee in London which was certainly where we sourced jackets later.*

Finton Lawley: *I played with the Saint's skiffle group at the WI hall. The hall was built on top of the old public baths. Rexy Webb I knew very well. Later he played drums with Manny Cockle.*

Under the headline TEENAGE DANCE or BEATNIK ROCK AND ROLL DANCE the adverts would usually mention one of the up-and-coming live acts.

Within a year or two most of the skiffle bands had started playing Rock and Roll. Finton Lawley: *Manny's band started as a skiffle group and they were damn good. Once they played in the City Hall. I went to a fatstock show when I was 13 or 14 with my uncle, and they used to have cattle in the City Hall there - can you believe - and during the interval they introduced the first Truro skiffle group, and it was Manny on stage. He was singing an Elvis song and it was really good. Then after that they changed and they bought electric guitars and they became one of the first rock groups in Truro. At the same time a few others were starting up, like the Staggerlees in Redruth.*

Redruth is eight miles from Truro. It is a town that was once at the heart of Cornwall's industrial revolution: the place where, in the late 18th century, the steam locomotive was invented. In fact Redruth can also lay claim to having its own famous drummer as, in 1947, Mick Fleetwood of Fleetwood Mac was born there.

In October 1957 'The Flamingo Club', a huge venue two miles out of the town, opened on a site now occupied by a Morrison's supermarket. By 1958 its dance hall boasted a 'super-sprung floor'. At the time it was promoted as 'The largest ballroom in the South West' though by the mid sixties, when it was hosting concerts by the likes of Pink Floyd, it had become known as Cornwall's largest pub.

Initially The Flamingo took business away from Tabb's Hotel on Redruth high street. Approached from street level via an arcade of shops, Tabb's own ballroom had, thoughout the 50's, been a popular venue for dances. But in 1959 the hotel became the setting for 'Youth Request Nights' instead. They were organised by an enterprising seventeen year old MC, Roger Brokenshire who would later sing with The Reaction. Roger: *Tabb's weren't getting much business because they were still doing ballroom dancing, so I suggested putting on Rock 'n' Roll dances instead. The hotel was four storeys high and much bigger than the current building. We would use their 30's-style ballroom which had a floor that would vibrate. Initially it was all just dancing to records, but later we got bands involved and brought some quite big names down from outside Cornwall.*

Eric Langman, who was later in partnership with Brokenshire, remembers Redruth becoming overrun with teenagers during the heyday of Tabb's Hotel: *So Tabb's dance hall is empty. Not good news.*

Then Roger comes along, and suddenly if you're in Redruth on a Saturday night the streets are chockablock with teenagers! They've come from all over Cornwall: Truro, Penzance, St Austell. That was the first regular teen dance that people traveled to. Starting at 7 and going on until 10 or whatever. They're 14 to 17 years old, so the dance is not going on late because mothers aren't going to let their daughters out after that time. And of course there's also no bar and no alcohol.

Truro Cathedral Choir singing near the War Memorial on Boscawen Street, Christmas 1959

Brokenshire doesn't remember any trouble: *They used to come over from Truro and try their luck with the Redruth boys, but there wasn't really any serious trouble. The 'teddy boys' in Cornwall were just interested in the clothes.* Graham Hankins was guitarist with The Reaction, and remembers the venue as it was later in the 60s: *We don't want to talk about Tabbs (shudders). Rough is not the word. And it was a big staircase if you got pushed down it!*

Rough it may have been, but Rex Webb, Eric Langman and Roger Brokenshire and the bands they worked with blazed a trail in the early days of Rock 'n' Roll in Cornwall. Based on their experience of Tabbs, over the next five years Brokenshire joined forces with Langman to form 'Teen Promotions'. They became active promoting dances and concerts by emerging local bands. Foremost amongst these acts were The Staggerlees and The Manny Cockle Four. Reflecting the rapidly changing musical landscape during the late 50s The Staggerlees, who took their name from a blues standard 'Stagger Lee', were billed in different adverts as a 'skiffle group', then 'rhythm group' and then 'rock unit'. The Blue Aces, featuring Rick Penrose, played at Tabbs as well.

1960: Beatniks and Truro School

During the summer of 1960 Alan Whicker made a short film documenting the arrival of 'beatniks' in the holiday resort of Newquay. Their spokesman was the long-haired folk guitarist Wizz Jones, who, during the summer months, made a living busking in the town. Wizz: *I knew people in Soho like Malcolm Price. I think he was the first London folk singer to visit Cornwall - in 1958 - and he suggested I visit.*

Beatnik pioneer: Wizz Jones in Newquay circa 1960. Wizz, his hair, and his 'rebellious' friends were the subject of a now celebrated documentary by Alan Whicker.

Wizz continued to perform at the county's folk clubs throughout the following decade, often bringing other musicians like Ralph McTell with him. He would also, with Roger Taylor's girlfriend-to-be, Jill

Johnson, briefly be a member of the Famous Jug Band. Jill, who was much younger, moved to Cornwall in 1960. Jill: *My family moved to Truro from Chichester, Sussex when I was about 10 and I remember my father - taking up his new job as Town Clerk of Truro - mentioning problems with beatniks in the county!*

Roger Taylor took and passed scholarship exams to Truro School that year, such that under the direct grant scheme he was able to start at the other boys' private school in Truro without having to be committed to a rigorous schedule of choir-singing.

Truro School itself was founded in 1880 and is now a co-educational school that retains its Methodist roots. Perched high on a hill, its classrooms overlook the City of Truro which nestles in the valley of the Truro River, its skyline marked by the spires of its Victorian Cathedral. The Cathedral seems to dominate the town, not because it is a big Cathedral, but because the town itself is not large, and in the sixties would have had a population of less than 15,000.

Many Methodists were, and are still are, teetotal. Les Brown, who later lived with Roger Taylor in London, remembers the school and its headmaster: *I bumped into Derek Burrell once in a pub in London, he was up for the Methodist Conference, and he said ' I can't drink in Cornwall - it's more than my job's worth'! Truro School was a relaxed school and I don't remember any corporal punishment at the time I was there. Certainly not me or anyone I knew, though we would have lines occasionally.*

Mike Dudley and Geoff Daniel who played in The Reaction, were also at the school. Mike: *Truro School had good facilities, and it was a very pleasant school to be at.* Geoff: *Of course it was smaller then and there were no women! I don't think any of us liked school much and just endured it. Looking back on it, though, it was a superb school and we could have all contributed a lot more - as Roger later did. We'd all been playing in bands of one sort or another since about the age of 13 so spare time was spent on that rather than anything else.*

Neil Battersby and Pete Gill-Carey started as 11 year olds in the same year as Roger. Neil: *We went to school on Saturday mornings and had Wednesday afternoons off. We had to wear black shoes to school, then*

(33)			1 S (23)			
ES. Room 17.			MR. M. A. L. CUMMINS. Room 29.			
I. D.	Sm.	12.10.48	Pol	Samuel, J. A.	V.	
T.	W.	21.10.49	*	Sandercock, C.	V.	
M.	V.	21. 3.49	*	Shearing, C. D.	V.	
n, R.	Sc.	7. 6.49	*	Shingler, C. P.	V.	
Hiley, J.A.N.W.	W.	23. 4.49	*	Sperritt, F.	V.	
H. R.	Sc.	23. 1.49	Pen	Stanier, P. H.	W.	
J. S.	Sm.	9. 2.49	*	Stephens, P. R.	Sc.	
R. J.	V.	12.10.48	*	Stetheridge, P. C.	V.	
L. A.	Sc.	16. 1.49	Pol	Stevenson, D. A.	W.	
M. J.	W.	29. 7.49	*	Taylor, R. M.	V.	🟊
le, P. J.	Sc.	7. 2.49	*	Teagle, W. D.	W.	
V.	Sm.	13. 9.48	*	Thomas, P. M.	Sm.	
C. D.	V.	16.12.48	*	Thorning, R. J.	V.	🟊
V.	Sc.	9. 3.49	Pen	Tierney, S. H.	V.	
B.	W.	6. 9.49	*	Treberth, W. D.	V.	
A.	W.	23.10.48	*	Treseder, C. P.	Sc.	🟊
C. J.	W.	5. 3.49	Pol	Trethewey, M.	V.	
D.	Sc.	12. 6.49	Pen	Uglow, J. T.	V.	
J.	Sc.	25. 5.48	*	Vage, P. J.	W.	
P.	Sc.	17. 9.48	Pen	Vickers, P. J. A.	Sm.	
	Sm.	21.11.48	*	Webb, G. H.	V.	
on, R. J.	W.	25. 6.49	Pen	Webb, T. R.	Sc.	
A.	W.	20.12.48	*	Webber, P. J.	V.	
M. A.	W.	21. 3.49	*	Wellington, J. J.	V.	
C.	V.	27. 8.49	*	Wheatley, N. C.	Sm.	
V. J. P.	Sm.	13. 9.48	Pen	White, D. C.	W.	
-Allen, N.	Sm.	26. 6.49	Pen	Willmett, A. M.	W.	
I.	Sm.	23. 1.49	*	Wright, A. P.	W.	
K.	Sm.					
S. C.	Sc.					
D.	Sm.					

Roger Taylor's first year class at Truro School. The columns include date of birth, boarding house and house.

change into brown ones when we arrived. There were three classes in each year, and in the first year the classes were alphabetical. 1A and 1H and 1S. We were in Poltisco which had three ex-world war II shacks in which we were based. For most of the lessons we had to go up to the main school.

Pete: *Initially I was in the same class as Mike Dudley, guitarist with the Reaction, and Roger was in another one. In the second year we were put into 'streams'. Truro School had the usual oddball masters wandering around the place, but it wasn't a bad place when I was there. At the time you think school is a pain but looking back on it you realise it wasn't so bad after all.*

Toni Carver was another contemporary. Now editor of the St Ives Times and Echo, he didn't know Roger well but remembers him clearly: *His school reputation was that of a bright academic. When we both were in the sixth form common room we were listening to Bob Dylan's 'Masters of War' and talked about the song and Dylan. I was shocked by how keen this academic kid was on Dylan. Years later when Roger started The Cross there was a TV snippet of him covering the song. I remembered the special nature of that conversation which carried the nature of the man's ambition and conviction.*

Neil: *You can see from the school photos that Roger was very pale and small and always looked anaemic! There wasn't an ounce of fat on him. He was a pretty boy, a bit like Twiggy when she had that 'waif and stray' look. I had to work hard to hold my own at Truro School, but Roger was one of the boys who did OK without having to try too hard. He was like our friend Les Brown, who was really clever but had to cope with being born with a finger missing.*

Detail from school photograph 1965. Top row left to right: Mike Dudley, Dick Halliwell, Pete Gill-Carey, Malcolm Broad, Roger Taylor, Dave Dowding. Headmaster Derek Burrell is lower left. Roger and his friends joined the sixth form in September 1965.

These days at around four o'clock Truro School boys - and girls - are often seen at the busy Trafalgar roundabout heading home in their dark blue blazers. In the early-sixties, when Roger Taylor started at the school, this roundabout on the east side of Truro near the school didn't exist, and nor did the busy dual carriageways or inner relief road coming away from it. Instead there were two garages (a filling station and car showroom), several small shops and a pub called The Admiral Boscawen which has since moved location. A holiday job at the filling station paid for John Snell's first saxophone.

Two other pubs, now also long gone, were located nearby at the bottom of Mitchell Hill: The Hope, where the Six Squares skiffle group rehearsed and performed, and The George and Dragon.

Trafalgar Garage filling station near Truro School, Truro. John 'Acker' Snell of The Reaction had a holiday job there as an attendant. In the late sixties this junction was replaced by a large roundabout. Photo courtesy Christine Parnell.

At the time the only possible route driving from Falmouth to St Austell was through the centre of the town as there was no bypass. The road where it crossed the river was quiet enough for the whole school to assemble there for an informal celebration at the end of each school year. Called the 'caps ceremony' the upper sixth, having processed noisily though the town, would say goodbye to the school by throwing their mortar boards into the river. Richard 'Dick' Halliwell was another of Roger's close friends: *We all went to the ceremony on Boscawen Bridge where the leavers would throw their mortar boards in the river. By the time we left this ceremony (and the bridge) had gone. I can remember watching it though - the buses back to St Agnes used to park where the car is on the left hand side. Then there were separate school buses for boys and girls.*

Aerial view of Truro in 1961: Trafalgar Roundabout with dual carriageways leading off it was built in the late sixties at the junction visible in the top left hand corner. Most of the houses bordering St Clement Street on the left side of the photograph were demolished later in the sixties to make way for car-parking and a wider road.

The whole area was redeveloped between 1966 and 1969. Richard: *That part of Truro has changed completely. I remember a chip-shop near the end of Malpas Road. We'd buy chips there after school, and at lunchtimes too and sometimes see Bill Cockle, Manny's uncle - who was a glazier - cycle along with huge sheets of glass under his arm. In the sixties Truro was a sleepy place. They still used to drive cattle up through the middle of the town, up Pydar Street, to the cattle market. The most exciting event of the year was the fair that took place on Lemon Quay.*

As well as being sleepier Truro was less commercial. Rick Penrose, bassist with Roger's first band The Reaction, saw the town develop in the post-war period. During the early sixties the music shops were very different and electrified instruments were not for sale anywhere: *Normally it would pay to go out of Cornwall because they just didn't have the stock. You'd go to Plymouth or Exeter. Because the music shop in those days is where you'd get a grand piano or a trumpet, they had no idea about electric basses or whatever. They might have just had a Hofner six-string or something. John Fry in Cathedral Lane had some good stuff, so I'd pop in there but that was a bit later on.*

Truro School gathers at the old Boscawen Bridge for the end of year 'caps ceremony' in 1963. The old bridge was removed during 1966/67 when the new bypass or 'relief road' was built. The work on the new road was not finished until Autumn 1969.

This was also a time before major supermarkets and out of town shopping. The town centre still had several green-grocers and butchers, including one run by Lord Paul Myner's family. The bakeries, all of course selling Cornish pasties as they do now, have changed relatively little.

In 1959 there were more skiffle competitions in the City Hall in Truro, but by 1960, the skiffle craze had largely run its course, and the competition was revamped and replaced by the Rock and Rhythm Championship which followed a similar format. The new competition would provide an invaluable springboard to Roger Taylor's career as a musician. Peter Boggia, who owned a clothes shop originally opened by his grandfather was the compere for several years: *The Truro Round Table would always support a charity each year. There were groups playing all over Cornwall, and they decided the best thing they could do off the cuff was to get these groups together. So we advertised and got them all. They turned up and had six minutes on the stage. I would go there for the night as compere and try and get all their names and then just go on the stage. After it was finished we would give the proceeds to the finance committee and all the money was given to charity. I did the first one in 1960. It was one of the biggest. The City Hall was full and we were having to turn people away.*

The winners in 1960 were The Druids from Bodmin, and a photograph from the time suggests that the bands' equipment was still fairly rudimentary, with one of the guitars playing though a Grundig gramophone just visible on stage. Also visible in the photograph is the table at which, in 1960 at least, the judges sat.

The Druids in the City Hall, Truro 1960. Photo courtesy Bryan Nicholls.

There was no write up in the paper for the Rock and Rhythm Championship that year, but in March 1960 the West Briton carried a picture of staff and pupils at Camborne School of Mines protesting at the Sharpeville Massacre. The shootings had been of innocent protesters in South Africa, and The School of Mines was recognised as a centre of excellence with close links to African Commonwealth countries.

1961 Dave Dowding and Kenny Pelmear

Dave Dowding, who now works in Truro as a solicitor, first moved to the city in 1961 when he was 12. He started at Truro School in the second year, where, as members of class 2B, Roger Taylor and he became class-mates: *You went up Trennick Lane to the second entrance. There was a big quadrangle and our classroom was downstairs on the left. Ken James was our first class master. Roger and I got together, I think because we shared the same taste in music.*

They soon started playing together: *He had a single snare drum and I had a very cheap Spanish guitar and we practiced initially in the garage. We even improvised amplification using a microphone in the guitar and an old gramophone.*

The quadrangle at Truro School in 2010. On the right is the building containing Roger Taylor's second year form-room. During the first year there were form rooms near Poltisco boarding house, further down the hill.

They were never able to rehearse at school. Dave: *Rock 'n' roll was a bit taboo. Kenneth Pelmear was our music teacher. He used to suggest that we brought our own records in to listen to in music lessons, but*

Truro School on the tennis courts at Epworth in 1962. Kenneth Pelmear is the teacher in glasses sitting next to the matron. Roger Taylor is the small boy standing at his left shoulder. On Roger's left are Mike Dudley and Malcolm Broad.

Derek Burrell (Headmaster) was a classical music lover, and so if we saw him coming we used to turn all the modern records off and put something classical on instead.

So Ken Pelmear taught us all to appreciate music of different styles. He'd say 'I know this is classical but just listen to what's going on'. And he used to play brass band music as well. We have him to thanks for opening our minds up and enlarging our musical interests. He was a nice guy. Very personable.

Geoff Daniel also remembers Kenny Pelmear as their music teacher: *His attitude to Rock 'n' Roll was not great but then most of us did, and still do, appreciate classical and read music well so I don't recall any big problems.*

Roger Taylor's efforts did not go completely unnoticed by teachers at the school. Peter Boggia, compere at the Rock and Rhythm Championship recalls being given a tip by one of them: *Later, I was warned by Dick Taylor who was a master at Truro School 'You want to watch this group. You watch the drummer. He's a most fantastic drummer'.*

Derek Burrell, the headmaster, was at least aware of the music of the time, and later in the sixties he brought a record into assembly. Peter Gill-Carey: *Derek Burrell started playing this song by the Monkees: 'I'm a Believer'. Everyone was keen on the music, and was singing along with it, but then he stopped the record and started talking about being a believer and 'seeing is believing' and so on. We all groaned because of course he was interested in the deeper meaning, the religious meaning.*

Roger Taylor is thought to have been given a cymbal, bass drum and tom-toms for Christmas 1961 so completing his first rudimentary drum-kit*. AIB

---

*Dave Dowding considers it may have been the following year that Roger first had a full kit ie closer to the time that they started performing live together.

1962 The Staggerlees

In the early 60's The Deadbeats became the Manny Cockle Four Big Beat Combo, with Rex Webb their self-appointed manager taking them to dances all over Cornwall. Manny was working in Blackford's printers in Truro: *Rex used to cram us all in his car and we never knew if we'd have enough petrol to get home again so he'd knock it out of gear to save petrol with the tank showing empty. In those days it was big business. I could earn as much playing my guitar as I did at the printers. My diary was booked out a year in advance.*

Manny Cockle with brother Peter. Finton Lawley is the other guitar player. Photo: Manny Cockle.

One of the regulars at Manny's gigs in the early sixties was Pat Johnstone, who would later run the Queen fan club with her sister, Sue. Manny: *We were all good friends. We used to drink in the Royal Tap, the bottom bar of The Royal Hotel. There was always a scene in there on a Saturday night/Sunday lunchtime in the early sixties. Later I had a son that was disabled, and Pat, who was involved in the music business arranged for Stevie Wonder to make a tape especially for him.*

Pat Johnstone had eclectic tastes: *I was into folk music like my sister, and followed John the Fish and Brenda Wootton etc. But then when Jayfolk came along later I was into other stuff.*

The Rock and Rhythm Championships ran successfully throughout the sixties. They were eagerly anticipated by teenagers across Cornwall, and in 1962 the young Dave Dowding and Roger Taylor went to see the bands perform. They would also have witnessed, and been inspired by, the hysteria of the audience.

Manny's band entered on 3 or 4 occasions, but by 1962 Pete Bawden had defected to their rivals The Staggerlees, and was replaced on guitar by the bespectacled Finton Lawley of The Saints. That year The Staggerlees won the competition.

The write-up in the Cornwall Gazette that year is particularly good: *NEARLY 1,000 TEENAGERS AT TRURO CONTEST. It was standing-room only at the City Hall, Truro on Wednesday, when the largest ever audience seen there really let their hair down for a night of Elvis Presley, Cliff Richard-style mass hysteria. Nearly 1000 teenagers were rocking in the gangways for the 1962 Rock and Rhythm Championship of Cornwall, and had the time of their lives. Alan Freeman disc jockey and star of BBC and Independent Television, made an express trip to Truro to help with the judging and make an appearance on the stage. Rhythm groups from nearly every principle town and some from Plymouth and Exeter, competed for the title of 1962 Cornish champions.*

So many people crowded into the hall that the Annexe had to be opened out and still crowds stood at the sides and back of the hall. Many of the groups had powerful modern amplifying equipment and the combined noise of electric guitars, drums and the screaming, clapping and stamping audience raised a pandemonium the like of which can never have been heard before in the old hall.

Ambulance men stood ready for fainting females. It was strictly a session for the young and healthy, with no room for tender ear-drums, even at the back. Anyone who thinks that Cornish teenagers lack the spirit of get-up-and-go had an object lesson to the contrary that night.

By 1962 The Staggerlees had started working more regularly in the dances organised by Eric Langman, Roger Brokenshire and 'Teen Promotions'. Eric: *When they won the Truro Competition in 1962, The Staggerlees were professional and smart: they wore suits, and were talented musicians. I was knocked out by them. They'd been getting better and better, and after they won the championship they decided they wanted to go professional.*

The Staggerlees were probably the first Cornish beat group to tour widely outside of Cornwall, which they did later in 1962 but, given Cornwall's geographical isolation and the travel costs they incurred, found that they struggled to make a decent living. Eric: *The thing that saved them was the Summer season the following year. It was May and I booked 6 halls in the holiday resorts: Perranporth Memorial Hall, Drill Hall St Mawes, Memorial Hall St Ives, Blue Lagoon in Newquay, St Johns Hall Penzance. I booked them up for 11 weeks. I think it was the first time anyone had done anything like this in Cornwall.*

Detail from Truro School photograph in 1962. Middle row L to R: Colin Sandercock, Roger Taylor, Mike Dudley, Malcolm Broad

So say we were playing in Perranporth on a Wednesday we would arrive about 11 o'clock and have about 50 boards with our posters on them and we would stick the name of the venue on the bottom: a bit of hardboard with string though it that we'd tie to lampposts. The circuses

do it now, but then it was a major innovation. We even had a sandwich-board man walking around. We would also print 2000 handbills that we would distribute on the beach. We ended up making a lot of money that year.

Roger Taylor, with his band The Reaction, would adopt the same promotional techniques later in the decade.

1963: Hurland Road, Cousin Jacks and Little Canaan.

In February 1963, after staying temporarily in a flat in Bosvigo House, Roger Taylor's family moved to a newly built bungalow on Hurland Road, a quiet cul-de-sac with views of Truro Cathedral to the North and Truro School to the East. At the time, the entrance to the house was from Northfield Drive, and it had a more generous plot than it does now, because Hurland Road itself was not constructed until later.

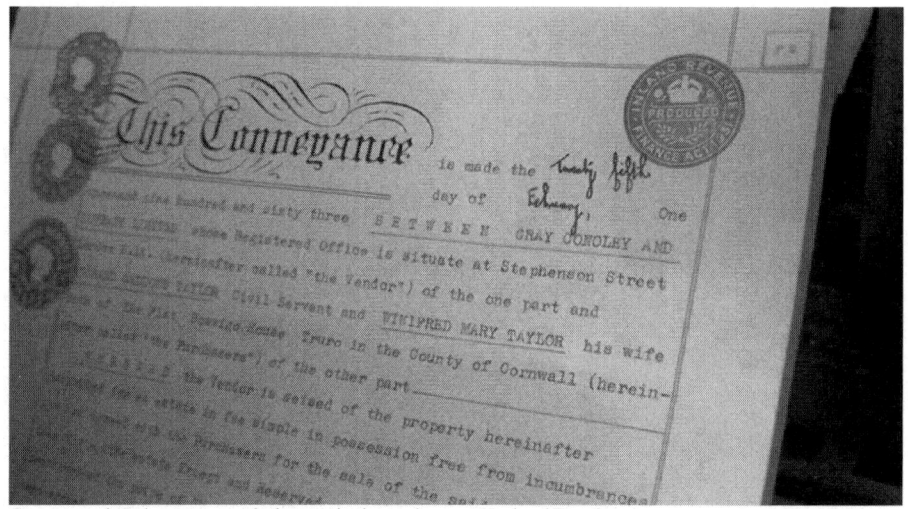
Conveyancing documents relating to the bungalow on Hurland Road

Keith Harding, now nearly 80, lives in the same house immediately opposite the Taylors' old one: *When they lived there, Hurland Road hadn't been built, and so there was a patch of land next to their house which they had flattened, where they put a badminton court. I would play there with my wife and daughter, 'Big Clare', with Roger's mother, Win, and his sister who we called 'Little Clare'. Roger would play as well. It was a lovely on a still evening.*

Keith became friendly with Michael Taylor, Roger's father. Keith: *Mike was quite the lad. He had a really nice Bristol car, and this Matchless 600cc motorcycle with a big M on the tank which - just fooling around -*

he would drive around this patch of land, and up the bank to the side of the badminton court. And once he came a cropper and fell off. He worked as a driving examiner in Penzance all the way through the sixties, so had to drive down there every day from here in Truro. He used to drive his bike like hell on the back roads through Redruth and Camborne, and despite his job didn't worry too much about speed limits either! He was about to go off to work once and he said to me that he was going to have an interesting day because he was going to have to test a steam-roller driver! I said 'I don't suppose they have to do an emergency stop'. He said 'yes they do actually'.

Hurland Road in Winter 2010. The road and wall to the left was built on top of the Taylors' badminton court after they had moved out. The roof of 1, Hurland Road is on the left, and Truro School is just visible on the hilltop in the distance.

Roger Taylor's boyhood home retains many of its original features. The cramped single garage where he practiced still has the original up-and-over door, and the parquet floor throughout is the same floor on which, later in the 60's, the members of Queen slept. Roger's old bedroom is very compact and looks towards Truro School, whilst the living room has big windows that would have overlooked the badminton court.

Current neighbours remember, with mixed emotions, the sound of his drums emanating from the garage at all hours. The neighbour who lived adjacent to the Taylors had a young baby at the time, and although fond of Roger and his family didn't like the noise. But Keith, who lived opposite, didn't think it was that bad: *When I knew Roger he seemed a very ordinary, normal young man. He was very dedicated and would practice most evenings. He'd be there in his garage, with the door closed, but you could still hear it all the way up and down the road. It wasn't objectionable. I don't think anyone ever complained about it. I certainly wasn't bothered.*

Roger was still close enough to school to walk, but he often cycled, sometimes with school friend Paul Treseder who lived nearby. Vaughan Hankins was another neighbour who attended Truro School: *I was 60 yards around the corner. I was into sport at school, but Roger didn't have any interest in it. Neither of us were big or well-built - but I enjoyed it and he didn't.*

Vaughan also played the drums and once experienced a strange sense of déjà vu on hearing Queen's first UK top 20 hit: *Roger was superior to me as a drummer and I was always rather struggling in his wake. I didn't practice as much as Roger: he was much more into his music. I used to watch, and listen to him practicing. Some years later in 1974, I heard 'Seven Seas of Rhye' on the radio for the first time, not knowing it was Roger or Queen. It was very strange, almost surreal: I felt the hairs rising on my neck because I recognised it. I thought 'I know this'. I realised that I had recognised the style of drumming that I had heard so much when I was younger.*

By the beginning of 1963 Dave Dowding and Roger Taylor were preparing to play to a live audience themselves, and their embryonic group had acquired a name, 'The Cousin Jacks', which is a colloquial term for a Cornish tin-miner. They had moved their rehearsal base to Dave's parent's farm at Little Canaan, in New Mills, an idyllic spot traversed by the River Kenwyn about a mile from the centre of Truro. Dave: *It was a small-holding: a mixed farm. Initially my father moved down and he farmed it. We had cows, pigs and all sorts really.*

They tended to use a smaller room upstairs in one of the barns: *As you go past the main house which is on the left going down the hill, the long building on your right is the original barn. The steps were removed,*

The ford at New Mills (2010). The Kenwyn River runs through the garden at Little Canaan Farm.

and it's a house now. We never performed at Little Canaan as I remember. My mother used to say that it was a terrible noise when we started in 1962-63! When we were The Cousin Jacks we played at parties and there's one I remember in particular. We played at Restronguet, indoors, at the yacht club at Mylor. Just Roger and I.

The boys shared instruments that night, as Dave could keep a basic beat on the drums: *I played all the tunes I could play on the guitar, then we swapped over and he played all the tunes he could. As people got more drunk they seemed to enjoy it more! We had a great evening. It was the Summer and everybody had a great time. In the early days, with a limited repertoire, Roger had plenty of scope to develop his skills with fill-in solos. The trick for me was cutting in otherwise he would just continue - great stuff.*

Roger was showing a natural aptitude at drumming: *I remember Roger drumming on anything that made a sound. It was a nightmare in class, as he was always being told off for tapping on the desk and so on. I only knew him when he wanted to play drums. But occasionally at that time I would play drums when he played guitar.*

At the time the biggest influence on them was The Shadows. Dave: *Tony Meehan had left and Brian Bennett was the drummer, and he was a classical percussionist. That year we went on the bus by ourselves to see The Shadows in Plymouth: Roger and me and a few of us. And we were very impressed by their professionalism. They all had these new Gibson guitars and they were so slick. They were playing Glenn Miller stuff that was extraordinary.*

Dave also remembers Roger being impressed by another live performance: *There was a famous jazz drummer who came to the City Hall. Roger was fascinated by his technique and solos. I am sure it wasn't Gene Krupa but possibly someone who played in his band. He was American and I remember Roger's eyes lighting up when he saw this amazing array of top notch drums, and the guy showed off some basic technique. It was really an informal masterclass. He was a classic big band drummer - very controlled - more a percussionist as I think Roger turned out to be.*

On Friday evenings in the early sixties teenagers in Truro could attend ballroom dancing classes at the same WI Hall that was used to stage Rock 'n' Roll dances on a Saturday. During 1963 Jenny Doble, Roger Taylor and mutual friends Mike Dudley and Malcolm Broad, were all members of the same class. Jenny: *It was Miss McGowan's school of dancing. There were about 20 people in the class, and not many boys. All of us had been sent by our parents to be 'socialised'.*

Malcolm: *I remember we had to put on extra-shiney dancing shoes and cavort around the Hall...*

It became an opportunity for girls and boys to come into close, but awkward, physical contact with one another. Jenny: *At the time it was all too excruciating. I was tall, so dancing with Roger was always clumsy and embarrassing for me! I was at least a foot taller than him! Waltzing and quickstepping felt a bit old hat anyway. Maybe we were behind the times in Cornwall...*

Neil Battersby was also at Truro School: *The two main girl's schools in Truro were the High School and the Grammar School and because of the colour of their uniforms the girls nicknamed each other The Brown Cows and The Black Cows. I remember there were old-time dancing classes at the High School as well as the WI Hall.*

Mike Dudley: *Rock 'n' Roll and ballroom dancing were not mutually exclusive. The main idea was to meet young ladies. We were 14 or so then.*

The lessons coincided with formal dances that they had all started to attend. Dave Dowding: *Around that time Truro School and the High School for girls started putting on dances. They were quite formal at first, with ballroom style-dancing. It was only later that groups like The Reaction would get invited.*

One of three photos taken inside the barn at Little Canaan with new band member Mike Dudley (right)

Jenny had known Mike for five or six years and they both travelled on the school bus from St Agnes. Suddenly on November 22nd they learnt that the US President had been assassinated. Jenny: *One night after the dance class my mother picked up myself and Mike and another friend, Malcolm Broad, and his parents came out to the car and said that JF*

Kennedy had been shot. I remember us all watching the footage in stunned silenced, then driving home to St Agnes in shock.

For Pat Johnstone, as for many of the older Cornish teenagers, President Kennedy had symbolized everything that was glamorous about America: *Kennedy being a young, sassy, sexy guy turned everything on its head. America had such a strong influence on all of us. It seemed to be bursting with energy and freedom. We were all listening to American music back then.*

That year the folk singer Donovan was inspired to become a musician after spending the Summer in the artist's colony of St Ives. The picturesque seaside town had, like Newquay further up the coast, become a magnet for 'beatniks', and some of the older teenagers from Truro - beatniks or aspiring beatniks themselves - would visit. Pat: *We were young people and we wanted something that wasn't just a boring job and a pension! Once we took some cider and our guitars and harmonicas and sat on the beach near The Sloop pub having a great time, singing and dancing, but the local fire brigade came round the corner and hosepiped us! They turned their hoses on us and hosed us out of St Ives! They thought us 'beatniks' were evil!!*

Perhaps not surprisingly Pat became the first of Roger Taylor's older friends and associates to leave Cornwall to find work in London. Pat: *Cornwall seemed like the end of the world. Nobody came down, and it felt really cut off. In the winter the greyness of the land and the sea and the clouds and the rain can be overwhelming. But then when the spring comes, the bluebells come out and the mood changes completely...*

1964: Folk music evenings, Mike Dudley and David Penhaligon

In the spring of 1964 the woods around 'New Mills' outside Truro would have been full of bluebells. With his father's blessing Dave Dowding used the barn at Little Canaan to put on folk music evenings in a larger downstairs space. Dave: *There were about half a dozen altogether. No-one famous sang there, they were all just local singers that we knew. There were lots of people around who could play and sing. It was very informal. Jill Johnson, who was later Roger's girlfriend, sang with her sisters. There was a guy called Richard or 'Oscar' Carveth who played, and another called Pete Baron. They were a bit older than us.*

Beat Unlimited on the steps of the barn at Little Canaan. L to R: Roger Taylor, Mike Dudley & Dave Dowding

Pete Baron was at Truro School, two years ahead of Roger Taylor. In 1964 the first of many Cornish folk clubs opened at Botallack on the cliffs over-looking the Atlantic Ocean nearly an hour's drive from Truro. *Richard (Carveth) and I used to turn up at Dave Dowding's carrying our two guitars on my 'Norman Nippy' 49cc moped. Along with a guy called Pete Wilton, we used to play as regulars or itinerants at most of the folk clubs west of Truro. We used to sing at the Count House at Botallack particularly. At the Count House sea shanties and Cornish folk songs were the accepted thing at the time, and various Scottish folk songs. So we would do all sorts of American country blues songs just to annoy people. Or at least we would do one or two that suited them, and one or two that suited us. And we'd do Lonnie Donnegan skiffle stuff which also wasn't really the done thing.*

Recorded on 31st October, 1964 a rare copy of the Count House EP featuring performances by John & Tel and Mel & Miles. The club tended to support traditional English/Cornish music.

Jill Johnson: *I remember Pete Baron's little moped ... it's awfully difficult to look cool on one of those! He used to go out with one of our classmates and friend Cathy Sharp. She later went out with and married, Richard Thorning who played bass with The Reaction later in the sixties.*

Manny Cockle: *The local music scene splintered when the folk thing started up down at Botallack. All this folkie stuff: I used to hate it!!*

Meanwhile Roger Taylor and Dave Dowding of Cousin Jacks were joined by Mike Dudley from the dance classes on rhythm guitar. He was also at Truro School, and was several inches taller than Roger. Dave: *Mike was very serious, and very bright. He was in the same class as us and he joined because we were looking to beef our sound up.*

He was still new to the guitar. Mike Dudley: *I started guitar at 14. When I started with Dave and Roger we were very much still on three chords, E A and D, or we did Shadows stuff, which was pretty easy except there was no sheet music around so we had to do it all by ear...*

Mike, who was living on the north coast in St Agnes nearly 10 miles from Truro, had had less exposure to live music than Roger and Dave, but remembers seeing a gig in the village in about 1963: *The Staggerlees and Manny Cockle Four did a performance in what is now the Pendeen Hotel, halfway up Rosemundy Hill. Then it was a home for unmarried mothers. They were the first live groups I'd seen.*

With Mike now involved, the band's name changed to Beat Unlimited. Dave: *We thought Cousin Jacks was a bit old hat and that it should be something a bit more dynamic. Actually I thought Beat Unlimited was a really good name.*

Beat Unlimited in Dave Dowdings barn, Little Canaan, Newmills. L to R Dave Dowding, Roger Taylor, Mike Dudley. Roger's bass-drum skin was painted by Roger himself.

One day in July 1964 Dave's mother took a series of photos of the group in Little Canaan, shortly after they'd acquired some new instruments, some bought from Moon's in River Street, Truro. Dave: *The photos show Roger's first drum set. It was Roger who would have painted the logo on his drum. He was very artistic. His art was colourful and expressive, and he had a good eye for detail. In the photo there is a tom-tom hidden behind Mike. It's very posed: for example, Roger's not holding the drumsticks as he normally would have.*

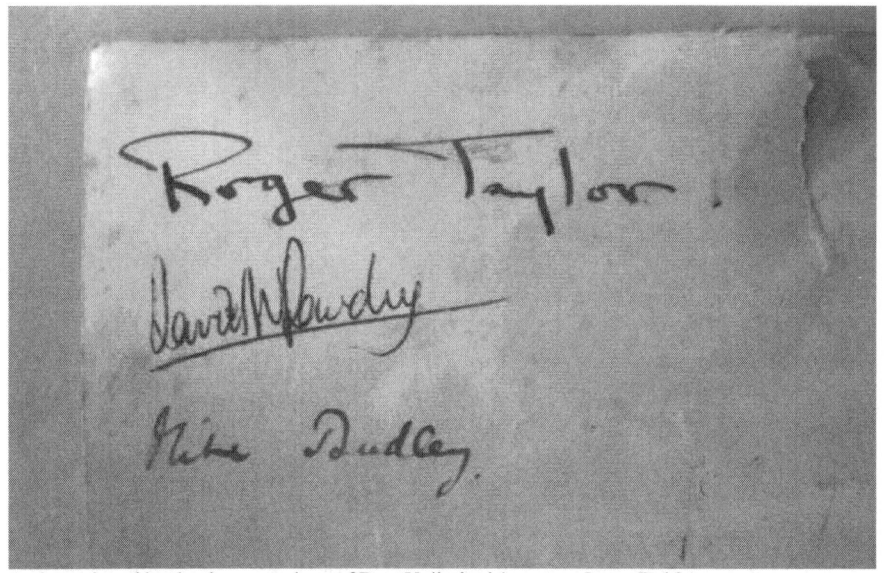

A photo signed by the three members of Beat Unlimited (courtesy Jenny Doble)

My guitar was second-hand. I think it was called a Futurama. It was a red and white guitar which only had two pick-ups. But I had a new 15W amplifier. My father, was, incidentally, mortified at the thought of his son ending up as a rock star!

Mike: *The first guitar I had, I got from a boyfriend of my sister's which was a Hohner semi-acoustic. Then I bought a Watson's Rapier, which I got in Plymouth.*

At least one of the photos taken that day was used to impress friends and admirers on the school bus. Jenny Doble was lucky enough to be given a copy signed by Roger and Mike in fountain pen, and Dave in a biro. Though dog-eared and torn it is still in her possession. It can be safely said that Roger's autograph, though bold and confident, appears considerably less practiced than it is now, though the flourish on the T has n't changed a lot. Jenny: *Mike would have given the photo to me. We used to come into school in Truro together from St Agnes on the bus. He also gave me my first valentine card at around the same time!*

The photos do not really reflect the look that the band had when performing live. Dave Dowding: *It was around the Kinks era when people were wearing winklepicker shoes. We had these matching smart olive green shirts with button-down collars, and cuban heels to play in - this was our performance gear. This would coincide with the Shadows being very smart and very slick. The look was definitely pop-inspired. If you look at 'A Hard Day's Night', the Beatles have got button-down collars, so I think we were just following a trend. The hair was getting longer and fringes were in. Mike's hair, though, is still slightly teddy-boyish.*

Although The Beatles had their first number ones in 1963, instrumental music using the electric guitar as the solo instrument was still popular. 'Apache' by the Shadows had reached the top of the charts in the UK in 1960, and it was one of several such numbers Beat Unlimited had in their repertoire. Dave: *Any of them could go on for ages. We had another instrumental, 'Wipeout' by The Ventures, that we could make last 15 minutes! We would just play it with lots and lots of drum breaks. It sounded like the recording, though I actually thought Roger's drum breaks were better! Can't say the same for my solo, but ours moved along quite nicely and we always opened with that.*

Though a couple of them had good voices Beat Unlimited didn't have a vocalist because, at least initially, their voices had n't broken. The three-piece played at lots of private functions. Dave: *I'm sure we played in St Mawes. We were popular at parties. We just made a big noise and everybody danced and had a good time. There were lots of parties in St Agnes. We did an outside one at Chapelporth Beach in the evening in the Summer. And that was the 3 of us. The weather was horrible and misty. It was hopeless really. All the sand should have wrecked our kit. My fingers and my guitar strings went green because of the salty air.*

We started off with very basic primitive strings that obviously corroded easily. Later we discovered you could get smooth better quality strings that altered the tone and speed you could play. It was a strange evening. The Round Table had organised it - it was very boozy and everybody got very drunk.

Roger's parents were supportive of these early efforts. Dave: *We thought we were very cool. We had a generator that Roger's father had organised. I think they were keen to help him. They could see he had a talent.*

Jenny Doble recalls a couple of parties that friends organised. One was at the Masonic Hall in St Agnes, and the other was the Young Farmer's Club at Threemilestone. Richard Halliwell was a Truro School boy who lived near St Agnes and, later, became an enthusiastic follower of all of Roger's bands. *I remember the performance at the Masonic Hall just up from Rosemundy Villa, which was Mike Dudley's house. They were still a threepiece then.*

On the 18th December 1964 they were booked by the Truro Liberal Association to play at the City Hall Annexe at a 'Xmas Party and Variety Concert'.

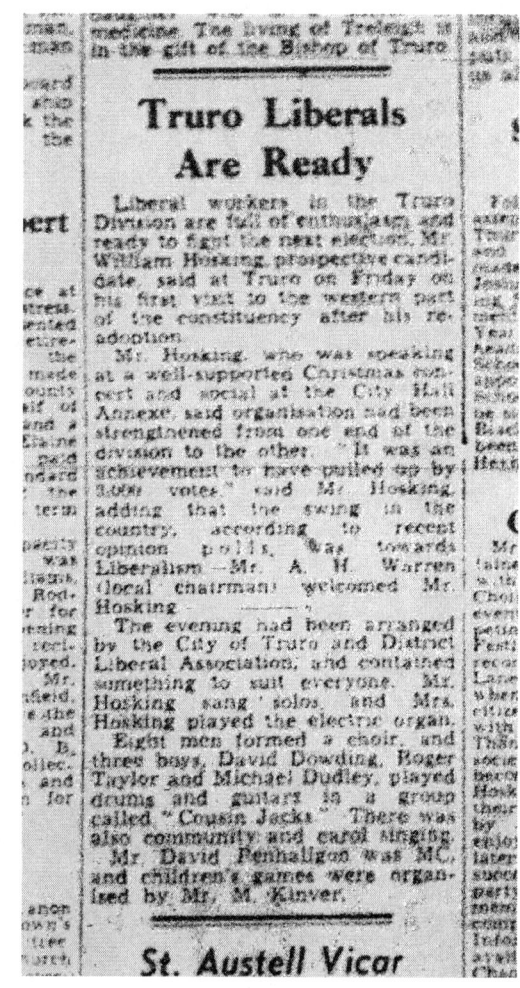

Dave's father was very involved with the local Liberals, who would meet in his office, next to the Truro Bookshop in Frances Street. By that time Dave had a Watkins guitar with four pickups. As the lead guitarist the spotlight was often on him: *I managed The Rise and Fall of Fingle Bunt (The Shadows) all the way through - in public - that night.*

The newspaper article one week later (see picture), describes the three boys playing as Cousin Jacks. Linda Roach, who was later a regular visitor to PJ's nightclub, was there as it was her uncle Morley Kinver who organized the children's games. By coincidence the MC was the twenty year old David Penhaligon who was destined to become one of Cornwall's most celebrated members of parliament. Shortly before he died in a car crash, Penhaligon, who was 5 years older than Roger, was interviewed for a documentary: *It was always alleged that he ruined five or six academic careers at school because he got other people involved in the group! I remember him doing a gig for the Young Liberals, and we lost money on it which might be more a reflection on the Young Liberals.* (TMY)

Some of the Little Canaan folk singers taking part in an English Folk Song and Dance Society competition in 1965. Jill Johnson is on the far left, sitting next to Sue Johnstone. Jill's two sisters are wearing the paler dresses. Pete Wilton and Richard Carveth are holding guitars.

Just before mock 'O' Levels Dave Dowding had appendicitis, and partly as a result the City Hall concert was the last time he played with Roger and Mike.

In the year above Beat Unlimited at Truro School, were two classmates with musical ambitions. They were bass-player Jim Craven and saxophonist John 'Acker' Snell. The band that became The Reaction started to form at about this time, and two of the folk musicians were involved as Jim Craven explains: *Acker and I founded the band: we were the two that got it going and we had various line-ups to start with. All sorts of people came and went. In the first gig we played, we had Oscar Carveth, who sold me the bass guitar that I had. Oscar was at the Cathedral School. Pete Baron was the drummer.*

Now working as manager of Simpson's clothes shop in Truro, Graham Hankins had just left school, and had been a member of the Blue Aces skiffle group along with Rick Penrose. Graham remembers attending sea scouts on Strangways Terrace with both him and Acker Snell, and having been briefly in a band with Pete Baron: *We used to all meet on a Sunday night in St Mary's Hall at something called 'The Cathedral Fellowship', which was a kind of youth club, and The Reaction came out of that originally, when Acker Snell and Jim Craven approached me to help form a group.*

Graham in turn suggested they talk to singer Johnny Grose, who had been at Truro Tech with him: *I got hold of John Grose. He was a wonderful performer when he was on form, but he had a problem: he was very nervous.*

Jim Craven: *The first gig we did, we had Johnny Grose and Graham Hankins, with Oscar on rhythm guitar, Pete on drums and me and Acker.*

Graham: *We played at the Youth Club at Kea. It was a hut in Playing Place on the Old Coach Road. I think we were involved with other youth clubs in Truro too. We did a bit at the Cathedral Fellowship on a Sunday night too.*

Jazz clarinetist Acker Bilk's 'Stranger on the Shore' was a world-wide hit in 1962. John Snell: *The nick-name Acker was, I think, coined by Johnny Grose after the Reaction had started. I didn't mind. I just put up with it. I first heard of Johnny before the Reaction was formed because my mother came back from an event in the Drill Hall in Moresk talking very excitedly about this young lad with a tremendous voice. Not long after that I met him through Graham.*

St Mary's Hall (2010). 'Johnny Quale and The Reactions' formed as a result of youth club evenings here.

In the official photograph of Truro School of 1962, many of the boys are sporting Elvis-like quiffs. Dave Dowding: *I remember the prefects at school were constantly combing their hair back, and had their caps sat at the back of their heads. They took liberties with the uniform. The trousers got narrower and the ties got narrower and the house-masters didn't like it. People would take the cardboard out of the caps. Everyone had to wear caps, even in the sixth form. People would wear winkle pickers if they could get away with it too.*

By 1964 The Beatles had already had several hits and some of the boys had been inspired to start growing their hair into bushy mop-tops instead. Pete Baron: *For a time all of us involved with the band were told, at school, that if we continued to have hair the length we had, we would have to wear hair bands to tie it back with! Which we did! The*

Beatles all had their own cut that was much longer than the standard short back and sides. At the time they were influential in terms of their look and their lifestyle, as well as their music.

Viv Hendra was also at Truro School: *Hair-length was a really big issue at the school throughout the sixties. Derek Burrell had just started as headmaster and he had his reputation to think of. Long-haired Truro school boys were the talk of the town. For some long hair was a symbol of moral decline!*

Dave Dowding remembers some of these older, long-haired boys watching Cousin Jacks at the Liberal Association gig. *There were one or two people who used to come to the folk evenings and did some rock and roll that wanted to play too. The guys I remember muscling in at the Liberal evening itching to get on stage were older and sang quite well, so you then had the makings of a much more versatile group.*

John Snell and Jim Craven, who were scouting for a drummer, were amongst them. John: *We had been to see The Rimshots earlier in the evening but considered that Roger was more effective than their drummer. At that time his drum kit was very limited but he played it very precisely and consistently - there wasn't much in the way of flashy drumming but it was a good steady rhythm and he had the ability to make the drum set sound better than it was. He was also aware of the audience whereas his two colleagues (Mike and Dave) were concentrating on their playing to the exclusion of all else. Roger was never tall but at that age he looked very small sitting behind his drums compared to the other two! But Roger made sufficient impression on Jim and me that we thought it worth making an approach...*

1965 Johnny Quale and The Reactions

On 7th January 1965 the West Briton explained that the City Council had agreed on *'a project that will result in the razing and rebuilding of properties on nearly 11 acres of the Pydar Street area'*. By providing them with one of their most significant early venues, this same project would contribute to the history of the rock group 'Queen'.

At around the same moment the group that was to be called Johnny Quale and The Reactions finally came together. Graham Hankins recalls meeting new recruit Roger Taylor for the first time. Graham: *I was in the main street in Truro one day and Oscar Carveth introduced me to this young kid. He said 'this guy is Roger Taylor'. And I looked at this little skinny kid y'know? Then John Grose turned up and said 'Hello. What are you called? Titch or what?' That's true. He called him Titch. John Grose always called him that!*

Roger was ultimately able to benefit greatly from playing regularly alongside boys who were older and more mature. John Snell: *Jim Craven would have persuaded Roger to join us. Roger was two years younger by academic year and nearly three in age, but the age difference wasn't really an issue. Roger was a confident character. Plus it was obvious from the beginning that he was talented and that's why Jim was so keen to have him in the group. Mike Dudley came along as well, but he needed a bit of tutoring and I think Graham brought him along a bit.*

Graham: *Roger brought along his tall mate called Mike Dudley who I remember at the time couldn't hold a guitar let alone a plectrum, but he learnt fast and he learnt good. In Johnny Quale and the Reactions he ended up mainly playing keyboard which gave a bit more width to the music. We'd heard about a contract in a hotel in Newquay, the St Brannock's Hotel, and we were trying to get enough musicians together to do it, but I also had a thing in my head about the Rock and Rhythm Championship. I wanted to enter that and win it.*

The band had to have a name with which to enter the competition. John Snell: *Jim and I were sitting in Truro School library during a free study period. We were trying to decide the name of the group, and having been told to be quiet, I scribbled 'Mighty Atom and the Reactions!' on a piece of paper and threw it over to Jim. A little while afterwards when we were outside he said 'Let's go for The Reactions' and the name was agreed.*

The Reactions' first rehearsal base in Truro (2010)

Rehearsals started in earnest. Graham: *We used to practice in the old Boys Club in the yard of the Royal Hotel. There were rooms there. But we mostly practiced down at the village of Malpas which was Jim Cravens' place. His parents had a market garden there. His mother was a school teacher. They used to have a cottage that they would rent out in the summer, but we used to have the run of the place during the winter for rehearsals. His Dad never took a penny off us and used to bring coffee down to us and all sorts. They lived in a cedarwood bungalow right at the top. They had a beautiful view. These people were wonderful!! We had wonderful times.*

Malpas is a picturesque village about a mile from the centre of Truro, perched downstream on the banks of the Truro River. It features in the Celtic legend of Tristan and Isolde and it overlooks trees in which nesting herons are often visible: *We would leave most of the gear, like*

Roger's drumkit, down there. I would travel on the bus to Malpas, because I was living on the opposite side of Truro, in Highertown.

Jim Craven was old enough to drive. Graham: *Jim Craven's Dad had a beautiful old car: an MG Magnette, a big square car like the police used to have. His father would let him take the car and he would come to pick us up. Acker Snell had a van that his Mum would drive for us.*

John Snell: *We needed a secluded location for practice because we didn't want any publicity until a workman-like performance could be assured! The secrecy worked for some weeks but one night faces were spotted peering through the cottage windows. A chase in the dark revealed that the intruders were not spies from another group but local girls who had been intrigued where the nightly music was coming from...*

Johnny Quale and The Reactions: John Acker Snell, Johnny Quale Grose, Roger Taylor, Graham Hankins, Jim Craven, Mike Dudley.

The band had to prepare two numbers to play. One was 'What'd I say' by Ray Charles. Graham: *We took the original riff and we did an instrumental version of it, which I put together, giving Roger Taylor a lead break in the middle of it. So he did a drum solo in the middle of the song. And it was obvious. I would say he was as good then as he is now.*

It was there in the beginning. It was there and he had it. He was incredible. For the other number Johnny Grose and myself sat down one afternoon and I worked out some music and he put some words together, and we wrote a song.

View of the Truro River from Malpas (photo 2010)

Pete Stanton, of Truro rivals Al Scott and the Klan, was one of the other drummers at the City Hall that night, and is less fulsome in his praise. *I don't remember Roger standing out as a drummer back then. He was a little bit cocky, but not overconfident. I think precocious is the word. Roger was four or five years younger than me, so when we did the contest he looked to pick up some tips. He asked me: 'How do you do this, how do you do that?', and I taught him some basics. But you kept a lot of it under your hat in those days. There were no drum teachers. You had to teach yourself by just listening and listening and listening.*

Pete recalls the atmosphere backstage: *You'd be in a line waiting to come on – you could hear all the cheering and screaming in the hall - and you'd be set up behind the curtain, all tuned up behind it and just waiting nervously...*

The Reaction was less casual than the other acts. John: *Graham had persuaded the group that we should have a strong identity: as an outfitter he arranged that everyone except Johnny appeared in smart charcoal grey trousers, orange long sleeve shirts and black knitted ties. Which we combined with some well-rehearsed stage moves reminiscent of the Shadows.*

The new group's appearance in the championship was literally their first formal engagement. Graham: *There was a fantastic atmosphere. The City Hall was packed. What else was there to do? They'd all be in there doing the hand-jive. It was wonderful stuff. There were 16 or so bands from all over Cornwall but no-one had heard of us because we hadn't really played anywhere else.*

There was a band from Bodmin called the Druids and they did 'FBI'. I remember that distinctly because it blew me away. And Manny Cockle was there. He was a wonderful singer, but he got disqualified. You were told to do two numbers in a set time. He did three but ran two numbers into one and they didn't allow it. They were that strict! The Strangers were in it, and another Truro group, Al Scott and the Klan. Their drummer, Pete, later covered for us if Roger couldn't make it.

The Reactions' own composition went well: *It was a ballad, which was right up Johnny's street. He had his hair in a bow at the back like PJ Proby...The whole band played along, then in the middle eight I played muted guitar, and Johnny got on one knee and begged for this girl to come back, you know.*

Despite The Reactions' lack of experience they came a respectable fourth, and though not winners they had the compensation of knowing that their 'kid' drummer's ability had been recognized by the judges. Graham: *Everybody was looking at this kid with a pair of drumsticks whose hands were moving so fast they didn't know what was going on. We'd made sure when we did the number that he had a drum solo in the middle because it was pretty obvious. He was that good. That night Roger Taylor got voted best musician of the evening. And our singer got voted best singer. Pete Baron gave me a lift back that night. My mother came to the door and asked how it went and I remember he said 'they were as hot as mustard'.*

```
                    COMPETITORS
        THE STRANGERS (Truro)
            J. BLEWETT     ..    Lead Guitar
            H. PENROSE     ..    Rhythm Guitar and Vocalist
            R. PENROSE     ..    Bass Guitar
            P. TONKIN      ..    Drums
        JOHNNY QUALE AND THE REACTIONS (Truro)
            G. G. HANKINS  ..    Lead Guitar
            M. DUDLEY      ..    Rhythm Guitar
            J. CRAVEN      ..    Bass Guitar
            J. R. SNELL    ..    Tenor Sax
            R. TAYLOR      ..    Drums
            J. GROSE       ..    Vocalist
        GEOFF AND THE CLIMATES (Penryn)
            A. BLACKETT    ..    Drums
            R. EDWARDS     ..    Guitar
            R. GAYE        ..    Guitar
            M. GEDYE       ..    Guitar
            G. DAVIS       ..    Vocalist
        SHADES-OF-BLUE (St. Austell)
            B. PASCOE      ..    Bass Guitar
            A. LLOYD       ..    Lead Guitar
            S. TUCKER      ..    Drums
            A. MARTIN      ..    Rhythm and Vocals
        THE MISFITS (Mevagissey)
            DAVE TUCKER    ..    Drums
            RON HARRIS     ..    Bass Guitar
            JOHN CLOKE     ..    Guitar
            STEPHEN KELLY  ..    Guitar
            NICK GOUGH     ..    Harmonica
        LITTER (Truro)
            A. HALL        ..    Rhythm Guitar
            C. K. VINCOE   ..    Lead Guitar
            G. PILSLEY     ..    Bass Guitar
            R. DUNCAN      ..    Drums
        THE GUNSLINGERS
            MIKE BLACKBOROW      Bass Guitar
            DENNIS PHILLIPS  ..  Drums
```

Annotated programme for the 1965 Rock and Rhythm Championship. Collection Jill Johnson

The winners were The Individuals, a group that included future Queen bassist Mike Grose (who, incidentally, is no direct relation to Johnny). Mike recalls: *At the beat contest of 1965, our first song was 'Up & Down' which Spike (Nigel Hooper) and myself sang, the second was 'Gloria' a Van Morrison song which Phil Bassett sang for about half a minute until the PA packed up. Luckily for us Spike played a blistering solo which I feel impressed the judges. Later, in 1970, Spike played sax with 'Marvelous Kid' at PJ's.*

Mike Grose - future Queen bassist - playing with the Individuals. Venue unknown.

The Fender Precision Mike played with the Individuals that night is the same one he played with Queen, albeit with modifications. Mike: *It was imported from the States. I bought it in 1963. It was pink at first, but I had an uncle who resprayed it black, then white. Then, when I played with Queen, it had been sanded down to a natural wood. I still have bits of the original guitar in my possession.*

Although they didn't win, people took notice of Johnny Quale and The Reactions. Graham Hankins: *None of these other guys knew us. They'd all been on the circuit for a while, and they looked at Roger Taylor as if to say 'who is this skinny little kid?' Suddenly all these strange people came in and it turned out they were agents. And they said 'Have you got an agency? No? Well you should join up with me'. I think there were three lots that approached us that evening and that's how we started to get work.*

One of them was Pete Brown of BCD, based in Queen's Crescent, Bodmin. *Mr Twelve and a half per cent! We met him early one evening in Bodmin after I'd finished work and the boys had finished school.* Another was Roger Brokenshire, who as a teenager had been involved with Tabbs Hotel, but by then was 24. Graham: *He was one of the people that came into that dressing room in the City Hall and - we didn't sign up for him so much - but we said yeh we'll work for you. He was very enthusiastic.*

> EASTER MONDAY
> Truro City.
>
> BEAT SPECTACULAR
>
> **THE INDIVIDUALS**
>
> (1965 Cornish Champions), also Truro's own top gear "In" Group.
>
> **Johnny Quale and the Reactions.**
>
> Dancing from 8 to 11.30 p.m.
> Admission: - - - - 5/6.

Two members of Queen played in Truro City Hall's 'Beat Spectacular' in Easter 1965. The advert was the Reactions' first.

Sure enough offers of other gigs came their way. On 19th April they played as support to The Individuals in an 'Easter Monday Beat Spectacular': *We came fourth in the '65 Championship and then they wanted us to support the winning band some days later, but we only had about five numbers that we could do!*

As well as developing their repertoire, the band quickly resolved to work on their image. Graham: *It was decided we'd have some publicity photographs done. There was a photographer in Truro called Cameracraft. He was brilliant with us and he charged us peanuts.*

A test photograph. Top: Graham Hankins and Roger Taylor, Bottom: Jim Craven and Johnny 'Quale' Grose

They did a test shoot with four members of the band, before the other two had turned up, and the unique print marked 'proof' in Graham's collection was the result. The better known image of all six of them (p. 61) was taken in the same studio shortly afterwards. The black and white photo does not do justice to their shirts, three of which were a matching bright orange, but it still conveys something of the camaraderie of playing in a band.

One of the earliest pictures of The Jays. Seven of their eight initials were J. Picture: Jill Johnson

That March Jill Johnson had been in the audience of the 1965 Rock and Rhythm Championship, and her profusely annotated copy of the programme (see photo) suggests that she both noticed and approved of Johnny Quale and the Reactions. Two months later she met drummer Roger Taylor, and became his girlfriend. Jill: *I met Roger at a folk concert at Dave Dowding's farm in New Mills in 1965. It was in his barn, all bales of hay and candles. I think Sue Johnstone was with me, but I can't be sure. Roger was sitting next to us in the back row (of course) and we left together. It was that night, or the next, that he took me to the local funfair in the field that used to be where Moorfield Car Park now is. And I believe the next night I went to one of his gigs with him. From then on it was a pretty regular thing.* Johnny Quale was *doing most of the singing when I was first with Roger, but then he left pretty soon after that.*

The Folk Music Evening that night appears to have followed closely on from another advertised on February 27th. On both occasions newspaper adverts placed by David Penhaligon and the Truro Young Liberals offered free transport from Frances Street and Victoria Square in the centre of town roughly one mile away.

Jill Johnson was a year younger than Roger and was herself active as a musician in a band she called 'The Jays': *The Jays started in 1964. I was 14. The first line-up was myself, my sisters, Janet and Jennifer who were twins and my best friend Sue Johnstone, who later ran the Queen fan club with her sister Pat before going to EMI. We sang mostly at special events, hotels, concerts, etc. The folk club scene wasn't really established at that time.*

I was never very fond of the English Folk Music - all finger-in-the-ear, and out 'a-walking' stuff. I always preferred something with a beat. I think my mother started it by giving me a guitar and a book of American songs. Sue also got a guitar and we taught ourselves some chords. We also liked blues - which was probably influenced by Sue's sister, Pat. Then Joan Baez became popular and the folk music scene grew, so we started seeing other people performing American songs - and went with that.

Sue Johnstone: *I met Jillian at St George's Methodist Church in Truro. We first formed a group when I was about 11, and my teenage years were then spent with the Jays (later Jayfolk). It was great fun.*

Jill: *We went to St George's for years. They had a strong youth group, and Sue and I joined the choir, mainly so we could sit in the balcony and see the Truro School Boarders on Sundays! It's where we got into the folk thing with the English Folk Song and Dance Society.*

The Jays sang more than once at Dave Dowding's folk evenings. So did members of The Reactions. Graham Hankins: *Pete Baron and I got kicked off the stage at Little Canaan for playing electric folk which offended the purists! The audience used to sit on straw bales. It was a lovely spot by the river, and you had to walk down all the country lanes to get there.*

> **The Atlantic All-Stars**
>
> # FOLK MUSIC EVENING
> ## at
> ## Little Canaan Farm,
> **FRIDAY, MAY 21st, 7.30—11.**
>
> Signposted from Truro Fire Station and the new hospital.
> Lifts from 19, Frances-st., 7.30-7.45.
> Organised by Truro Young Liberals.
>
> Princess Pavilion, Falmouth

An advert from The West Briton for one of the last of the folk music evenings at Little Canaan. Part-organised by future MP David Penhaligon, Jill Johnson first met Roger Taylor there.

Les Brown was at Truro School: *I remember Dave's house by the river in Little Canaan. My God it was beautiful there. They grew lots of exotic trees and plants that I remember getting zapped one winter by the frost...*

Mike Dudley: *I wasn't interested in folk music, but I would have met Jill and Sue around that time and, actually, I went out with Sue Johnstone, for maybe a year, a bit later when I had a car.*

Jill Johnson's contribution to the story has been underplayed in other biographies. These same books have been misleading, with a Record Collector article even describing the Jays as being 'large-bosomed'. Jill: *This would fit my sisters, but not so much me, and definitely not Sue Johnstone who always had a slim and boyish figure (much envied I might add!). There were 4 not 3 of us in the group, no flute until 1968, and Pat Johnstone was definitely never a member. Roger and I were together from mid 1965 to early 1969, though with varying levels of commitment and 'exclusivity' during that time.*

In fact during part of 1965 Roger is thought to have been seeing a girl from Flushing, a village that is a short trip by boat to Falmouth. Jill vaguely recalls their rivalry: *I knew one or two girls that he was involved with. One tried to beat me up at a dance in Falmouth!*

Jill, who was 15, and Roger, 16, would tend to meet in café's in the town. Jill remembers two in particular: *The Riverside and The Galleon were both café's. The Riverside was a little hang-out behind the Cathedral - Old Bridge Street I think. Right next to the bridge over the River. It used to have fishing nets from the ceiling and candles in bottles - very moody! I think we had some impromptu music things in there. The Galleon was the café that used to be in Victoria Square where Argos is now.*

The cafés became places where musicians from different bands could meet. Pete Stanton: *I remember the Riverside Cafe. I used to go there on a Saturday morning and have chips and coffee. All the bands went in there.*

John: *The Riverside Cafe on Old Bridge Street was the only real meeting place in Truro. It was either that or the Wimpy bar opposite the museum…*

Graham: *With us lot, we'd go in to The Riverside, and have one cup of coffee and make it last the whole afternoon! They used to do great corned beef sandwiches too. It was handy for the Truro School boys. Not many from my school went in there, but I could get away with it because I was a musician so I was 'accepted'. We used to meet there to discuss the latest records and the fact that Bob Dylan was going electric. All this sort of stuff we'd sit down and debate in great detail.*

And there were girls there too. In fact wherever Roger was there were girls. He was baby-faced, with long blond hair, jeans a size too small, high heeled boots - Cuban heels - and a black velvet jacket. Roger was always very conscious of his image. He would customize his drumkit too. He covered it with black and white sticky-backed plastic from Woolworths at one point.

Malcolm Broad: *He was always fashion- conscious. Tight jeans were very fashionable and I remember him sitting in the bath at his house in Park View trying to shrink his pair!*

Graham Hankins saw a lot of Roger Taylor during this period: *I recall Roger in my mother's front room in Highertown putting a copy of the West Briton over some cushions and playing it with some knitting needles.*

The harbour in the coastal village of Mullion as it appeared in the West Briton May, 1965

The earliest Reactions concerts were organised with the help of Roger Brokenshire and the 'Teen Promotions' gang. Graham: *We did a lot with Roger Brokenshire and his business partner Jack Pascoe. They would go and hire village halls: Mullion, Coverack, Helston anywhere, and they'd poster them up, then have groups like us go and perform. And of course in those days they used to just fill up.*

Jack Pascoe had been at Trewirgie School with Brokenshire, and by then both had jobs at Tom Mutton's butchers in Truro. They had been involved with organizing Rock 'n' Roll nights since the late 50's. Jack Pascoe, who still has a broad Cornish accent, recalls gigs with The Reactions: *Mullion on Thursday night was fantastic. We used to have to refuse entry it was so busy there. We did it for 2 or 3 years, once a week. Roger (Brokenshire) and I used to book the groups. We did all the running and organised it for everybody. Couple of nights a week we had to go out with posters. We would go over to Jolly's when they were at Carharrack and get the pop. We'd get their home-made pop and so on and take that over. I ran dances at Perranporth, Mullion, Hayle for years, and a few at Penzance with Eric Langman.*

Early that Summer Roger and Mike took their O-levels. Then on 17th July Johnny Quale and the Reactions played in Launceston at a barbeque organised by the North Cornwall Conservatives. Graham: *Johnny had bought this new fangled PA with echo on it and the Conservative party candidate wanted to speak through his microphone. Johnny deliberately turned the echo up so his voice echoed around the field. It was funny...*

John: *By then Jim had passed his driving test so the group's transport for these far-flung venues was his father's MG Magnette and my mother's 5 cwt Ford Thames van, driven by either her or by me with an accompanying driver. On one occasion I remember my mother had to make a hurried journey from St Merryn, near Padstow, to Truro and back when Roger found that he had forgotten to pack his drum sticks before the van left Truro!*

The Reactions were eager to accept opportunities to perform, and, through a misunderstanding found themselves booked to appear at St Ives Rugby Club where they were expected to provide the music for a night of ballroom dancing. In order to fulfill the commitment John Snell's Uncle Vic, who was a pianist, was asked to help. John: *The club had clearly thought it was booking a mini-dance band. Vic was persuaded to become an honorary member for the evening. Most of it saw Roger delivering strict tempo for waltz, quickstep, cha-cha and foxtrot whilst Vic did most of the work! Only at the end were The Reactions able to play. The club did pay up, whilst muttering that the evening was not what they had expected.*

During Summer 1965 the band traveled to Devon for their first mini-tour. Graham: *We went on to work for Lionel Digby in Devon because Roger Brokenshire had done it all before. I remember him one night we played in the Bamboo Club in Redruth (part of Tabbs), and coming to me and saying 'Do you know what's happened tonight? You guys have now clicked. Before you were individuals and now you're a band'. I always remember him saying that.*

Lionel Digby with Screaming Lord Sutch and The Savages. On the far left is Ritchie Blackmore later of Deep Purple and Rainbow. Collection: Roger Brokenshire

It seems Brokenshire felt confident enough to recommend them to the promoter who in turn booked them into some large venues on the other side of the Tamar. Graham Hankins: *Lionel had organised for one of the local bands in Torquay who had a Commer van and a driver to chauffeur us around with our kit. But Acker Snell's mother drove up from Cornwall with it and went off and stayed in lodgings whilst we went up in Jim Craven's Dad's Magnette.*

John Snell: *Lionel Digby was obsessed with the Wild West. He used to go round Torquay dressed in cowboy gear complete with six-guns. The very first time we met him we'd arrived in Torquay where there was no sign of him, we did the gig, and were sitting around on the amplifiers wondering what to do next, when suddenly there was a crash and a bang from downstairs as he let off his guns and the door was thrown open, and Graham found himself staring down the barrell of this six-gun!*

Graham: *We played St George's Hall, Exeter and I'd never been in a place so big in my life, and Johnny, the singer, was petrified! We lost him in the toilet for about 3 hours! He was prone to nerves and I wasn't much better. So he'd have this tonic stuff for his throat and would get in some state. We played St George's as headliners, with a band supporting us. Roger Taylor and Mike Dudley were only 15.*

They'd had Peter Jay and the Jaywalkers there the night before and we pulled a bigger crowd than they had.

John: *St George's Hall was a bigger than the City Hall in Truro, and was really beyond the capacity of our amplifying equipment.*

Graham: *We then went on to the Lansdowne Club in Torquay, which I think was run or owned by Lionel Digby. We had orange shirts and black ties and the audience were fascinated by us. Lionel Digby, though, was mad as a hatter. He was off his trolley! Absolutely off his trolley! He looked after us mind, but he was unbelievable. He had a bugle that he used to blow out of the window as we drove along in the van!*

John: *On these visits to Devon overnight accommodation was spartan, ranging from sleeping in vehicles in a lay-by on the Exeter by-pass to the lounge floor of some friends in Plymouth.*

After their escapades that summer the boys in Roger Taylor's year entered the sixth form at Truro School. Roger and Mike, together with Les Brown, Pete Gill-Carey and Malcolm Broad were in a class of twenty predominantly studying sciences at A-level. In the lower sixth their form master was Mr Taylor (no relation) who was, for many years, deputy head at the school.

Roger Taylor 1965. Detail from Truro School official photograph

Roger took Biology, Chemistry and Physics. Malcolm: *Roger wasn't into sport at school. He was self-taught as a musician and so he wasn't even involved with music at school either. I remember doing endless dissections of dogfish as part of A-level biology with him. The teacher was Brian Jackson. Roger was very adventurous and lively, and when it came to chemistry, he would always jump ahead with experiments and would mix up the reagents more enthusiastically than he ought to! He was naturally a bit of a risk-taker, but very likeable with it. He didn't* exactly get into trouble at school - that would be putting it too strongly - but he was often the one to get a verbal 'whiplashing' from Colin Taylor, Brian Edwards and Alan Plester who were the Chemistry teachers.

Richard Halliwell and Roger shared a passion for following the latest musical trends. Richard: *Later, in the 80's Roger said that, back then, I knew more about music than he did. We would sit and yack forever about bands and what was going on. The prep labs were in-between the physics labs (then rooms 9 and 10 I think) on the ground floor near where the form room was. I seem to remember there was a kettle and an old toaster there that we used during break time. Thursday was the highlight of the week, because every Thursday Roger and I would get the Melody Maker and we'd sit and get a coffee and scan through it. We were both deeply into music at that time.*

Bert Biscoe, now a city Councillor in Truro and about three years younger, remembers Roger and Richard, or Dick, acting as lunch monitors: *Most of the sixth formers had to sit at tables with the younger kids. There were 12 boys on each table, and everyday Roger would be there as our table head, with Dick as the deputy. Roger and Dick were best buddies. Roger would have had to stand up whilst grace was said to the whole school. Then they'd help dish the food out, after helping themselves. I'd eat all the semolina. Roger didn't really talk to us younger boys, though he'd shout 'pass the peas Biscoe' in his high pitched voice. Dick and he would talk to each other from each end of the table about music, and what they'd done the previous night. Roger struck me as being rather self-contained, whereas Dick was more jovial - on the whole.*

Richard Halliwell: *There were two sittings - boarders and day boys. We all stood while one of the masters on the top table said grace, then sat down and the head of table served. Food arrived in large rectangular aluminum pans. It was probably just the sort of food you would expect for the period, so puddings were custard-based: roly poly and custard, spotted dick and custard, banana custard etc. There was one main dish and one pudding - no alternative choices - it was eat it or leave it. And we ate it - especially after PE or games!*

Neither Richard or Roger enjoyed winter sports: *Games in the winter could be more than a challenge for those not of a sporty nature. Taylor and I were n't interested or any good, but skiving off was quite difficult. One particularly cold, windy day our obvious lack of interest in rugger was rewarded by being told to run round the field. At least we generated some warmth that day…*

View of Truro from the rugby pitches of Truro School. The Science Block, where Roger Taylor studied for A-levels, is visible behind the trees.

Cross-country involved running up Trennick Lane, over several ploughed fields to Malpas and back. There was one point where a stream with a steep slippery bank beyond had to be negotiated, and there were speedier boys who waited at the top ready to push the stragglers back down into the water! Showers and changing were pretty primitive - a wooden hut across from the entrance to the Science Block. There were no fancy trainers or branded sports wear then. Still we all survived and I expect it was 'character building'…

Away from school Richard and Roger had become regular partners for concert-going. On October 14th the two of them went with Mike Dudley, John Snell and others to see The Who perform at The Skating Rink in Camborne, then used as a large roller-skating disco. Still fresh on the scene, The Who had had their first top ten hits that year, and their drummer Keith Moon became one of Roger's idols. Richard: *We arrived early enough to catch the sound check. I well remember the sheer volume, it was like nothing we'd heard before! We must have persuaded someone to give a lift as none of us were old enough to drive in '65.*

The popular story is that the volume blew out the rear windows of the venue! Certainly The Who were in full flight - massive drums and stacks of feedback throughout the night. The high energy singles 'I Can't Explain', 'Anywhere, Anyhow, Anyway' and 'My Generation' all featured. Plenty of windmill guitar playing and Moon drumming as only he could: it was electrifying! I could hardly hear a thing until about lunchtime the next day!

Mike Dudley: *The Who were loud. Roger tried to model himself on Keith Moon, but actually the way he played was much more like Mitch Mitchell. He could play Hendrix drum patterns beat for beat...but Keith Moon used to wear a suit, and he inspired Roger to buy a mohair suit because, for a while, that's who he thought he was!*

School-friend Peter Gill-Carey describes a more sedate performance in November 1965. Peter's father was a GP in St Agnes, and the family lived in a large house called Penkerris at the entrance to the village: *The Reactions played at a birthday party – either mine or my sisters – and we had the drums and other instruments in the lounge. My mum was apoplectic because Roger tried to drive nails into the floor. They'd have played for about an hour, and we cleared out the furniture, rolled the carpet up and invited lots of people round.*

It is likely to be a stripped down version of the Reaction, as members like John Snell do not remember being there. John: *Roger would use the nails every time to stop his kit moving forward, as he would hit the pedals very hard. I remember an instance when the bass drum actually went off the front of this stage...That's when the nails first appeared...*

Peter's mother Dorothy, now in her eighties, describes other aspects of Roger's preparations: *Roger was a charming boy. We always used to have a nice blazing fire going in the drawing room and I remember him at the party asking very politely if he could warm up his drum skin in front of the fire. How many other boys would have even noticed that their drum had gone out of tune?*

At the suggestion of Dorothy Gill-Carey the band also played in the Wesleyan Hall beneath the chapel in St Agnes at an evening organised by the WI. *They were playing to the WI ladies, some of whom were quite elderly, and they thought it was a bit loud. I remember some of them taking out their hearing aids. But the president was rather taken with Roger. 'That little drummer was wonderful' she said afterwards.*

View of the Truro River from Trennick Lane: used for Truro School cross-country running during the sixties.

Dorothy tried to help the band in other ways: *I used to design their posters. I had a school certificate in lettering and I did it for well over six months.*

There were gigs in more formal venues too. Graham: *We did a lot of work for The Flamingo that year. The one that sticks in my mind is Jimmy Powell and the Five Dimensions. They were a tremendous band. Back then not only did we struggle to get enough numbers to play but we were struggling to get enough decent amps and mics and so on together. We ended up using their kit, and we had a fantastic evening with them.*

Joy Simpson (nee Hone) was the manageress. She was a right hard case. 'Come on my lovelies its time you started' she'd say. And the bouncer was Fred Sinclair whose sons went on to become professional wrestlers. Lovely old boy, he was, with two cauliflower ears.

Graham Hankins also remembers regular visits to Falmouth in 1965: *We did a lot with Monty Banks, manager of The Princess Pavilion. His normal job was working with the gas board, in middle management. There again, fabulous man, who always put on a dinner suit. Half the floor would be fighting down there but he'd still be there in his dinner suit!*

Advertised gigs in 1965 at The Princess Pavilion include 14th August (support to The Dowlands), 25th September (support to the Couriers) and 20th November (support to Rikki and the Layabouts - advertised as 'The Reactions featuring the original Sandy'). The November gig was one of the first without Johnny Grose. Graham: *Johnny left the band because he wanted to watch an Elvis film. That is true. We got a booking on a Saturday. He said 'I shan't be there because there's an Elvis Presley film on, so if you do it, you'll have to do it without me'.*

Jim Craven suggests that, actually, his nerves may have finally got the better of him. It seems Roger 'Sandy' Brokenshire, who wasn't the sort to get nervous, willingly offered his services instead. John Snell: *Roger Brokenshire first sang at short notice at a Saturday dance in St Keverne that he was organizing with Jack Pascoe. Johnny Quale's increasingly erratic voice frustrated him and affected his confidence, as well as causing tensions in the group. Matters came to a head in November 1965 when Johnny decided that it was more important to see the latest Elvis movie than sing at the booking in St Keverne. Roger Brokenshire (Sandy) was persuaded at short notice to come out of retirement for the evening. And an extraordinary night followed! Sandy had dusted off his gold glitter jacket and gave an object lesson on how a singer should engage with his audience, digging out every stage trick from a long career of talent shows, tours and study of other artistes. The audience loved it, and the group found it exhilarating and strangely liberating! After that there was no going back...*

Roger Brokenshire for the best part of a year, became The Reaction's singer. Graham: *Roger Brokenshire stepped in and he was a showman. Gold lamé jacket and black drainpipes and all the gear. He was really*

One of the first Reaction gigs after Johnny Quale had left the band.

good. We called him Sandy, because he'd originally been Sandy and the Beachboys.

As well as being involved with music promotion Roger Brokenshire had had experience as a child singer. Holman's made heavy machinery for the Cornish tin mines, and at the time was still one of the major employers in Cornwall. Roger Brokenshire: *I've been singing all my life. In 1952 I won the Holman's Canteen Championship for Cornwall. Then I went on the Carroll Levers Discovery Show recorded on BBC Radio that came down to the City Hall in Truro.*

As a teenager he went on to sing regular spots at the Flamingo Ballroom. As a result Brokenshire was recommended to Lionel Digby: *I was with Lionel for about 4 years. I knew him when he first started his agency business in Paignton.*

Lionel suggested Brokenshire adopt the stage-name 'Sandy' when he first sang with his backing band 'The Beachboys' who were based in Bodmin and North Cornwall, but played further afield.

At the time that he joined The Reactions, however, Sandy was also holding down his day job, as well as organizing dances with Jack Pascoe: *I was working T. Mutton's in Victoria Square. I'd have been in my early twenties. They would have been younger. They were still school lads.*

The earliest surviving photograph of The Reactions performing live was taken that Christmas at Truro School, and for some reason Sandy was not actually taking part. Graham Hankins: *If you look at that Christmas photograph it's me singing, and Roger Taylor. Roger and I actually started doing a bit of harmony together. I remember doing The Searchers 'When you walk in the Room', and 'Route 66' that was The Stones' version, and 'In the Midnight Hour'.*

The photograph is one of many taken by Louis Pascoe, a lab technician who worked at the school and was friendly with the boys. The school had a room that was often used for dances, as Geoff Daniel recalls: *It was the old common room on the right as you go through the main entrance. We played there a couple of times after the gig with Graham Hankins that was photographed. It caused a bit of a problem as many of the local girl's schools turned up, and Derek (Burrell – headmaster) wasn't amused by some of the goings-on in dark corners!!*

As the image shows, during 1965 Mike had switched to playing keyboard. John Snell: *He initially played an electric piano that was a very temperamental thing, then he invested in a Vox Continental. The piano was unreliable. It would sound like it was going out of tune and it wasnt really robust enough for moving around.*

We never practiced at Truro School. Although most of the people involved in The Reaction were at the school, the group basically grew up separately from it. The staff were sniffy about the band at first, until later when we played at that dance. It was quite a revolution, actually, to have a dance at the school. We were the first rock or pop group to play there.

The Reactions playing at Truro School, Christmas 1965: L to R Jim Craven, Graham Hankins, Roger Taylor, Acker Snell, Mike Dudley

Richard Halliwell explains the Esso tiger in the photograph: *The common room was fairly near the chapel. We were allowed to decorate the room with posters and so on, hence the tiger in the photo. We were given fairly free reign in that respect - within reason. The school was still rather traditional. Bear in mind we all still had to wear caps, and the prefects wore velvet caps with tassles.*

The same common room had a record player, which during the day Roger and Richard would monopolise. Richard: *Roger was very keen on a band called The Creation. The thing that attracted him was that their guitarist was the first to play his guitar with a violin bow. He liked the theatrical element involved. We had a sixth form common room and Roger's copy of that Creation song got played there again and again.*

That same December The Spencer Davies group had a number one hit. Richard: *There was a record shop called Fords and Roger went to buy two copies of 'Keep on Running' by Spencer Davies, one for each of us. I also remember him bringing the record that The Reaction made into* school. *He'd have played it in the common room and I later I borrowed it.*

During the time Roger Brokenshire was the singer, Roger Taylor's house at 1, Hurland Road had become The Reactions' centre of operations. Roger Brokenshire: *We used to rehearse in Roger Taylor's Mum's garage, in the bungalow at the end of a cul-de-sac. Roger used to come around after school and wait for me to finish work. He was really keen. He was quiet, a smashing guy though. I liked Roger. I remember walking up Lemon Street with him.*

Despite being the youngest member of the group Roger Taylor was, by force of personality, gradually becoming more influential. Richard: *I think he'd already decided music was what he wanted to do and so it mattered to him more than the others. Roger became the driving force behind the band. Mike was not far behind him, but Roger would have done most of the bookings.*

1966: Rock and Rhythm Champions

Graham Hankins left the band soon after the Truro School Christmas concert, and was replaced by Geoff Daniel, also known as Ben, who was a Truro School boy in the year above Roger Taylor. Graham: *My last gig with Reaction was at Truro High School for girls. We did an instrumental number that night by drummer Sandy Nelson called 'Let there be drums' which gave Roger the focal point. When Paul Rogers and Queen did their big concert in Sheffield - which I've got on DVD - Roger Taylor does a version of it then. And I sat in my chair at home as a 60 year old and thought 'I remember the first time he did that. I played it with him then...'*

Mike Dudley's friend, Jenny Doble from St Agnes, arranged the dance at the girl's High School and would have approached Mike beforehand. *We would have had teachers invigilating so nothing got out of hand. 'The Reactions' were the main attraction, and they played for at least an hour.*

John: *Geoff's arrival brought a new sound to the group that suited some of the other changes that were taking place. Sandy was very taken by soul music and considered that it suited his voice and the new line-up. He had access to records that had not yet been released so much new material was introduced, particularly from James Brown, Wilson Pickett and Otis Redding.*

Advertised dates early in 1966 included more dances in Coverack, at Lambeage Hall, and St Brannock's Hotel, Newquay. Then, having come fourth the previous year, the band started preparing for the '66 Rock and Rhythm Championship which was scheduled for the 7th of March. Much now depended on their new singer. Jack Pascoe: *I remember them practising in Malpas. I helped them choose the songs they sang that night. Roger Brokenshire has a particular style, and 'The Midnight Hour' suited his voice perfectly.*

The band also made use of the old Boys Club at the bottom of Lemon Street, and during their preparations, considered every detail. John: *Firstly the group's name was changed from The Reactions to The Reaction. Plus our appearance was changed: we all wore black polo neck jumpers and dark brown trousers, whilst Sandy wore a sheepskin jacket that had been custom made for him at the Morelands sheepskin factory in Redruth, dyed orange, blue and silver. Finally the group name on Roger's bass drum was replaced by a black and white bullseye which pulsated hypnotically at every beat. Following Graham's departure Roger was also now providing the backing singing for Sandy.*

The Reaction on the night of their success in the Rock and Rhythm Championship, 1966. L to R: Jim Craven, Geoff Daniel (Ben), Roger Brokenshire (Sandy), Roger Taylor, Mike Dudley, John Snell (Acker). Photo: Geoff Daniel

I remember the dressing room used by the Reaction that night was thick with the odour of Right Guard deodorant and Cossack hair spray! Plus some judicious stage make-up that Sandy considered necessary to counteract the lights. The hall was packed and very noisy as competing groups of fans screamed for their favourites.

Roger Brokenshire: *The atmosphere at The City Hall was electric...The groups came from all over Cornwall and they all had their own fans. They were mainly teenagers. They were meant to be seated, but they were jumping around, shouting and screaming and dancing, and they all had their boards and banners up!*

John: *The Reaction were in a league of their own that night. As the curtains rolled back Roger Taylor launched into a 13 second drum solo as a prelude to the group's own interpretation of 'In the Midnight Hour'. After the first two riffs Sandy bounced up to the microphone wearing his extraordinary jacket and the hall was alight! This was swiftly followed with Carol King favourite 'Will You Still Love Me Tomorrow?'*

The West Briton reporter was struck by the sheer amount of noise generated by the audience. Under the headline *'Beat Night is a Screaming Success'*, the article continues: *banners, streamers, whistles and cat-calls greeted every group, and emotions ran high as rival supporters clashed in vocal battle.*

John: *When the group repeated their set at the end of the evening there was mayhem at the front of the stage as disappointed girl supporters of the St Austell groups confronted their gleeful counterparts from Truro! The last publicity photographs show the stage strewn with discarded banners.*

The paper goes on to suggest that The Reaction's success may have been due to their unusual choice of instruments: *'Thousands of pounds-worth of equipment was used for the contest, but there was little originality or variety in the choice of instruments. The Reaction, a group that had been playing in its present form for only ten days was judged the winner. The five instrumentalists are all sixth-formers at Truro School, and their vocalist, Sandy, is a one-time professional singer. The group...gave a highly polished performance...Their vocalist, Sandy, wore a tricolour sheepskin coat and rainbow trousers, and at the end of the performance was mobbed by young girls'.*

The judges in 1966 were Joy Hone from The Flamingo, John Adams of The Winter Garden and John Curnow leader of the Ray Allen band, with whom Manny Cockle had started working.

The night was not without controversy, and emotions ran high. The point was not missed by The Cornish Guardian in an article that singled out their guitarist, Tony Coxon, for praise: *When the judges announced that The Dissatisfied had not been been placed disappointed fans who had travelled from St Austell, Mevagissey and Par went wild. Paper was thrown and insults were hurled at the judges.*

The Reaction's prize for winning included a cup which Roger kept proudly on the low slate mantelpiece in the bungalow at Hurland Road. John: *After the cheering had subsided there was no doubt as to who would be the winners, and the silver cup spent the next year on Roger's Taylor's mantelpiece. It was like a totem to him!*

The band was also given a support slot with Gerry and The Pacemakers at the Flamingo, which took place on the 17th of March. The Reaction would have bumped into Mike Grose again because by then The Individuals had split, and he was with The Smokey Joes: the other support act that night. Mike: *Yes, I was there. Although Gerry's music wasn't my thing, the guy had bags of charisma: a true people's person and a very entertaining gig.*

The other prize, an audition with the BBC, never materialized. However the group came close to appearing on television when, in the spring not long after the championship, they were considered for Opportunity Knocks. John: *The Opportunity Knocks auditions were advertised on Westward TV and we were slotted into a Sunday morning session. We presented 'Midnight Hour' at the Ballard Theatre in Plymouth and Roger Taylor's entry drum solo followed by Sandy's bound on to centre stage caught Hughie Green's attention. We received a letter from the producer at ABC TV to say that our audition had been successful and that we would hear further from them. But we didn't...*

Later in March an advert was placed proudly referring to The Reaction as Cornwall's champion Group. It included a four digit phone number. John: *The telephone number was Jim Craven's house in Malpas. Household phones were much less common in those days. I think*

Roger's family was on the phone because of his father's employment as a driving examiner, but at that time most Reaction bookings would have gone through Jim. My mother didn't have a phone until the mid-seventies, so I used phone boxes on the Moorfield car park or at the bottom of Lemon Street.

The Reaction's enhanced status was exploited in many of the subsequent advertisements, such as one in May for a gig at The Penmare Hotel, Hayle: *'Friday Night is Beat night with The Reaction, Cornwall's champion group'.*

With the increasing frequency of bookings, it became sensible for the Reaction to have their own transport. They ended up buying a well-worn Bedford Dormobile - in Jack Pascoe's name - from a private seller.

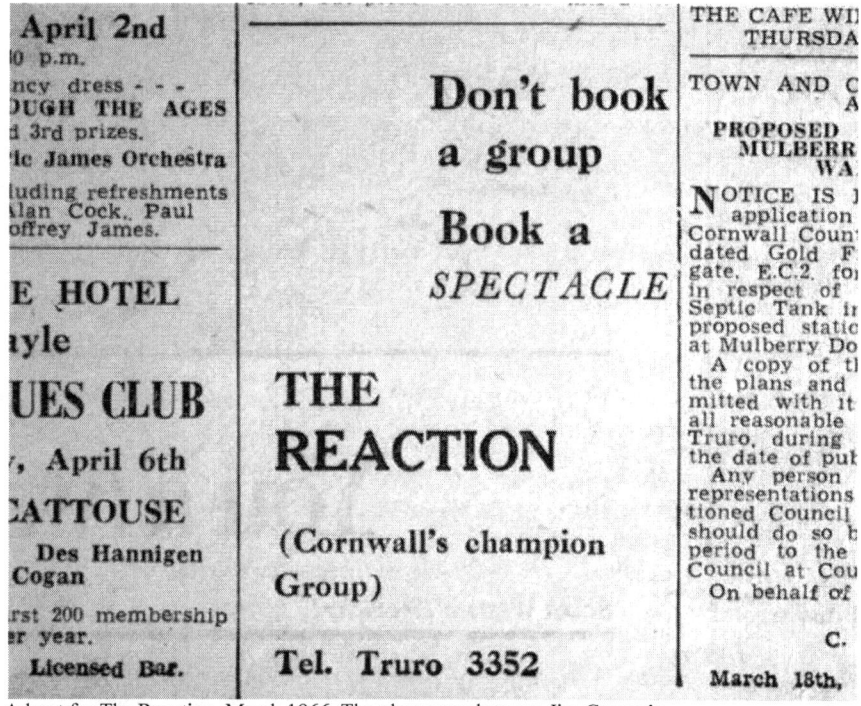

Advert for The Reaction, March 1966. The phone number was Jim Craven's.

John: *I usually drove the van. I would have to get up lots of speed going downhill in order to get it up the other side! When the windscreen wipers stopped working we tied them both to a piece of string which we fed through the side-windows so we could operate them manually!*

One of the private bookings at this time came from St Eval American Air Force air base near Newquay. John: *Towards the end of the evening it all turned sour. A young coloured man had obviously overstepped the mark by dancing with a white girl from the camp. There was much shouting and a knife was pulled. The commander's wife tried to intervene, but in the uproar and brief mêlée that followed she was upended and very publicly lost her knickers. The band just played on. Order was restored but it was quite disturbing, and it gave us all an insight into some of the tensions that were still present in America during the sixties.*

Another private booking saw the group playing in a barn in Idless, near Truro. John: *We arrived to find lots of teachers from Truro School in the audience! The night ended noisily with the teachers proving that their bread-roll throwing could match that of anyone else! The following Monday nothing was said, other than the odd surreptitious smile and wink.*

That summer the band was reunited with singer Johnny Quale who, having arranged to make a four song EP for promotional reasons, needed a backing band. Whilst they were there the Reaction also recorded two songs without him.

Everyone involved gathered together one quiet Sunday morning in the cinema in Wadebridge: John: *The stage of the cinema was festooned with microphones that led to a fully equipped control room where the mixers and tapes were located. The group was playing into an empty hall but the sound balance was under the control of the recording engineers. Overall the performance was somewhat restrained and only the final track really came to life.*

When Johnny's session was complete there was still some time left. The engineers suggested that Reaction might wish to make a further recording on their own - for an additional fee. Roger agreed to sing and drum on the basis that as the backing singer he remembered the words to most of the songs. So, with no preparation, tapes were laid down of

'Midnight Hour' and 'I Got You' that formed the A and B sides of the resulting pressing. Both were completed within two takes.

Only a few dozen pressings were produced of each record and after everyone had kept their own copy the remainder was sold through the Riverside Café in Old Bridge Street in Truro.

In St Mary's Sunday School building opposite the Riverside Cafe, other recording sessions, this time involving The Jays, took place. Recording enthusiast Rod Wheatley told Record Collector in 1995 that he remembers Roger Taylor accompanying the girls, and it is thought the tapes are still somewhere in Truro.

Early in 1967, there was also recording session in the Plaza Cinema in Truro but the tapes appear to have been lost. Mike Dudley: *That was a great shame because we did a very, very good session then by chance. It was recorded by the Truro tape recording society and I guess those tapes are around somewhere. They were very good quality and we managed to play reasonably well on them.*

Having played in 1965, the Conservatives invited The Reaction back for their BBQ on July 29th 1966. This time the speaker was a certain Michael Heseltine, who, before becoming a member of Margaret Thatcher's cabinet was the the MP for Tavistock.

The end of the 1966 summer term saw the Bedford van sporting a prominent 'Reaction' logo executed by Roger Taylor in Egyptian-style lettering on the bonnet below the front windscreen.

In August, after a Saturday booking at Carharrack Carnival on the 13th, the band returned to Torquay. The first date was in August supporting Jimmy James and the Vagabonds in the Town Hall, but it coincided with bassist Jim Craven going to College and therefore dropping out of the band. A temporary replacement was found in the form of Rick Penrose, an older boy who had a day-job that he would continue for several years at Peter Boggia's clothes shop in Truro. Rick was about four years older than Roger Taylor, and had been at Truro Cathedral School. After playing with the Blue Aces skiffle group, he had joined The Strangers, another Truro-based group.

One of The Stranger's first concerts had also been one of their biggest: supporting Frankie Vaughan in Truro City Hall in 1962. Queen would make their first ever appearance in the hall in 1970, then go on to play there twice in 1971. Rick: *I used to love it there. It was in need of repair even in the sixties, they'd let it go downhill. But it had wonderful dressing rooms. You had the main auditorium and then they could open up the Annexe to one side. High stage. Orchestra pit. And all the way up the side of the theatre, behind, were the dressing rooms. At the end of the corridor were steps up, and the main dressing room for the stars was up there. The audience would sit on red velvet chairs, that were fixed but could be moved.*

The Strangers posing with Frankie Vaughan in the West Briton. Rick Penrose is the first of the three boys holding guitars.

Whilst The Strangers acted as a support band for other big names coming to Truro, such as Adam Faith in 1963, they also organized their own dances, like a regular spot in the nearby village of Grampound. Rick: *We ran a coach out to Grampound Road where we played every Saturday, and it ended up so popular that we needed three coaches eventually. But sadly John Blewett (guitarist) died aged 20 or 21. The*

Strangers had got to the state where we'd been going for some time and people were falling by the wayside, and Roger asked me to do a weekend in Torquay as a stand-in bass player. He has a wonderful way with people: before you know it you've agreed. I'd always wanted a Fender Precision bass, and he said 'I'll get you that and an amp if you come up and play for the weekend'. That made my mind up.

After a single rehearsal at the old Boys Club Rick traveled up to Devon on a motorbike with his wife-to-be, Valerie, whilst Acker Snell drove the Bedford van.

The Torquay gigs were once again organized with the help of Lionel Digby. John: *In 1966 Lionel had requested that the Reaction appear in Torbay ahead of the Jimmy James gig for a 'Westward TV publicity opportunity'. This turned out to be a publicity stunt at the Totnes Horse Show. We were dressed up as Red Indians and had to follow the horses around the arena, whilst being announced as 'Lionel Digby's new signing for the summer'!*

Jimmy James and the Vagabonds were a difficult act for us to support because they featured the same soul-based repertoire but done in greater depth because they had a full brass section, as opposed to the Reaction's single sax. Not only that, they were also very competent clowns and acrobats with a tremendous zest for life!

Rick Penrose: *We played with Jimmy James and the Vagabonds then went back to the lodgings in Paignton with them. The landlady, Mrs Burt, came down because they brought some women back and at about 3 in the morning they were running around in the garden naked. They got thrown out: 'Everyone out! This is a respectable boarding house!' she said.*

John: *In 1966 Mrs Burt offered the use of a large garage at the back of her property for rehearsals which we were grateful for because the time spent on the road gave us little opportunity to strengthen our repertoire. By this time there was a core of easy-dancing soul-based numbers including: 'Ride your pony'; 'Down in the Valley'; 'Mr Pitiful'; 'Shake'; 'River deep mountain high'; 'Dancing in the Street'.*

The Reaction didn't get to see Cream perform on the Saturday, but did meet guitar legend Eric Clapton in different circumstances the following year. On the 6th August they were booked to play at the Flamingo but ended up spending longer in Devon than they had originally planned: Rick: *We'd finished the gig at Torquay Town Hall, and we had all the stuff to pack up. Roger said 'I'm going to take the van because I've got these two girls and I'm going to run them home'.*

We said 'How far is that? He said 'Oh not very far' and off he went with the van. And of course it was hours before he returned and the caretaker said you've just got to go: I want to go home now! So we're out on the street and we're a tad pissed off with him and he eventually comes back and he's like 'sorry, sorry…'

I think that same night, and by then its very late, Mike Dudley noticed that the palm trees in Torquay city centre were lit with these giant red lights. He decided to stop the van, get out, and saw through the electric cable that was attached to one of the lights, so that we could nick it to use it in our light show!

The following week The Reaction returned to Devon this time as support to the Kinks. This time Lionel Digby found them a local bass-player called Geoff Hawkey. Geoff already knew Roger 'Sandy' Brokenshire, having played with him in a band called The Rockin' Rockardo's. Geoff: *Lionel Digby said 'Sandy has been asking after you, saying they want a bass player'. So we practiced in The Old Cop Shop in Torquay, next to Lionel's shop, for 3 or 4 hours one Saturday afternoon, then that it was it. We were off to a gig. Lionel did a lot for the teenagers in Torbay. He is a great character.*

The following night the band played further up the coast in Dartmouth, and Mike Dudley still has one of the flyers made for the occasion. Mike: *Roger probably designed it himself. Although it would have been a joint effort and someone would have printed it off cheaply. We charged around in a van, and stuck up posters and handed out flyers ourselves. We spent most of one Summer and part of two other summers up in Devon.*

John Snell: *Geoff Hawkey was a very competent bass-player who had a remarkable ability to fall asleep. As soon as we finished we'd get the van and I'd be the mug driving off and Geoff would be snoring away, sleeping like a top! The van was a very unreliable and it consumed quite a lot of our income in keeping it on the road. In those days there was heavy holiday traffic on unimproved roads, only the A38 between Plymouth and Exeter had any appreciable lengths of dual carriageway, and journey times were significantly longer than they would be today. One night in the darkness of the early hours after a session in North Cornwall the van was crossing Dartmoor towards Torbay when I realised that I'd fallen asleep at the wheel. The van had veered across the road, and I'd only been woken up when it hit the verge on the opposite side.*

As Geoff confirms, the 'Westcountry Tour' took in venues all over Devon and Cornwall: *We played at the Queen's Hall, Barnstable, and I went back to this girl's house and I was an hour or so with her, and when I returned they were just pinning a notice on the stagedoor saying 'see you tomorrow in Wadebridge'. I supposed they expected me to walk there! Then, as well as Wadebridge, there was the Headland Pavilion in Bude. I had a little starting gun when I was in The Reaction, and the two Rogers took the gun down onto the beach at Bude and lost the bloody thing. We were basically living in the van so we had lots of time on our hands. And yes, quite often we slept inside it, and would bring girls back with us. Five of us: Mike Dudley, Acker who had a goatee beard at the time, Roger Brokenshire, me and Roger Taylor. It was not very comfortable, as we had all the gear in there too.*

Sandy and the Rockin' Rockardos, Torquay, 1962. Geoff Hawkey and Roger 'Sandy' Brokenshire are the two looking at the camera. Sandy is wearing socks and an old-fashioned bathing suit. Photo: Geoff Hawkey.

There was a village hall, in South Brent. I remember we had military uniforms, like the Beatles on Sargeant Pepper, which we got from Lionel Digby. For several years afterwards he asked me where they went but we must have lost them. We wore them for a couple of gigs at least.

Whilst in Bude The Reaction met Heinz Burt who had a number one hit with 'Telstar' in 1962. Joe Meek, the legendary record producer is reputed to have fallen in love with Heinz, before going on to kill his landlady and then himself. John: *I remember coming back from Bude where we'd performed with Heinz Burt who had been drinking a lot of vodka. We heard all the Joe Meek stories that later formed a TV documentary. I didn't believe them at the time.*

After the gigs in Devon in 1966, Roger Brokenshire was eased out of the band. Jack Pascoe, his friend at the butcher's recalls: *I think they thought he was necessary to get them a bit further at that stage, but he was always slightly outside the group. The feeling was probably mutual, as Roger had other irons in the fire.*

Rick Penrose: *Roger (Taylor) had a thing about picking people up. He knew we'd have a booking and he'd go 'Let's not pick him up. Let's say...we've forgotten' and we would drive off without them. That's really what happened with Roger Brokenshire.*

John Snell: *Roger Brokenshire left early in September, before the gig supporting The Creation at The Blue Lagoon. The Bedford van left with him, because his friend Jack Pascoe was the registered owner.*

He had a strong voice, and he could really draw an audience in. But I think people felt that his stage performance - which was always animated and lively - was getting a bit over the top. Roger Taylor had only ever filled in and done backing vocals before then. He had to learn how to sing and play drums at the same time. It took him a while, and it was difficult. He always used to sing with his head up leaning forward, and I never quite knew how he managed to do that and play drums at the same time...

After losing the Bedford, The Reaction opted to buy another van, and during September, John found a second-hand Ford Thames. Mike Dudley: *We bought the van for 70 or 80 quid. It belonged to the band, and it was a 6 or 7 year old van near the end of its life.*

Peter Gill-Carey and Neil Battersby, who were in the same year as Roger and Mike at Truro School, were drafted in to help drive it. Pete Gill-Carey: *Neil used to keep it out with him quite a lot because he had more space. We passed our driving tests before the others so we used to drive them around to gigs and things, and I used to go on the door.*

Neil Battersby: *Acker drove a Bedford CA Dormobile. The van Pete and I drove was a navy blue Ford Thames, registration 116 KCV.*

Pete doesn't remember getting a cut of the money: *I didn't do it for money. I was just happy to be there. I enjoyed the music that they played, and if I wasn't on the door, I'd spend the evening dancing with Val Burrows (Ricky's girlfriend).*

Neil was involved with The Reaction for more than a year, and remembers gigs on the water near Restronguet next to Falmouth at the entrance to the Devoran River: *Roger tended to organise things. He had the ambition and the appetite for it, and he wanted to succeed even then. The Reaction played on boat trips up the Fal. I think they may have been birthday parties on a large ferry boat. The boat would have had its own generator for lights etc. It may have been moored at Restronguet, because I remember Roger being down there with his mother's Triumph Herald, and he left the lights on so that when we got back the batteries were as flat as a pancake. We didn't have any jump leads, so had to take a battery out of another car.*

After leaving Geoff Hawkey in Devon, The Reaction hooked up with Rick Penrose again, and the band, increasingly spurred on by their singing drummer, were busy. Rick: *It seemed to me that once I'd joined them I seemed to be working all the time. We were under Pete Brown of BCD so for any of our bookings we were meant to pay him a commission. Of course we would 'forget' to tell him where we were booked, and sometimes he would find out, and sometimes we would change our name and do it under different name. So we played a lot more bookings than are listed.*

It was a hectic schedule: *I was very, very tired. I was working in the day as well. I remember in 1967 getting in at 4 in the morning from Taunton. And I literally couldn't sit down at work because I'd fall asleep. It was that bad. It was a pretty hectic life.*

Keith Harding: *Once Roger was stuck on Bodmin Moor and he phoned me in the middle of the night. There was some reason why he couldn't get through to his father he said 'Could you get Dad please Mr Harding? I can't get hold of him and we're stuck'. So I went over the road and woke his father, Mike, up. It was something like 3A.M. He said 'I'm not going up there now they can wait' And they did. He didn't go up there until at least an hour or so later!*

> **B.C.D. ENTERTAINMENTS LTD.**
> (Members of the Agents' Association)
>
> ## P. D. BROWN
> *(Managing)*
>
> 114 QUEENS CRESCENT   BODMIN 2614
> BODMIN   & 2144
> Cornwall   *(24 hr. service)*
>
> Sole Representation of:
>
> # The REACTION

Both sides of Pete Brown's business card. Collection Rick Penrose.

Despite the disruption and the frequent late nights the Truro schoolboys' parents seemed generally supportive of their efforts. Rick: *Roger's mum definitely was. They all were. They were young lads doing something they wanted to do. There were quite a few gigs we organized ourselves that also didn't go though Pete Brown. There were gigs at Perranporth Memorial Hall that went all through that Summer: might have been a Wednesday evening. We put in some money towards the cost and Roger got people from Truro School to run the door and so on.*

Neil Battersby: *During 1966 the last number was always 'Land of a Thousand Dances', when Roger would do a drum solo and I would flick the lights on and off, and we managed to fuse the electrics at Perranporth Memorial Hall on at least two occasions.*

The steps from the high street up to Perranporth Memorial Hall (2010). Built in 1957 and largely unchanged since.

Newspaper ads were not used for Perranporth gigs. Neil: *If I remember correctly we made fluorescent posters and Roger used to go out and stick them up on telegraph poles using wallpaper paste, and put them in shops and that kind of thing. It cost money to put ads in the West Briton.* Mike: *There's a captive audience in Perranporth. The tourists wouldn't read the papers, so no ads, but we did leafleting and flyers instead.*

Pete Baron: *They were playing in Perranporth in the hall in the middle of the town when Roger exchanged a very fine leather jacket for his first Zildjan cymbal. There was a band down from Sheffield (the Staggerlees?) that night, and they used to play at Perranporth each year, and Roger swapped bits of clothing for bits of their kit!*

In 1966 Jill Johnson's group, by then renamed 'The Jayfolk', were also busy and frequently performed at the Tell-a-tale Folk Club, Chapel Street, Penzance where Cornish stalwarts John the Fish and Brenda Wootton were regulars. Notable visiting musicians included Arlo Guthrie - son of legend Woody - who also sang there. Jill Johnson: *I think Des Hannigan used to play there a lot. The Jayfolk used to sing some of the songs he wrote - great guy! Jayfolk didn't sing many original songs, just a couple of Des's, maybe one of John-the-Fish's and a couple of our own. In 1966 we were also on Westward TV Folk Wave series, with Martin Carthy and Dave Swarbrick.*

Jayfolk on the Hoe, Plymouth at the time of their appearance on Westward TV, November 29th 1966. They were billed as The Johnson Girls.

Jill was at school with Gill Wilton, a girl who was going out with and would later marry Vaughan Hankins, Roger Taylor's neighbour and classmate. Vaughan: *The two Jills were at school together so we used to go out as a foursome to places like Flo's Bar in Devoran. There was a real character who sat at the bar called Blossom. Tregye Country Club was another in-place. It had a cellar bar with huge pillars, candles in VAT69 bottles and a ceiling that was yellow from cigarette smoke. I was always the driver. Roger hadn't passed his test, so it would have been late 1966.*

John: *Because Roger was going out with Jill Johnson, her group The Jayfolk sometimes came to Reaction rehearsals and joined in on the* soul numbers. The result was very effective and on one occasion they were persuaded to be backing singers at a concert, which turned out to be the Flamingo. When the girls arrived they were not comfortable with the big hall compared to the folk venues where they normally sang. So we agreed they could have a microphone backstage and sing behind the curtain. They took up their position behind the curtain, and the sound balance was being checked when there was a loud shout from the hall: 'Hey you misseys, get off my stage - no groupie girls backstage in my hall!' It was Joy Hone, the owner, and she was in full flow. The group had forgotten to inform her that there was going to be an experimental line-up with girl singers. There was no remonstrating with Joy, her word was the law in the Flamingo, and that was the end of the idea of the Jayfolk singing in public with Reaction, as the very embarrassed girls returned to the dance floor...

Rik Evans had bought Penrose's marquee company in January, 1966, when he was 21 and he and his company helped provide opportunities for both The Reaction and Queen. Rik Evans: *Not sure how Roger and I very first met. The first thing we did together was when he still had The Reaction, and, that year, I booked the band for weddings and things. We got to know each other once I'd taken the business on. Back then Roger used to spend a lot of time sitting on the railings outside what was WH Smith down at the bottom of town whistling at girls. That was his main pastime, when he should have been at home doing his homework! I think he was a bit of a rebel, old Roger. But there's nothing wrong with that.*

Later, Led Zeppelin became a big influence on him. I remember, after Queen had formed, being down at Hurland Road playing one of Led Zeppelin's early albums and a group of us all sitting round listening to it.

Roger, Mike and their contemporaries entered 'Sixth Science' in September 1966, with Mr Scales (known as Fishy by the boys). Growing in confidence, that autumn they hired out a large hall in the middle of St Ives on more than one occasion, describing themselves proudly as having *'recently returned from their West Country Tour'*.

Dave Dowding: *A couple of times we hired local halls like the Guildhall in St Ives. I used to go on the door and take the money. Roger was singing and was very much the front man by then.*

Truro School Yearbook 66/67

The town, which for at least a decade had enjoyed an international reputation as a leading centre for modernist art, was now subjected to a poster campaign orchestrated by Roger Taylor. John: *I think the posters were designed by Roger. They were a Dayglo base colour: orange, pink or green, with black printing and a space for the venue to be written in felt pen. We would go to an area and set off in different directions armed with paste and brush or drawing pins, generally choosing convenient telephone poles. The campaign nearly came to grief in St Ives when Roger spotted a good site on an electricity sub-station that had clearly been used for promoting every event in the locality! He used copious amounts of wallpaper paste to ensure that the carefully aligned dayglo poster would last until the event was over. But as he stepped back to admire his handiwork a voice from behind said 'Very nice sir. Now take it down'. Such was his concentration he had been unaware that the local constabulary had been observing him for the past five minutes!*

Richard Halliwell: *I remember going to the Guildhall. In those days you could book those halls for next to nothing. Godolphin Hall, Helston was another. There was a bit of a circuit, and there was a gang of us who* were on the door. And I did their lights several times too. They had a battery of lights with different coloured acetates over the front.

Paul Treseder was another Truro School contact who was able to help. He met his future wife at one of the gigs: *John (Acker) Snell roped in his cousin Pamela Dunstan to sell the pop and crisps at these gigs. Pamela and I subsequently got married.*

Les Brown, who later brought Roger and Brian May together, also assisted backstage: *I remember gigs when we used to help with basic light shows. Once we had this mad idea of setting Roger's cymbals on fire. We did it with a rag soaked in petrol which we squeezed on the cymbals, and we nearly burnt the house down. It was in front of an audience somewhere in mid-Cornwall and it was really bloody dangerous! We didn't do it again!*

Rick Penrose: *We used to like to start the concert in total darkness, and for a while Roger put a single light bulb inside his bass-drum so it was the only light on stage. But the bulb kept smashing, so we tried to set fire to the cymbals instead. It was St Blazey where we nearly set fire to the place...*

Later in 1966, probably on 28th October at a Halloween Dance in the City Hall Annexe, Neil Battersby made a recording of The Reaction playing live: *One day I thought I'd take my reel-to-reel along to a Reaction gig and I tried it in the hall and it had a magic eye on it and it distorted because it was far too loud. The microphone was a plastic thing that had a pause button on it with six pins that went in the back of the tape recorder so I put it in the canteen and kept my finger crossed and recorded it. And it was fine until Dick Halliwell came in and started drumming on the table!*

The Guildhall St Ives (2010). In the foreground is a sculpture by one-time St Ives resident, Barbara Hepworth.

In the recording Roger's drumming, whilst driving and strong, is not as flamboyant as it became later and it is his singing that stands out more. His voice is very expressive, and he makes light work of potentially difficult high-pitched soul numbers by the likes of James Brown. Mike Dudley's organ is also prominent in the recording, and Acker's saxophone adds character to two or three of the songs. The concert, which has plenty of raw energy, finishes with a lighthearted 'Looney Tunes'style instrumental finale that the boys had composed themselves.

No guitar is audible. Mike Dudley: *When we decided to become a soul band we thought it would be a good idea for me to play organ because I'd studied piano. We ended up doing a lot of gigs with just organ, bass and Roger, and for a while we played as a threepiece without a guitarist.*

Although not apparent in the recording, on 'Land of a Thousand Dances' by Wilson Pickett, Roger Taylor would improvise by playing an old piano frame. Rick Penrose it recalls ruefully: *It really pissed us off because it was heavy and we had to load it into this damn van every night! He would play it with these soft gong sticks. We carted it around everywhere and wired it up to the PA. We would take it down to the front and Roger would say 'Thankyou very much for coming we hope you've enjoyed it it's been wonderful playing here at whereever', if he could remember where we were which he didn't always. Then he would then go and hit the piano frame for quite a long time. He would do it at the end of the show as part of Land of a Thousand Dances, and it could go on for up to 20 minutes.*

Reaction contract with BCD signed on 28/11/66. Collection Richard Prest (kernowbeat.co.uk)

John Snell *New material started to be introduced after Roger Brokenshire left: the piano frame for Land of 1000 Dances finale appeared not long after this.*

On 28th November the five members of The Reactions signed a contract with BCD entertainments witnessed by Rick's girlfriend, and future wife, Valerie. Lasting a year, it would have followed on from the contract signed in 1965. It promised, but probably didn't deliver, their agent 12½% of their earnings.

In the second half of 1966 The Reaction played at The Blue Lagoon in Newquay five times as support to artists from outside Cornwall. As well as one of Roger Taylor's favourite bands, The Creation on September 17th, this included Screaming Lord Sutch on New Year's Eve.

Lord Sutch, who also worked with Lionel Digby in Devon, was a pioneer of theatrical rock and in the mid-sixties his band included Ritchie Blackmore of Deep Purple. Later Sutch would become the founder of the Monster Raving Loony Party. Rick Penrose: *Lord Sutch couldn't sing, but what a showman! Phenomenal. 'I'm a hog for you baby'. Heavy rock. Solid. Incredible.*

The Blue Lagoon, Newquay 1961 photo Peter Hicks.

John Snell: *Sutch delivered his trademark manic performance - uprooting the ballroom's plastic palms to taunt the audience - and his backing band was very impressive, despite being dressed as Roman legionnaires, complete with helmets, breastplates, kilts and sandals. Afterwards, when Reaction were packing their equipment into the van, Roger was observed in intense conversation with the Roman Legion's organist. Afterwards he told us that he had been invited to join a newly forming band. The organist was Matthew Fisher and by May 1967 the new group, Procul Harum, was known internationally for its record 'Whiter Shade of Pale' that held the no.1 spot for 6 weeks.*

The Reaction also played on Christmas eve in the Flamingo. Rick Penrose: *Acker Snell was dressed up as Father Xmas and shaving foam got sprayed about the stage! It was real party time and the Flamingo was packed from the front of the stage to the back. They'd have buses that would come from around Cornwall.*

1967: Jimi Hendrix, Doug Puddifoot and the accident on Goss Moor

Many of the houses in the Moresk area of Truro were demolished in the latter half of 1966. Work on the relief road or bypass below Truro School had also started in earnest, and continued beyond 1967. By the end of the decade the new road had become Cornwall's first dual carriageway.

Whilst Roger Brokenshire was their singer, The Reaction's set had been dominated by soul numbers. Roger Taylor: *We used to do a lot of soul things. Otis Redding and James Brown classics amongst others: I Feel Good (James Brown), My Girl (Otis Redding), Johnny B Goode (Chuck Berry), I'll Go Crazy (Don Bryant), and Around and Around (Chuck Berry).*

Richard Halliwell remembers the band then: *One favourite was Martha and the Vandellas 'Heatwave' with Roger doing very high backing vocals. It sounded like the 'Scaramouch' bits on Bohemian Rhapsody.*

After 1966, however, partly under the influence of The Who, heavier guitar-based rock became a bigger part of their repertoire. This coincided with saxophonist John Snell moving away from Cornwall to start a course at Portsmouth University. He would, however, return to play with the band on an intermittent basis over the following year.

Rick Penrose: *Do you know 1,2,3? It had a lovely sax intro. He didn't have to play the whole number just parts of it and the sax gave it a certain something. But he always had trouble with his reeds splitting which used to annoy people because they would squeak!*

Neil Battersby: *Acker was a nice bloke but he often managed to set the mics up so they howled, so Mike or Roger would have to go round resetting them so everyone could take their fingers out of their ears!*

One of the first engagements of 1967 was a return visit for The Reaction to the Rock and Rhythm Championship in Truro City Hall this time billed, in an advert of the 12th January, as 'guest artistes'. Peter

Boggia was the compere, with Joy Hone and John Adams again, and Dusty Dunstan (Blue Lagoon) the judges. The West Briton describes an audience of 600 teenagers, and The Reaction as being *'extremely well received'*.

Penmare Hotel in late 1990s (photo Richard Prest www.kernowbeat.co.uk) Now demolished.

27th of January saw the first of a series of bookings at the Penmare Hotel, in Hayle, in the West of Cornwall, followed the next day by another concert in St Ives where the venue and publicity were organised by Roger and Mike. The light-hearted advert, as well as offering OAP's half price entry, referred to cult American band The Electric Prunes. Mike Dudley: *That was just a tongue in cheek ploy to attract attention to the poster! We did think of putting Jimi Hendrix or the Beatles but thought that a relatively unknown but progressive-sounding name was better.*

On the 11th of February the members of The Reaction were picked up from their homes by Peter Gill-Carey, the designated driver that evening. Pete: *I was driving at first. The van was at my house and I'd gone around collecting everybody, but then I swapped seats with Roger in Truro because he had said he wanted to drive. He'd just passed his test.*

The Electric Prunes were an influential psychedelic rock band from the U.S. who at the time of the advertisement had had a minor hit with 'I had too much to dream last night'.

The band, accompanied by two girlfriends, set off to a gig in Dobwalls Village Hall, near Liskeard, when they hit a lorry parked on the main road on Goss Moor, about 5 or 6 miles outside Truro.

Rick Penrose: *You had the driver's seat and the metal engine cover, I was sitting on that. Valerie and Pete Gill-Carey were in the passenger seats. And there was the kit behind us and Mike Dudley was in the back too with that damn piano.*

Neil Battersby: *Val was on Pete's lap in the passenger seat. I was sitting on an amplifier. Mike was with Marian Little, who was his girlfriend at the time. She always said she was a princess; related to the royal family of Hungary.*

Rick: *It was a straight bit of road. The lorry we hit was sticking out and its tail was out in the road. It had no lights on and the reflectors were coated in mud so we didn't see it till it was too late. Roger went right through the windscreen and landed on the road. The van turned over.*

Valerie, who was my first wife, was sitting on the seat with Peter Gill-Carey, who was the one most seriously hurt. But the joint in Valerie's shoulder was also smashed. I think Mike Dudley went out the back doors. The van landed on its roof then slid up the road upside down. And there was the screeching sound of metal on tarmac. It was awful.

I dragged Valerie out but Pete was so bad. He was in a pool of blood. It was early evening, 7 o'clock, and we were blocking all the traffic. I pulled Valerie out because I was afraid the van was going to catch fire so I got her out to the side of the road, but Peter couldn't move. We were just, like, kneeling there with him. I remember being in the City Hospital later and they said 'Don't wait in the waiting room. You're frightening people'. My face was covered in cuts and there was blood everywhere.

Pete Gill-Carey, who suffered severe injuries, was in hospital for almost exactly a year: *I went in in February 1967 and came out in February 1968. In the old days there used to be a hump-backed bridge going over the moor and that's where the accident happened. It was because of the humped-backed bridge that we couldn't see the lorry, which was just the other side, until it was too late.*

The 1967 gig that never was: The Reactions' van crashed en route

A navy blue Ford Thames van like the one in the accident. Picture match by Neil Battersby.

Dorothy Gill-Carey: *They gave Peter 9 pints of blood and, that night and for several days after, they said to me and my husband: 'Don't hope, don't hope'. The injury took all the flesh away from the area under his right arm. And his lungs had collapsed. He had to go to Frenchay in Bristol for skin grafts. They didn't discover until he was in Bristol that he had also lost the movement in his hand.*

I sat with him in the hospital every single day. When he was feeling really bad I used to say 'When you're better, Peter, we can buy a sailing boat and take it down to Carrick Roads and you can learn to sail'. It gave him something to look forward to. And when he recovered we went and bought an Enterprise (sailing dinghy) for him. Peter had to take his A-levels with his left hand. Then a few years later they operated on a muscle in his hand so that he could move his thumb. The court case took several years to sort out. But the driver of the fish van was found guilty and Peter got paid damages.

Since the accident Peter Gill-Carey (pictured in a detail from school photo) has continued to have limited movement in his right hand, and has learnt to write with his left one. Forty years on he isn't bitter or resentful about what happened. Peter: *It wasn't Roger's fault even though he was driving. We were fortunate that a person just before us had reported the van for being badly parked, so the police were already on their way and got there almost immediately. The main problem with the accident was that I was really enjoying life and it put a stop on*

things. Also originally I had been hoping to be a doctor like my father which wasn't then possible. But otherwise I remember those days with much fondness.

Peter recognizes now that if they had not swapped seats, Roger might have been the one that was injured: *Being in the right place at the right time, or the wrong place at the right time. It's just one of those things.*

Geoff Daniel: *I drove myself to Dobwalls that night, so didn't know anything about it until the police arrived and took me to Truro City Hospital that night. I went to Summercourt garage the next day (may have been with Mike Grose who I knew from primary school) to unpack the equipment and assess the damage.*

Roger was driving the van and hit an unlit truck. He was fined and the group paid the fine. It's not a good memory. I was the only one who made it to school on the Monday and the headmaster, Derek Burrell, made me address the assembly and tell the school what had happened.

A few weeks later I was away (ill or on a school trip, I can't remember) and I think Mike Grose - Queen's first bassist - stood in. That was a fairly normal practice among the bands then: bitter rivals in public but mutually supportive in private.'

The accident was reported in the West Briton on both the 13th and 16th of February. Peter Gill-Carey is described as critically ill in the first report, and as slightly improved but still very ill in the second.

Jill Johnson: *Thinking about that dreadful accident brings back memories. I was the one that usually sat in the van where Peter sat. But I was out of the county at a hockey match and didn't get back in time, so they went without me. It could have been me. Very scary. I only found out next morning when Roger's mother called.*

Jenny Doble was one of Peter's St Agnes friends: *I remember going to see Peter in hospital. We were allowed to walk down to the City Hospital in our lunch hour. It was only a day or two after the accident and, surprisingly, we were allowed into intensive care. I was doing A-levels then, and had to go back to double chemistry. But it was really shocking. Awful.*

None of the core band members were seriously hurt in the accident and although the van - and the piano frame - was written off, their concert schedule was not badly affected. Geoff Daniel: *I think we missed a gig or two. None of the band had more than cuts and bruises. But the biggest problem was transport. I think we all drove ourselves with gear to gigs from then on as we knew we were off to Uni in September. I think we stayed as a 4-piece until we went to Uni.*

Rick Penrose: *After the accident Valerie, my wife-to-be, was in hospital and I was under considerable pressure from her to stop playing. I might have taken a week or two off. The windscreen came in and afterwards I would wake up in the mornings and the bed would be full of glass. It would just come out of my skin. I'd have an itch and there would be glass poking up through my skin.*

We were due to get married in March and it was put off until May or so.

Mike Dudley: *The band continued, but with no van, so we managed then with cars. But the result of that crash was that there was a court case. And, wrongly, I believe part of the blame was put on Roger and damages were awarded against him.*

But the accident impacted on Roger Taylor in other ways. Dorothy Gill Carey: *When the accident happened Roger's father went a bit peculiar. He used to go walking on the cliffs. His father must have thought that Roger had ruined his career, ruined his life, and everyone thought that Peter was going to die.*

Advertised engagements in February included a support slot to The Quiet Five at The Flamingo on the 18th of February, and another

The Strangers and girlfriends at The Farmer's Arms, Newquay. Rick Penrose is seated with Valerie Burrows on the left. Photo: Rick Penrose

booking at the Penmare. Mike Grose remembers deputising for Geoff Daniel that night and John 'Acker' Snell temporarily joined them from Portsmouth too, having come to Cornwall to visit as a consequence of the accident.

At the end of February 1967, Roger received a postcard addressed to The Reaction, from Hughie Green inviting them to another audition for Opportunity Knocks in Plymouth. The Jayfolk were also involved.

Though neither group progressed in the competition, Jayfolk still made the front page of the West Briton the following week. As the article explains, Jill's sisters were emigrating: *'One of the most popular groups on the Cornish folk scene is to lose two of its founder members with the*

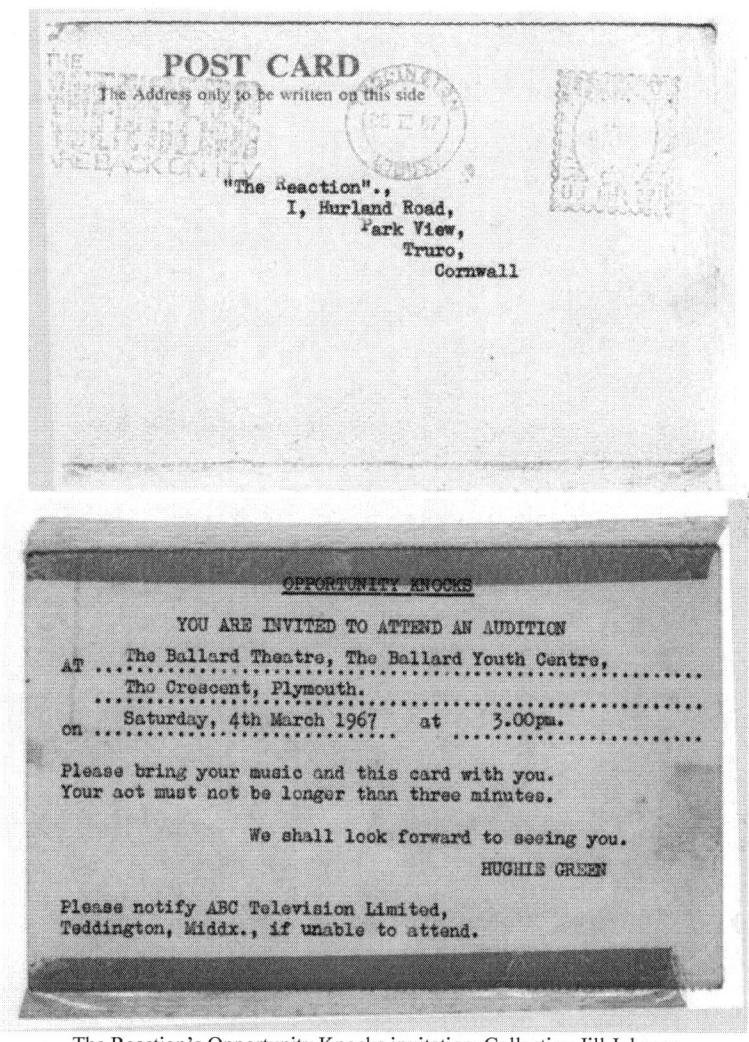

The Reaction's Opportunity Knocks invitation. Collection Jill Johnson

departure to Canada of twins Jennifer and Janet Johnson'. Jill: *My two sisters emigrated to Canada in 1967 and I brought in Penny North and Josie James. But frontpage news? I expect a lot of it had to do with my father being the Town Clerk, we couldn't do anything without being under scrutiny.*

The Jayfolk seizing a photo-opportunity after writing off their Austin van late in 1967. Their name is just visible painted on the side of the damaged vehicle. L to R: Jill Johnson, Penny North, Sue Johnstone, Josie James (driving).

The Jayfolk as well as The Reaction had an accident in 1967, as Penny explains: *I was at Truro Grammar School with Jill and Josie. Josie sang high and I sang low! We used the A35 van which I shared with my mother to travel to gigs, and eventually it had a banner saying 'Jayfolk', in colourful bubble writing, stuck on the side. Sometimes Josie drove it. Unfortunately this van was written off on Penpillick Hill near Tywardreath when we rolled over somewhere near where the escape lane is now. We were on our way home from a second, but unsuccessful, audition for Opportunity Knocks, with Hughie Green. The photo was taken at the top of the drive of Pengarth, my family home in Grampound which we ran as a guest house in those days.*

Jill: *In the photo Sue and I have matching coats on which we had purchased from our savings, after having worked our socks off sorting bulbs for some stingey farmer out Calenick way - during Easter vacation I think.*

The house had a shed that was used as a rehearsal space by Penny's friends. These included Trevor Mannell, Paul Moon and Mike Grose all of whom were later involved with PJ's: the club in Truro where Queen played.

Early March saw gigs for The Reaction at the Princess Pavilion, Falmouth, Penmare Hotel and Blue Lagoon (4th 10th and 11th). Then later in March the Torrey Canyon oil tanker hit rocks off The Seven Stones near Lands End and spilt its cargo into the sea. The story dominated headlines in both the national and local press for several weeks. The impact of the massive oil slick on the wildlife and on the beaches of Cornwall was of most concern, with The West Briton describing Cornwall as being *'all set for battle of the beaches'*.

The following night The Reaction were once again booked to play a Friday night at The Penmare, less than ten miles in-land from the stricken oil-tanker, and they returned twice more in April, also fitting in a gig in the Annexe of the City Hall in Truro on the 20th.

Doug Puddifoot, future Queen photographer, lived in Ruislip, but came to Truro to visit Jill Johnson in Cornwall in 1967. Jill: *I was the one who introduced him to Roger. He was a BBC cameraman and he took several photos of me with Roger at my parent's house one Summer when he was visiting. The picture in the garden was at my parent's house: Summerville, Crescent Road in Truro.*

I thought the garden was pretty big, but everything is relative. Roger used to spend quite a bit of time there - both in the garden and at my house. When my two sisters were there also, there was always a crowd, all our respective boyfriends and other couples. Roger was a regular and my parents and sisters knew him well - quite one of the family. He would come over to hang out, watch TV, listen to music - or I would go over to his house on Hurland Road.

In the 70's Doug helped design the first Queen album cover and took all the early promotional photographs of both Smile and Queen. Doug:

View of Truro from the overgrown garden of 'Summerville', Crescent Road circa 1967. The garden has now been built over. Les Brown's house is off-frame to the right. Collection Jill Johnson.

Although I lived in London, I did visit Truro quite a lot. My cousin was Town Clerk of Truro, and his daughter, Jillian Johnson, was Roger Taylor's girlfriend at the time. So I got to know Roger through Jillian, and also met Sue and Pat Johnston. Roger was in Reaction at the time, but I never saw them play. Then when he came up to London to college we used to meet quite often, and when he was in Smile I used to take photos at their gigs, and that carried on when Smile dissolved, and Queen formed. Then when their first album came out they asked me to take the photos for the cover.

During much of the time she sang with Jayfolk, Jill had short hair, as captured in the photograph. Like the RAF roundel painted on Roger's bass drum, it was inspired by the 'mod' fashions of the mid-sixties. Jill: *The short hair was a Mods style that started in 1964/65. Before that, for the girls, the fashion icon was Cathy McGowan (from the TV Show 'Ready Steady Go!') plus Sandy Shaw and Cher, and they all had long* straight hair. When the Mods came in it was all Lambrettas, short cropped hair and Marks and Sparks twin sets! That's why I had my hair cut. Also, of course, the Mary Quant look was in - mini skirts, very clean, angular looks with bold target patterns. It was great! The dress that I had on in the picture with Roger was a Mary Quant design I think.

Whilst visiting Truro, Doug also took some portrait photographs of Jill's best friend, Sue Johnstone. Later one of the resulting images would reappear, subliminally, in what is probably the first ever photographic print of Queen.

The schools and residential areas of Truro are on the outskirts of the town. Jill: *As regards Roger picking me up from school: it was a bit of a walk from Truro School to the Girl's Grammar School - so I don't believe he walked it that often (and he wasn't into exercise!) More frequently we would meet at each other's homes or downtown.*

When he started driving (1967), he would borrow his mother's mushroom-coloured Triumph Herald, and drive up. In fact, I don't remember him having his own car in Truro, except later when he had this weird station-wagon thing he called 'Matilda' or something. It might have been Mike Dudley's. Dreadful car! He would usually take the Triumph though - and we always ran out of petrol because he never filled it up. I can't tell how many times we'd have to turn off the engine and coast down hills out in the middle of nowhere just to save gas. I was frequently late home (and in dire trouble) because of it.

Access to cars, although owned by their parents, gave Roger Taylor and his friends more independence and they would share lifts and petrol money. On April 25th Dave Dowding drove Roger up to Bristol to see Hendrix at The Colston Hall. Dave Dowding: *We traveled to Bristol for concerts, a high spot being Jimi Hendrix live. I was driving and was just 18. It was unbelievable. Hendrix destroyed everything on the stage. Roger came with me.*

Richard Halliwell: *It was Roger and Dave and myself. We skived off school and went to Dave Dowding's place to get changed first. On the way we called in to see Pete Gill-Carey who at that point, poor chap, was in Frenchay Hospital in Bristol having skin grafts.*

Roger Taylor and Jill Johnson in Summerville's garden circa 1967. Photo Doug Puddifoot.

For all the members of Queen, including Roger, Hendrix was a massive influence. Rick Penrose remembers hearing Hendrix for the first time on Radio Luxembourg: *Right through the fifties and sixties they had a fantastic range of music. And a lot of the Radio Luxembourg DJ's went to Caroline and BBC and what have you.*

All the most interesting music was mainly to be heard on the pirate radio stations: *I was on Perranporth Beach when they (Radio Caroline) went by. That summer its boat sailed up and down the coast and everyone on the beach would be 'wow'. They were transmitting all the time. Saying 'we're just going into Perranporth Bay now and there's Newquay'.*

Truro's best record shop was Ford's opposite the library: *Ford's was a forward-looking record shop so they stocked a wide range of artists that young people wanted whereas the more sedate music shops like Moon's that sold records as well would only have bands like Victor Sylvester.*

Dave Dowding: *As a drummer Keith Moon was the biggest influence: the big drumming sound of The Who. The records were coming out and we just bought them from Ford's. You could go in and listen to a record on headphones before you bought it. I also remember us buying Shadows singles in there, and EPs.*

Having both survived the accident on Goss Moor, Rick Penrose got married to Valerie in May 1967, after the marriage had been postponed because of Valerie's injury. *We had the reception in the Carlton Hotel near the High School. I lived in Midway Drive, Uplands Park and Roger and some of the others came back.*

On May 28th, whilst Reaction played again at the Penmare, regular visitors to Cornwall, Maddy Prior and Tim Hart, who three years later formed folk-rock outfit Steeleye Span, played on consecutive weekends in Truro at the ancient Red Lion hotel. About a month later the front of the hotel was irreparably damaged by a run-away lorry.

Keith Harding was working in the SWEB (South West Electricity Board) offices on Boscawen Street: *I heard this almighty crash and all the phones on that side of the street stopped working. I went out to see*

what had happened and was one of the first on the scene. The lorry was carrying concrete blocks. It was very heavy and its brakes had failed at the top of Lemon Street. The driver sounded his horn all the way down the hill, then when he got to the centre of the town he tried to turn hard right to stop, but hit the Hotel, the front wall of which collapsed. It was amazing that no-one was killed, but his feet were caught up in the wreckage and it took ages to get him out.

In early May The Reaction played 'The Skating Rink' in Camborne, a venue that had hosted the visit by 'The Who' the previous year. Then on the 18th the West Briton announced: 'Cornwall's Battle of the Beaches has been won' as the Torrey Canyon clean-up operation drew to a close. The following week adverts appeared for Ralph McTell at the Folk Cottage and The Reaction supporting Danny and the Belmonts at The Winter Gardens in Penzance.

When it opened in 1964, The Count House was the first of several Folk Clubs that would emerge in Cornwall. By 1967 The Folk Cottage near Mitchell had established itself as the most influential. Opened in January 1966 by John Sleep and John Heyday and located in the countryside not far from the site of the accident on Goss Moor, The Folk Cottage drew nomadic musicians from all over the country, and Roger Taylor and most of the other younger 'rock' musicians visited it.

Mike Grose: *Yes I remember going to the Folk cottage at Mitchell. John the Fish and Ralph McTell were resident musicians I remember. Everyone would be stoned of course. That was the norm then. I went several times.*

Folk musicians in Cornwall undoubtedly smoked cannabis in the 60's, but beer was also consumed at the Folk Cottage. Clive Palmer, who had busked in Paris with Wizz Jones and had cult status as one of the founders of the Incredible String Band, lived there too for a while. Clive: *If you took a large bottle the guy at the local pub, The Plume and Feathers at Mitchell which was half a mile away, would fill it up with beer for you. And you could take it with you. It was ten pence a pint then. We didn't have a license or anything. The main road went through Mitchell, and you went down this lane to a place called Landrine and you'd be there. You wouldn't recognise it now. In those days it was a beautiful place. A wonderful place. It could have been any century, it was so lovely down there.*

The stage was upstairs, and on the wall behind the performers was a distinctive black and white mural of a naked woman, her hand reaching outward towards the audience. In many ways she epitomized the care-free bohemian spirit of the club.

Jill Johnson later made a record with Clive Palmer and The Famous Jug Band. Jill: *I believe Roger and I went to The Folk Cottage at least once together. I'm actually not sure what his views on folk music were. I*

L to R: Clive Palmer, Henry Bartlett and Pete Berriman on stage at the Folk Cottage, with nets and the mural behind. Jill Johnson would sing with them as 'The Famous Jug Band'

don't think it was his thing, he was definitely more a 'rock person', but I don't ever remember him making derogatory remarks about it.

Jill's group the Jayfolk also performed there. Sue Johnstone: *I remember it well. I remember it being cold! There was an open fireplace with armchairs downstairs as you came in, and you went upstairs to play. Pat, my sister, hung out with early folk musicians like John the Fish and Brenda Wootton, and so through that we got to play at the Folk Cottage. We sang there quite a few times in fact.*

Mike Dudley: *The Jayfolk played with The Reaction a few times, and they frequented the Folk Cottage. I went to the Folk Cottage a few times mainly because of Sue Johnstone when we were going out together.*

Les Brown was a reluctant visitor: *The bloke that played the jug (Henry) used to empty his jug, which was full of spit, out onto the head of a parrot that lived there! The Folk Cottage had a very pseudo atmosphere - you had to sit in stoney silence and listen - though you could sing along if the band would let you. I would have gone with Sue and Jill, I think.*

Tony Coxon of The Intruders who was later in a band with Mike Grose was more enthusiastic: *I saw the Jug Band at Mitchell Folk Cottage. That was <u>the</u> place to go. I saw Michael Chapman there, which was a revelation. He got me into playing acoustic guitar, and playing Naked Ladies and Electric Ragtime which was one of his top pieces. It was a really nice place to go, and very crowded. I remember Roger and my friend Paul Moon, then drummer with the Intruders, talking once when we were there.*

Bert Biscoe, who was living in Truro, was a regular: *I was heavily into Folk Clubs. I used to drive up to the Folk Cottage every Friday and sit on the sofa near the stage. I saw Eric Clapton up there one night with Maddy Prior and Tim Hart of Steeleye Span. He was one of Henry Bartlett's mates. Henry told me he was riding to Brighton on his scooter once in the late 50's to go the beach, and he took Eric Clapton on the back. They pulled away from some traffic lights, the scooter took off and Henry looked around to see Eric clutching his guitar, sitting there in the road. He wasn't holding on properly and had slid off!*

Tim and Maddy came down regularly. I remember Maddy dancing round the edge of Piran Round with the moon in the sky it was fantastic. They came down a lot because between the Folk Cottage and Piper's Folk, Cornwall had the two best, most creative, most avant garde Folk Clubs in the UK. For a 3 year period they were cooking! They were the best, alongside Les Cousins and The Half Moon in Putney.

The Reaction remained busy throughout the Summer of 1967. Increasingly organizing their own venues so as not to pay a middle man, they played several times at the village hall in St Merryn near Wadebridge. There was also a floodlit barbeque at Hayle Rugby Club. One of the last gigs that summer (August 9th) was as support to The Kinks, this time at the Flamingo Ballroom. Rick Penrose: *I'd had an ambition since I was 11 was to play there: it was such a massive place. It had what they called the Long Bar that ran the length of the dance floor. They would open that during the week and not open the ballroom as such.*

It was a big thing for Cornwall because The Flamingo brought down the big names of the time. Joy was lovely, but she was a business woman. So there was no fooling around about anything. She was very, very strict. When we played with The Kinks there, their PA didn't work so the roadie was really sweating. We linked ours up to theirs and they used our amp and speakers. We all helped but Joy was going mad. 'Come on dears what are you doing in there? Doors open 8 o'clock. What are you doing Reaction?'

Joy was strict about girlfriends too. Rick: *She didn't want you to bring in any girls. You had to sneak them in the back through the stage door. She thought girlfriends should pay! That night we opened the crowd were chanting 'We want The Kinks' but actually the band were stoned, and not very good, so they started chanting for us.*

Dave Dowding: *I remember picking Roger up and driving him over from Truro to The Flamingo the night they supported The Kinks. I stood backstage and watched Ray Davies looking vague as if going 'where are we? What are we doing here?' The Kinks were quirky and sort of tongue-in-cheek but didn't go down terribly well. I remember thinking the drummer looked really nervous. I got the feeling that The Reaction were going places. They were better than the main act by then.*

Towards the end of the summer of 1967, as the boys prepared to leave Cornwall to go to College, Geoff Daniel left and Mike Dudley moved back to playing guitar. The Reaction had become a three-piece modelled on The Jimi Hendrix Experience. Rick: *I got on really well with Geoff - we called him Ben. He had a beautiful guitar with a scroll neck. When he left our big change was from soul to Hendrix/Cream stuff. It was a significant afternoon. I remember it was late summer because it was hot and we rehearsed in Dave Dowding's barn. We were then doing Hendrix's 'Foxy Lady' and Cream's 'Sunshine of your Love' and stuff like that. It was very important and new to me, a big change musically. We'd just listen to the record and work it out from ear.*

Rick also remembers rehearsing as a threepiece at Hurland Road: *It was in Roger's living room in Park View with the curtains drawn to try to keep the sound in.*

Mike Dudley: *We mainly listened to music together at Roger's house. By then we did most of our practice in his front room. His parents were out in the late afternoon. But we didn't rehearse that much together. We'd listen to things apart and come together to play them. It was very hard to get the sheet music, so it was mostly learnt by ear.*

Mike invested some of the money earned into buying the best guitar he could find. Mike: *Hendrix arrived and so did Cream, and John Mayall was on the road, and so I wanted to play guitar again. I bought a Gibson SG. All we had as amplifiers were Vox AC30's and the sound wasn't right with the Gibson, so I ended up changing it for a white Fender Stratocaster like Jimi's.*

I ended up taking the group's money and dividing it up and occasionally paying the agent - not very often, actually, which irritated him. Towards the end of it Roger asked for an extra 10% which he got. The band's fee then was typically 15 or 20 quid. I'd earned enough money to buy a car, guitars and the organ. The SG was about £100.

Throughout the lifetime of the group, there were many concerts that were not advertised, and as a consequence the exact date and venue is unknown. Late in September there was a gig near Land's End in a remote village close to the Atlantic Ocean. It was probably The Reaction's last concert before the new academic year. Rick Penrose: *I had a friend who was Spencer Davis' roadie and he let us use his equipment one night: his PA and amps and mics. And we were playing down in St Just with amazing views overlooking the sea and we used all these Marshall amps. It was a little town hall it was a beautiful evening. I remember that. I was married then and I used to make homemade wine so we would all came back and drink it to the early hours, because you can't come back and just turn off...*

In 1985 Truro School's Magazine, Terraces, contained a short article on Roger Taylor, in which deputy head Dick Taylor owns up to having advised him to study dentistry, saying: *'there wasn't much money in drumming'*. Others to this day consider it to have been a strange choice. Rik Evans: *I can't imagine him as a dentist. I can't think what possessed him to think of that one.*

Jill: *Becoming a dentist? It always seemed really strange...I remember his mother campaigning for it ...wanting him to do something 'serious'...none of this music stuff! But for Roger it seemed to be more of a way for him to get up to London, rather than a burning desire to take care of people's cavities!*

Jill and Sue of Jayfolk performing with Penny North and Josie James after the Johnson twins left for Canada.

When they were younger the Truro schoolboys' parents had always been supportive of their sons' musical efforts, but Roger's mother now wanted a steady career for her son. Keith Harding: *Thinking about Roger's parents: I can imagine Mike would have encouraged his music, but Win, his mother, was the more sensible one, who would have encouraged his studies.*
Roger Taylor confirms this: *My mother wanted me to be a surgeon. She was convinced I'd make a good one, and tried to kid me I'd do well at it.* ...1974cutting

In fact, in October 1967 Mike Dudley went to Oxford University to read chemistry, but Roger's ambitions to move to London were put on hold. He ended up entering what was then called the Upper Sixth and staying on an extra year at Truro School for retakes. It is not surprising he needed the extra period of study. Not content to only play in his own band up to three or four times a week, he is also known to have deputised for drummers from other bands as well. Graham Hankins: *We had several agents, and always had bookings, and Roger just wanted to play. However he got through his studies I don't know.*

The Reaction continued to play in Cornwall as if nothing much had changed. Mike was down most weekends, and the band still had gigs booked up some way ahead. Mike: *It's not that far down from Oxford. I had a car and would just drive down. It was fun - and an ego-trip.*

In the late 60's there were 3 or 4 places in Cornwall that regularly advertised strippers. One such venue was the old Bodmin gaol which had been converted into a club. The Reaction played there in November and December 1967. Rick: *We got up to Bodmin and set up. We opened with some songs and were quite looking forward to this stripper, and she came up to us and asked if we'd do some light background music to accompany her. And it was very...interesting. She danced around and did the 7 veils type thing through the audience, in the middle of the floor. We were up on the stage. I also remember Bodmin Town Hall where a fight broke out. But we were OK. They used to put their hands up to the stage to try to pull off Mike's footpedals, and he would just stand on their hands. He was great big bloke anyway.*

In December the musical darlings of the London Underground visited Cornwall. Richard Halliwell: *I saw Pink Floyd with Sid Barrett at the Flamingo. Pretty sure Taylor was there. There was a full psychedelic lightshow, and plenty of dope etc.*

1968: Creatively weird light shows

On January 15th 1968 The Reaction returned to Truro City Hall for the 'Top Group Championship', which was the 'Rock and Rhythm Championship' under a new name.

The band went on to use a new name themselves on more than one occasion during 1968. Rick Penrose: *Peter Boggia was the compere. He was also my boss at work. If I remember he wanted us to compete and it was very last minute. The Fantastics name was my suggestion.*

Bert Biscoe: *There was a delay and then the curtains parted to reveal The Fantastics, and I was effing knocked out by them. I think they had a light show going as well, and a dancer called Joelle who was dancing in and out of it as I recall. She was a very shapely french girl with long blond hair. She was scantily clad for those days and was into a kind of dances that were more likely to be seen on the back street of Paris!*

Mike was very tall with long blond hair up and tight jeans up at the front of the stage. He was wearing what looked like a 1950's plastic table cloth cut into a kaftan, and Roger was sat behind this enormous kit on a rostrum. And they played 'Land of a Thousand Dances' and 'Walk me out in the Morning Dew' by Tim Rose. From that moment I thought of rock music in a completely different way.

Rick: *We talked before the contest about how, when the curtains closed and we moved our kit into position, we would not be rushed by the stage manager: as professionals we were going to make sure that everything was perfect. So Roger made sure he had his kit exactly as he wanted it.*

Actually that night there was a man who lived who lived at Malpas who used to go up and down the river in a venetian gondola! He made - among other things - shirts from silk, and they were off the wall even by the 60's standards, and he was behind stage at the contest and asked us if we would wear them. Which we did. And of course, there was a buzz as the audience found out we were really The Reaction.

The Reaction appear as The Fantastics in The West Briton in 1968

The West Briton's review omits Roger's name: *'In second place were the Fantastics, a group of three Truro musicians who decided to enter the contest only two or three days before. He and his colleagues Richard Penrose and Michael Dudley are members of The Reaction which won the championship two years ago. The group has temporarily disbanded because the other members have gone to college and university'*.

The winners that year were called 'The Peace and Quiet' and according to the West Briton they *'produced a lighting effect with a system known as liquid projection, (which) riveted the attention of the 600 teenagers who crowded the hall to watch and hear the 12 groups in the contest'*.

The Reaction played alongside The Peace and Quiet as The Fantastics in February and, after reverting back to their old name, were soon to incorporate the same psychedelic lighting techniques themselves. An advert probably placed by Roger for a gig on March 16th at the Godolphin Hall in Helston puts it thus: *Fantastic New Reaction: Light Show, oils etc, Records, best, latest, Go-go Girls, Cokes, in fact everything.*

Mike Dudley: *We got the lighting together for the marquee shows and we definitely had some coloured filters on a rotating disc that we made up ourselves. Acker was good at that kind of thing. He had a workshop attached to his home on Lemon Street. I think we also had flashing lights and oil and water mixes that were available commercially.*

Rick: *Acker would also have repaired the red light that we nicked from Torquay. I remember we used it outside at a gig at The Bluff Hotel in Hayle, when we had all our amps facing out towards the ocean.*

On April 11th Jill Johnson's father, who frequently appeared in the paper in his role as Truro City's Town Clerk, announced in the West Briton that he was 'glad to be seeing buildings going up'. The comments were referring to the protracted Pydar Street redevelopment that had started in 1965. Contracts worth nearly £3 million had been awarded to builders Dudley Coles Long.

The Reaction returned on three more occasions to the Penmare in Hayle in the early part of the year, then Easter Monday saw the first of a series of marquee gigs that Roger organized with Rik Evans.

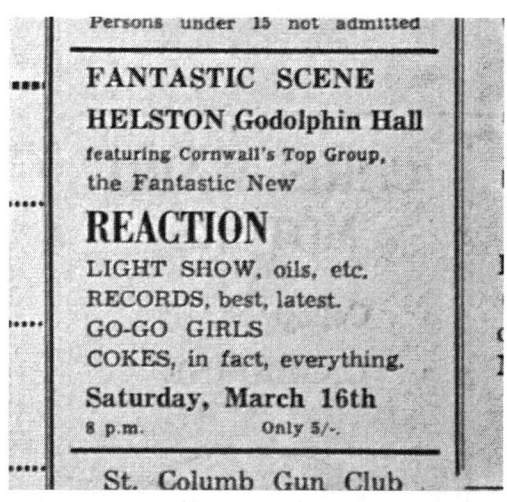

Rik Evans: *A year or two later after I first met Roger we set up the Summer Coast Sound Experience: both of us trying to make money out of it, me as part of my marquee business.*

The advert for the first gig promised *'Easter Monday Happening at Trevellas Cove...signposted specially...witness the sounds of the incredible REACTION...Creatively weird LIGHT SHOWS. Food and drink, all in the most LIT-UP MARQUEE ALIVE. We'll sell you this experience for only 6s'*

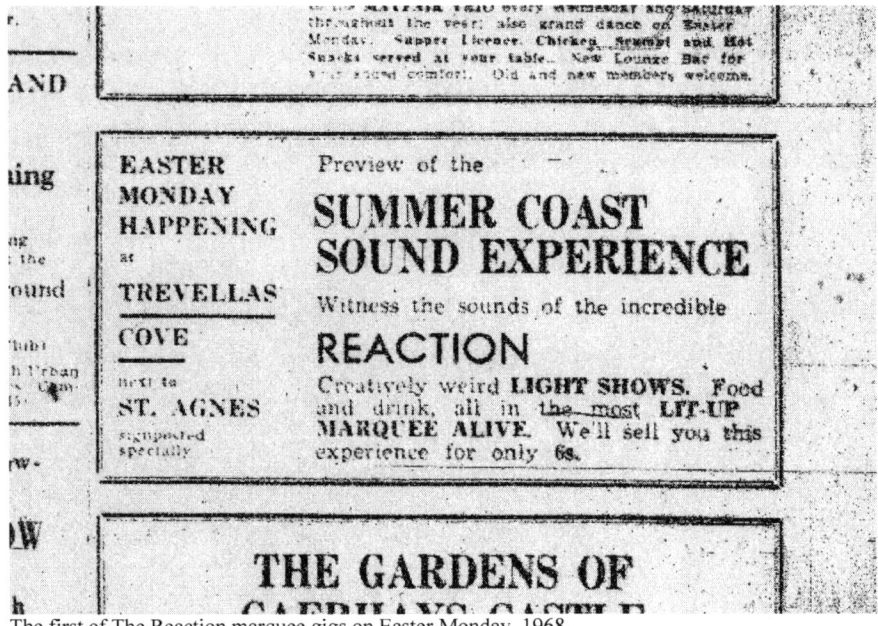

The first of The Reaction marquee gigs on Easter Monday, 1968.

Rick Penrose: *The oil light show was the only lighting on stage. We also had go-go dancers. We played records in the break which went on a long time so we didn't have to play so long, selling cokes etc. It was all self-funded. The oil light slides were displayed all over us and behind us, so we looked like the cover of Cream's Disraeli Gears. I always felt the record breaks were too long, though, and we would lose the punters.*

The marquee gigs were advertised using posters that the ever industrious Roger again designed and posted up himself. The first one just outside St Agnes was affected by bad weather. Mike Dudley: *The one at Trevellas Porth was notable for the fact that it poured with rain and we ran a cable from some farmer's kitchen window through the rain: sparks flying everywhere. And it was also a time when people wore dreadful paisley things so we've got pictures of me wearing appalling paisley trousers!*

The cable in question was obtained by Roger from his neighbour in Park View. Keith: *They had a gig planned for Trevellas Coombe and*

Roger came to see me and said 'Have you got a bit of cable please Mr Harding?', and they ran the cable from one of the houses on the Trevellas side of the valley.

The rough road leading down to the beach at Trevellas - also known as Blue Hills - is so steep and treacherous it had acquired a reputation as the most challenging stretch of the London to Land's End motor trial, an annual event organised since 1908 by the Motorcycling Club of Great Britain. There is a photo of the motor trial taken the same weekend that The Reaction played (see picture), and a report from 1929 describes Trevellas thus: *Of all points through which the trial passes Bluehills Mine is probably the most remote and desolate.*

Rik Evans: *It was ridiculous place to have it. This was the good old days when you didn't have to ask permission or get a license or all the nonsense that goes on these days. It was raining, and we had the marquee up on the flattest bit of ground we could find. It's all mine rubble down there. And the beach is a stoney beach that slopes, so we couldn't have had it there. It was a flat area back on the old mine waste.*

Easter in Cornwall — Competitors in the Land's End trial await their turn to attempt the tough cliff-road section at Blue Hills, near St. Agnes, on Saturday.

Mike Dudley went up to the house at the top. It was many hundreds of yards away, and he asked if we could plug in, and the lead came down over the hillside through the gorse. Hardly anyone came to it and frankly we lost money. I can recall the band playing at the back.

John Snell: *Somebody - probably not keen on pop music - living nearby had seen the cable and questioned its electrical safety. Fortunately Roger said that his neighbour who worked for SWEB had said it would be OK...*

Rik: *We set a little stage up. Because it was so wet there was a mud puddle in the middle where we put the marquee and I remember a couple of rockers dancing in this mud puddle to the band playing in the background. And Roger, halfway through, decided to go and snog his girlfriend in the back of his Triumph Herald outside while the band kept on playing.*

L to R: Acker Snell (partially visible), Rick Penrose, Roger Taylor, Mike Dudley. Roger's painting of Jimi Hendrix is on the bass drum.

Predictably enough there was a problem with the electricity. Rick Penrose laughs about it now: *There was actually a problem with the mains lead from the farm. We had mains ran up this huge cable, but the plug had to be changed. Roger said 'look I'll go down and see the farmer and get him to turn off the electricity. Give me ten minutes, then change the plug'. So he went off. He drove down and I waited ten minutes. Then I undid the plug and it was still live so it actually blew out of my hand. I had this shock go right up my arm. Roger had seen the farmer and had a chat with him but forgot to ask him to turn it off!*

Actually Trevellas Porth was poorly attended. It was so inaccessible. We ended up making a loss.

When Roger Taylor was n't performing himself he was watching others. On April 9th he and his friends saw a mixed bill at the ABC in Exeter. Richard Halliwell: *There was a girlfriend of Roger's called Maggie who worked in the old army and navy surplus stores in Falmouth. We used to go down there and buy sailor's trousers that had a flap that came up, then two flaps that buttoned across the front. They were baggy and flared, and we made them tight to the knee and they used to flare out so much you couldn't actually see your shoes! A gang of us including Roger drove up to Exeter and saw The Kinks, and The Herd and The Tremoloes all on the same night, and I remember walking up the main street with Roger both of us wearing these white sailor trousers which we tried desperately hard to keep clean. And we saw the Small Faces there or maybe in Plymouth.*

Penny North: *Jill and the Jayfolk knew about Maggie because once when we were performing in Falmouth we saw Roger with her…Jill was not best pleased!*

Perranporth in the West Briton (1966)

Perranporth, unlike Trevellas Porth is a huge, sandy beach a couple of miles or so further up the coast where the sun sets slowly over the ocean. When the Reaction reunited in the Summer the beach would have been full with a captive audience of holiday-makers. The group had been booked to play another marquee gig, this time as part of the Ladies Surf Championships. The Reaction ended up playing hundreds of concerts in Cornwall but this was, undoubtedly a high-point.

Mike Dudley: *The one at Perranporth was particularly successful.*

Perranporth 1968. The most successful Reaction gig?

Rik Evans agrees: *The Perranporth Beach one was definitely the most successful. We did it in league with the Surf Life Saving Club, so they could make some money as well. They put on a barbeque outside selling burgers and things. We packed a massive marquee out with people but unfortunately there were complaints locally about it, so the council didn't let us do it again, which is a shame because that could have become a really good, regular gig.*

Rick Penrose: *The life-guards had to take the kit across the beach in jeeps. We had to load them up and make several trips. I had sand in the speaker cabinet for ages after that. It just blew in. But it was really busy. It was a fantastic night. We had a lot of people from Manchester. People here at that time were playing pop stuff and we weren't and that's what appealed to them. We were quite unique in what we played* in Cornwall. We were doing Cream and Hendrix and we were heavy. And <u>very</u> loud. Roger had this amazing full sound. His bass pedal work was extraordinary. Well all of it was.

Roo Fairbairn was in the year below Roger and Mike at Truro School: *I remember seeing Reaction many times. They did the big one on the huge beach at Perranporth when everybody ended up sleeping wrapped up in the drop down sides of the marquees. Hundreds of people were left sleeping there overnight. It was amazing. I slept there with my girlfriend: we slept wrapped up in the canvas.*

As a singer and guitarist who played in the Red Lion and organised folk nights there, Roo also remembers Jill Johnson and was given an autoharp that had been hers. Roo: *Pete Gill-Carey, Roger and Mike Dudley were dayboys so we didn't mix socially till the 6th form because as a boarder you weren't allowed out. By the time I was getting to the end of my time at Truro School Derek Burrell the headmaster was allowing us out. I remember asking if I could go down to play music at the Navy Arms - I was going to play with Jayfolk – he said 'yes as long as you don't drink. Or let me put it another way: as long as I don't hear about you drinking'.*

Promotional postcard from Jill Johnson's collection

Actually I wasn't good enough to share the bill with them. The Jayfolk were almost an institution. They really were good. They did all the famous West Coast American folk songs. Lovely harmonies. Really Great. Everyone would try to copy them and I'm sure we tried to get them to sing at the Red Lion.

The best recordings of the Jayfolk were made at Penny North's living room in Grampound in 1968. On the tapes the girls give confident and lively performances of songs that range from spirituals, to blues, to doo-wop to 60's folk favourites, like Joan Baez. Their four blended voices result in arrangements that sound original, and often strikingly so. Josie James: *Jill and Sue were more into their music than I was and would usually work out the chords and the arrangements on their guitars then we would all come together to add our own harmonies. I mainly played tambourine!*

Jill Johnson: *1967 and 1968 The Jayfolk played regularly at The Navy Arms in Truro and the Roseland Inn in Philleigh, as well as a variety of concerts, holiday camps and clubs. In the summer Roger, with Reaction, ran a series of beach dances in marquees set up by Rik Evans. Reaction played the main set, and The Jayfolk would do the acoustic intermission.*

Throughout their years of singing in the pubs and clubs of Cornwall Jill and Sue of The Jayfolk were still at school and under the legal drinking age. Though they were both younger than the members of The Reaction, they would still get served. Jill: *Drinking in pubs…yes… sometimes we could hardly see our guitars by the end of the night! Age didn't ever seem to be an issue in those days. I could barely reach over the bar - I'm short - and they still served me. Also they didn't have a problem with our friends coming and not drinking, though to an extent the pubs relied on them for revenue…*

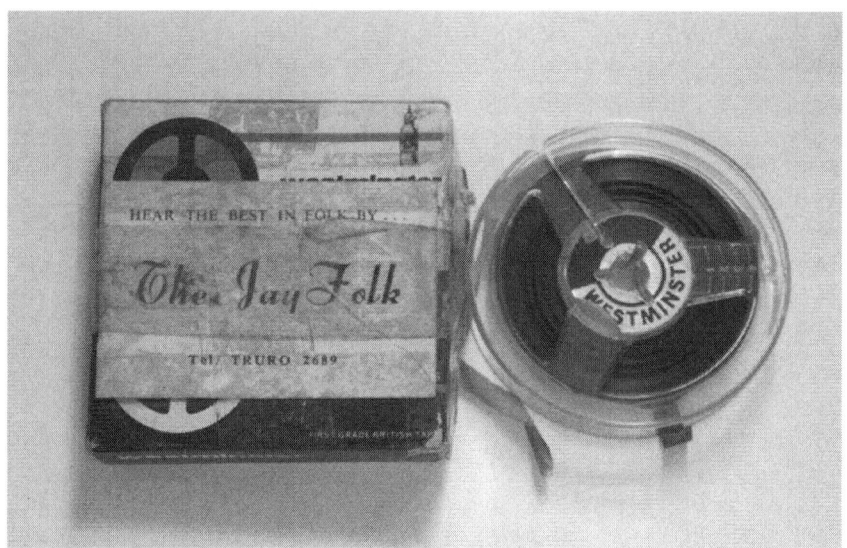

A unique reel-to-reel mono recording of The Jayfolk. Collection: Penny North

The Navy Arms became a regular haunt for Jill and Roger and their friends. It was midway between Roger's house and Truro School, and later it was somewhere the members of Queen visited on several occasions. Jill: *The Navy was always just a little sleazy and in that sense definitely different to the Royal or the Britannia. So it suited us really well. It wasn't a big pub. I think I remember 3 rooms. The front room - the lounge bar - had a window onto the street: that's where we would play. I think there was a public bar, and a room at the back that had a juke box, and darts. Mostly our crowd would hang out in the back room when we weren't performing.*

Later I do remember going there a couple of times when Smile came down from London. Sue and her sister Pat were also there. I believe it was after Roger and I had split and he was there with his new girlfriend Jo...a very nice lady.

Les Brown: *Jill was a neighbour on Crescent Road. I used to go to St George's youth club together with Jill and Sue, who I would have known before I knew Roger. I saw the Jayfolk and the Famous Jug Band performing lots of times, and I used to go to the Navy Arms a lot too, where I also saw them. The Navy was the best pub in Truro at the time. It was a magical pub - exactly as pubs ought to be.*

Sue Johnstone's sister, Pat, returned to Truro from London when her mother became ill, and she worked behind the bar in The Navy on most evenings. Pat: *I worked in the day in a boutique and the pub in the evening. It was a really fun place. Really crazy people used to go in there. My father thought it was a den of iniquity! The Cockle family were usually there, and my family and friends and other people could go there and just be themselves. You went there to have an experience! Everyone there was over the top including the owners.*

The Navy Arms on the north side of Fairmantle Street shortly before being demolished in 2000. The Jayfolk sang whilst sitting in the window on the left. Tabernacle Street which leads to Lemon Quay and stage door of The City Hall is just out of shot on the left hand side.

Les: *Bill Cockle, who was a regular, was the most georgeous guy you can imagine and he once said to me, after I'd moved to France, why don't you send me a postcard, Les? I said I don't know your address Bill. Just put 'Bill Cockle, Truro. It'll get to me'...So I sent him a card and it did get to him!*

Pat: *My sister's Jayfolk band were one of the best in Cornwall. If you're a musician you will recognise a good harmony and they had the best harmonies. They sang there at the Navy - and various other artists used to play there.*

Living in St Agnes, some 8 or 9 miles away, Richard Halliwell didn't go to The Navy quite as often. During the summer holidays he tended to meet Roger and the other Truro School boys at bars outside Truro: *I do remember that the Tregye was a popular watering hole - probably because there was a bar extension until (gasp!) midnight. It was pretty dingy, though, as I recall! The Daniel Arms was another popular haunt.*

His local pub, The Driftwood near St Agnes beach, was also a frequent meeting place and it is quite possible that two blond rockstars of the 70's were, unknown to each other, in the village at the same time. Richard: *Rod Stewart was a regular to Cornwall during 68 – 71, because he had friends in St Agnes. First time I saw him he had a blond girlfriend and a yellow Marcos sportscar. A year later things were on the up and he was driving a white Marcos. Then the last time he had an even more opulent (blond) girlfriend and a white Lamborghini. He stayed in Perranporth and was drinking in the Green Parrot resplendent in leopard-skin suit, when one night, after a row with the blonde, she went out and kicked the door of the car, creating quite a dent. In fact around this time (67-71) lots of musicians would come down to Cornwall on holiday. I saw Steve Marriott, John Mayall, Donovan, Manfred Mann.....*

Soon after the Perranporth marquee gig Reaction bassist Rick Penrose, finally called time on the band. Rick: *I remember I was really tired and I was thinking I could really do with a break from it all, so I was like 'come on give me a break'... I'll even let you borrow the bass. So I let them use my bass, and gave it to Roger. And he brought it back with the G string broken, so he still owes me for that!*

The Reaction continued to play, albeit with different bass-players, including Geoff Daniel: *I borrowed Rick Penrose's bass. We then had that great Summer of 68! I had to leave in mid-August to do an industrial placement as part of my Engineering degree. I think Rick Thorning took my place (and my girlfriend) for the last month or two.*

Mevagissey Harbour in the West Briton (1966)

At the beginning of July they played in a 'Beat Dance' as part of Mevagissey Feast Week, only to return a couple of weeks later to play another marquee gig. This time it was described as a 'Rave'. Rik Evans: *Mevagissey was pretty reasonable. That was down at the bottom of the hill approaching Mevagissey on the right on what was the football field in those days, but it's probably been built on now. Got permission presumably from the council for that one.*

There was another gig we did out near Carnon Downs in the middle of a field. Approaching Carnon Downs from Truro it's on the right. It's a gate onto a bus lane now but it would have been a gate into a field. People would have parked in the field, and paid at the door, and there'd have been posters out in the road.

In the sixties every village hall in Cornwall would have had a band in playing for a dance. There was a lot of work out there in those days for local bands and people would turn up. And it was halls rather than pubs: people are drinking younger these days. It wasn't so obvious that young people went into pubs.

> **MARQUEE RAVE**
> Mevagissey Recreation Ground, featuring
> **The REACTION, Light Show, Records**
> LONDON FOLK GROUP
> WEDNESDAY, 31st JULY

Another Marquee gig by The Reaction. It is not known who the London Folk Group were.

Richard Halliwell recalls being with The Reaction in Mevagissey that Summer when they were refused service in one of the pubs: *We were asked to leave because we were considered to be 'undesirable'. At that time Meva was a conservative little fishing village, and we were dressed unconventionally. I mentioned the very wide 'loon pants' we wore. We might also have been wearing some type of military jackets...*

Mike Dudley: *The Mevagissey one I remember. We did a gig there pretty well on the harbour and the strange thing was that Eric Clapton was there and came up and introduced himself in the interval. Of course we had been playing several Cream numbers!*

Between the two Mevagissey dates on 24th July Roger Taylor, Richard Halliwell and a couple of other Truro School boys went to the Flamingo to see 'Traffic' who later that year played on Jimi Hendrix's Electric Ladyland album. Richard: *We arrived late and the gig was sold out. Luckily the dressing room window was open and we managed to convince the band that we had travelled some distance to see them (which wasn't true) and were huge fans (which was). They were very friendly, opened the window and helped us in. So we ended up chatting with Steve Winwood and the other band members, and then walking through to the main hall. It helped that Roger already knew the layout of the place. We had previously seen the last tour of the Spencer Davis Group in Plymouth, before Steve Winwood left them to form Traffic.*

That Summer Roger, Jill and friends also had an outing between musical excursions. Jill: *I remember an overnight in a tent on the headland at Falmouth: the Reaction, myself and a couple of lads from London that had attached themselves to the band. Not sure where the tents came from - perhaps a loan from Rik's marquee company. It was all very innocent. Or it seemed so. But the police got involved when they came upon our little campout which just happened to be in a restricted area (a fact that I remember commenting on, but hey, I'm just a girl...). I think they ran the number plates on the Londoners' car and found that they were wanted for thieving or something like that. Luckily the rest of us managed to absolve ourselves of anything other than bad judgement! But I seem to remember that we had to report to the police station in Falmouth and, on the way there, Roger got another ticket for overloading the car!*

John Snell *I remember sitting with Roger and Jill in Jill's parents' kitchen discussing what had happened when there was a knock at the door and one of the London lads appeared (called Jerry, I think). He was looking relieved and announced 'It's all OK. The Cornish police were pretty good – they didn't beat me up like they would have done in the Met!'*

Jill recalls another Reaction gig: *There was one marquee gig in a field at St. Mawes. Roger's friend Rick Thorning was taking me and Clare, Roger's sister, home (late as usual) too fast, and we had a nasty accident. Then we had another one that same day when we went to pick up the damaged car with Roger driving 'Matilda'. Roger had the knack of getting us into trouble!*

Rick Thorning was one of the stand-in bass-players that summer and he traveled with Mike and Roger across the Tamar for at least one gig in Devon. There is a photo of the three of them in Dawlish (Teignmouth?). Mike Dudley: *His car – the one that crashed - was an old MG Magnette. Rick Thorning lived in Falmouth and went to Truro School. He was*

pretty late in the day and I'm sure he would agree, he wasn't a very good musician, but he knew enough to play bass. It's simple to play simple bass.

Symbolic of the times, in July 1968 Tabbs Hotel in Redruth was demolished to make way for a Tesco's store (see photograph p.149). It had been a decade since its heyday as a pioneering venue for Rock 'n' Roll dances.

Jill Johnson: *In September 1968, Josie and Penny left for college. Sue and I continued the band and added a flute. I was planning on joining Roger in London, so I got hired by the BBC and was supposed to start working for them later that year. Then the Jayfolk played a gig in*

The Reaction in Devon in 1968. L to R Mike Dudley, Roger Taylor, Rick Thorning. Photo: Mike Dudley

Wadebridge where I met the Famous Jug Band, and they recruited me for the band. I dumped the BBC offer, and started playing with them in

November '68 and then we went on tour early in 1969. One of the photos is of me and a fellow called Patrick Wiseman practising in an anteroom at that very concert before going on. The Jayfolk were breaking up for several reasons – one because Penny and Josie had gone to college, and two because I wanted to go to London to join Roger and also see if I could get into the music business.

I wanted Sue Johnstone to come with me, but her mother was ill and she didn't feel she could leave – so I determined to go anyway. I did the BBC thing to appease my parents and get them to agree to my leaving home, then I joined the Jug Band and went to London with them. Ironically, Sue did leave Cornwall the following year, hooked up with Roger and our other friends in London and ultimately started the Queen Fan Club with her sister...

Clive Palmer founded the Incredible String Band, which, in 1969, played at the iconic Woodstock festival. He was a free-spirited folk singer who had come to Cornwall to live in a caravan at the Folk Cottage. Clive: *I remember Jill at that time. She had one of those Afghani jackets and short hair and a little black car. I was impressed with her singing. It was a natural voice and very clear. It wasn't like an X-factor voice. There are lots of wannabe singers, but hers was special.*

Jill: *I used to drive a little black Austin A40. It had those indicators that actually came out on little arms...*

Bert Biscoe: *For three or four years Jill and Roger were definitely an item. And for a while they were at the core of the music scene in Cornwall. He was doing rock music and she was hooked into the folk scene, and between them they had the whole thing tied up. She was a brilliant singer, and they were young but they were both stars in their own right.*

At the end of Summer 1968, after the last of the marquee gigs, The Reaction finally split up. The last newspaper advertisement clearly bearing The Reaction's name was for a concert on 6th September in St Merryn Village Hall, but there was another in Bodmin on the 14th for a band billed simply and enigmatically as the 'Fantastic'. Perhaps it was intended as a cryptic way to say goodbye, but certainly this is likely to be The Reaction as they had been using the word throughout 1968: since appearing as 'The Fantastics' in the Top Group Championship.

Jill Johnson with Patrick Wiseman playing in Wadebridge, 1968 the night she was 'spotted' by Clive Palmer and The FJB. Photo Jillian Johnson

Mike and John 'Acker' Snell stayed involved with the Cornish music scene by joining The Bobby Knight Soul Band. Popular for a few years in Cornwall, the band also played at PJ's club. John: *Bobby Knight was Bob Peters. I introduced Mike Dudley to the band as lead guitar.*

Two weeks after The Reaction's last advertised gig Roger started dental studies at the Royal London Hospital Medical and Dental School. Before he went he suggested to bassist Rick Penrose that he come up to London with him, but Rick didn't feel he could: *By then I was married had a mortgage and a good job, and I was brought up that you had to have a proper job.* Rick, though, remembers a comment made by Roger's mother: *When he went to college, I do remember Roger's Mum saying 'you're not to go up there playing, Roger, you're up there to study'.*

Finally leaving his band and the life he'd known in Cornwall, Roger Taylor shared the momentous journey to London with ex-Reaction guitarist Geoff Daniel. They had planned to live together in a flat in Shepherd's Bush with Truro friend Les Brown: Geoff: *Roger came with me in my purple Triumph Herald to London in late September 1968. After the trip, which took about 8 hours in those days, we went down to The Kensington Arms. Les had found the ground floor flat in 19, Sinclair Gardens. Four of us moved in: Roger, Les, me and a bloke called Pete who was so into transcendental meditation he rarely spoke and just smiled a lot. He had a cupboard in the basement where he used to meditate...*

I was a year older than Roger - same as Jim Craven. I didn't get the right A-level grades so went into the Upper Sixth and retook, leaving in '67. Les and I were in separate digs or halls of residence for the '67/'68 academic year, but were fed up with the restrictions, which was why we decided to rent the ground floor flat in Sinclair Gardens after the brilliant Summer of '68 gigs.

The enigma of the final gig of The Reaction. September 14th 1968

Les, an academic year ahead at Truro School, had come to London the previous year to study at Imperial only two months after his 17th birthday. Les: *I still have nightmares about when I first arrived, met my 'personal tutor' and went drinking after hours in a pub in the mews somewhere behind the road that The Science Museum is in...*

Sinclair Gardens is a crescent-shaped terrace of large three-storey houses, and The Kensington Arms a ten minute walk over a railway bridge behind the house.

Sinclair Gardens (2010). The first black door on the left is the entrance to No.19. The junction with Addison Road is visible in the distance.

During the time he lived with Roger, Les does not recall many conversations about Dentistry: *Pete Kelsey and I were doing Mathematics at Imperial and we might have talked about our course, but otherwise the conversation at the flat was all sex and drugs and rock 'n' roll. And beer. The Kensington Arms was our local pub. It had good jazz in the back bar but we could hear it from the front bar, which had no entrance fee.*

I do remember a discussion with Roger about wisdom teeth operations though. He once explained that it is one of the most dangerous operations known to man, because there are 59 ways to die whilst you are having wisdom teeth taken out! As students it seemed that anything gross was worth talking about!

Roger caught the tube to college, and it was quite a way, but I never went with him. Another guy who lived in the flat later, little Dave, was on the same dentistry course.

Pete Kelsey later got a job as a sound engineer at the famous Trident Studios, after visiting Queen there whilst they were mixing their first album. He went on to work with the likes of Elton John, Brian Eno and disco-king Cerrone. Pete: *As far as I remember Roger was doing dentistry all that year and probably at least some of the following year.*

The flat was small. Les: *The flat was pretty tiny. There wasn't enough space for a full drum kit there. Roger might have had bits of his kit there. There were two rooms and a kitchen, and Pete and I were both vegetarians so we took turns to cook for each other. The flat was totally disorganised but I don't remember any conflicts over food etc.*

Downstairs in the basement there was a bathroom, a huge empty hallway that served no useful purpose, and two cupboards that we would use for meditation. We'd sit inside them and chant 'ohm, ohm' or whatever. We had a lifesized cut-out photo of a policeman in the basement too which we put down there to freak people out on the way to the toilet!

There was one huge bedroom and a smaller room at the front and whoever needed a bit of privacy - if a girlfriend was staying - would book the room at the front.

We had a cat that we called Jimi (after the guitarist of course) but he didn't survive. I don't think we fed him enough, and he went and found a more congenial home! We also had a Smile sticker on the flat's window (the big fat lips with the 'ting'). Quite large (at least 15 inches wide): it was designed and made by Tim Staffell and, I think, silkscreened in multiple copies as part of a college project. I think Doug Puddifoot took a picture of this, probably in black and white. He was often there and was always snapping away.

As a drummer he had never had lessons, but having played more than 300 concerts with The Reaction, Roger Taylor had perfected his craft by performing live. And barely before he had attended his first dentistry lecture he was auditioning for the group that became 'Smile'. Les Brown famously spotted a notice placed by future Queen guitarist Brian May on the student union notice board in Imperial College. It was asking for a 'Ginger Baker/Mitch Mitchell-type drummer'.

Les: *The Union Bar was smaller than it is now and more like the snug of an old-fashioned pub (although, for gigs, I think they also opened a bar along the back wall of the Concert Hall). As I remember, the first day back at Imperial College I went to the Student Union Bar, saw the 'Drummer Wanted' ad written in hand by Brian, and brought it straight back to the flat. I think the audition took place the same week.*

The Royal London Hospital in Whitechapel (2010).

Brian May was studious and gifted and two years older than Roger. During summer 1968 he had completed his Physics degree at Imperial - then as now the UK's leading institution for scientific teaching and research - and was involved in studying zodiacal light from an observatory in Tenerife, whilst preparing to start a PhD.

Brian had been playing in the band '1984', which was already familiar to Les: *If you were a member of the Imperial Union which cost about ten bob you could see bands playing there every week and they were often big bands - people like The Who for example. We were very spoilt. In my first year 1984 were very often the support band. There were n't many other college bands: we were all scientists and not many of us musicians.*

Pete Edmonds had been at school with Brian May and Tim Staffell, and his wife-to-be, Wendy, went on to design and make Freddie Mercury's most distinctive stage costumes. Pete became Smile's first roadie and soundman: *I'd known Brian from Hampton Grammar School. He was in the Latin A stream, the top stream, and I was in Latin B. I was involved with 1984 initially, and it kind of carried on with Smile.*

I remember when we were still at school, 1984 playing a church hall in Twickenham. The word got round that the 'Hounslow Boys' were coming down to cause a bit of bother. The bouncers on the door ran away and the Hounslow boys came in and a fight broke out. The band kept playing through all this... Later 1984 played a gig at Imperial College where they supported Jimi Hendrix. In fact I remember Hendrix trod on my foot, apologised and said 'Sorry man'!

The Imperial Union Concert Hall proved an excellent venue for Smile and Queen. Les: *You would sometimes get a thousand people in there. It would be standing room only - shoulder to shoulder and not always that comfortable. Mainly people from college and the girls at Maria Assumpta. Imperial Union was a bit like the Navy Arms – run- down but cosy and informal.*

Although '1984' had split up in 1968, Brian was still in touch with singer and bassist, Tim Staffell who was at Art School in Ealing. After Roger had contacted them via the number on the notice, Brian and Tim went to meet him in Sinclair Gardens, where, having left his kit in Cornwall, they played together, with Roger improvising using a pair of bongos.

It was several days later that they played properly in the jazz practice room at Imperial. Les: *The first proper audition was in one of the little rooms upstairs where people practised. I remember we were relaying booze up from the bar downstairs so it must have been one of the rooms on the first floor of the Union.*

Shortly afterwards the three-piece that later became Queen, was formed. Tim later explained what the drummer brought to the group: 'Roger was lively and exciting and ran on adrenaline. He was always up and Smile was enhanced by his energy' TEL.

The musical and personal relationship that Roger Taylor went on to form with Brian May has endured intact to the present day. In a very candid interview in 1998 Brian said: *'Roger and I hit it off like brothers, and we've been together the longest, which may be why now we fight so much. The sound of my guitar and his drums worked from the beginning. It gelled and it had that hugeness.'* MOJO.

Tim Staffell, lead singer with Smile, at his parent's house in 1969. Photo Ian Lynch.

Roger's involvement with Smile brought the friends from Truro into a whole new social circle. Les Brown found he got on well with Brian, but despite both being at Imperial they talked more about science fiction than real science. *I used to talk to Brian and Tim about science fiction: Tim particularly. Tim Staffell, I got on very well with, and we were both very keen on SF. We used to have endless arguments and discussions about it, and about books that we'd read and so on. Tim introduced me to Frank Herbert actually.*

Richard Thompson was someone else who they met through Brian and Tim. He had been the drummer in '1984'. Les: *Richard was there at the flat a lot. He used to drive Smile around. I remember the dashboard fell off once as he was driving along and he just slammed it back in place and we just continued driving along. He had a Transit later but originally it was a Bedford van.*

For a few weeks Smile included a keyboardist studying in the same graphics class as Tim Staffell at Ealing by the name of Chris Smith. He lived around the corner in Addison Road, where his flat had been used for more than a year as an occasional 'crash-pad' by a shy but exotic-looking fashion student called Freddie Mercury (then Bulsara) who had been commuting to Ealing College from his parent's house in Feltham. Freddie knew Tim from College, and soon became friends with Roger. Having both grown up in environments very different to London, they were also united by a shared passion for Jimi Hendrix.

Roger Taylor: *We came together through Hendrix. When we (Brian and Roger) spoke to Freddie, we discovered we had the same musical tastes. He was a complete Hendrix freak. He once saw him 14 nights in a row, in different pubs every time.* ITOW.

Les: *Although Tim introduced everyone to Freddie somehow they didn't really click with each other. I remember the first time I met Freddie, Smile were doing a short gig at Ealing College one lunchtime, and went to visit Freddie beforehand. He played us 'Heard it on the Grapevine'...I remember Freddie later coming round to Sinclair Gardens, and saying 'I'm starving. I'll just go into the kitchen and boil an egg. And then coming back three minutes later and saying 'How do you boil an egg?' He was a lovely guy though. People like Freddie often stayed overnight there, but they never lived there to my knowledge.*

When he wasn't playing with Smile Roger and the others would watch other bands. Les: *Roger and I had the same tastes in music, and we would see bands at Imperial like Taste.... Then there was an all-night thing with The Faces in the middle of London somewhere...*

Detail from one of Freddie Mercury's sketchbooks - completed whilst studying fashion at Ealing.

Photographer Doug Puddifoot worked as a cameraman for the BBC, and was one of the crew involved with filming the classic Monty Python series. Les: *We saw at least two Python shows, filmed at the White City studios, which were convenient for Shepherd's Bush. We usually walked there, if I remember correctly. Doug gave me the shooting scripts for the entire series. Even the screen directions were hilarious! One of them involved a rat in the wainscoting, which turned out to be a sheep with a machine gun!*

Pete Kelsey and Les occasionally assisted Smile. Pete: *Les and I would sometimes go with Smile and help unload the van and set up the gear, and after the gig do the reverse. There was one gig in Richmond where they opened for 'Yes' that I remember particularly. Brian was a very nice guy and very meticulous about his playing - he knew all of Hendrix by heart and could play the songs note for note. As I recall he would tend to go along with what others wanted to do except on the subject of his guitar playing where he had some very specific ideas.*

When I knew them, Tim Staffell was down on both himself and the band, though, and always criticized what they did even if they performed really well. He seemed to see everything that was wrong instead of what went right. It is that that ultimately broke up Smile as far as I know. Freddie was always the go-getter, the one with ambition and it was he I think who pushed Queen to the success it had. Freddie stepped in later and seemed to take the reins and lead the others to his concept of Queen.

Imperial Student Union (2010)

Roger Taylor arrived in London at a time when the college music circuit was becoming increasingly important. Thanks to Brian May's many contacts within the college, Smile's first concert is thought to have been at Imperial on 26th October supporting Pink Floyd. Only a couple of days previously Brian had received his BSc degree certificate from the Queen Mother.

Whilst still at Sinclair Gardens Roger Taylor had visitors from Cornwall including Jill Johnson. Jill: *I visited him in 1968/69 at least a couple of times, and stayed in the flat. I think Ben and Les were there then, and a chap called Pete.*

Ben (Geoff Daniel) found the comings-and-goings in the flat a bit too much: *I remember Tim Staffell would turn up at all hours, often with 2 or 3 girlfriends in tow. Lots of others would come and go, and I found it a bit chaotic and not conducive to study, so I moved back into halls of residence in 1969. But I went back to Sinclair Gardens at weekends, by which time Smile had been born and the flat had filled up with people sleeping everywhere. I went regularly with them to gigs. I remember one where they backed Berkeley James Harvest I think at Imperial. BJH got pissed off because the crowd preferred Smile!*

Jill Johnson: *Back then transportation was always a problem for Roger. I remember when he came back from London on the train - with his drumkit. He called up my Dad from Truro train station, and asked if he could get a lift home. My Dad drove over to pick him up, and there was Roger in a big girl's sunhat, a long army coat and a full set of drums, on the pavement waiting! I'm not sure how we managed to get it all in the car!*

David Bowie's appearance in Falmouth 1968

It snowed heavily that Christmas. Jayfolk temporarily reformed for one of the more interesting of the events to take place in the Duchy in the sixties. Roger Brokenshire was, indirectly at least, at the bottom of it. After leaving the Reaction he had returned to working as a promoter, but had become aware that live music was losing its allure. He advertised in Melody Maker for a DJ and he got Gerry Gill. Gerry: *Bands like the Reaction had been popular in the fifties and early sixties, but their popularity was dropping off and the dance halls were empty on a Saturday night. So on May 22nd 1968 I drove to Cornwall in a beat-up Thames van with my friend the DJ Adrian Love who I dropped off in St Ives.*

That summer Gerry found himself regularly working the halls with Brokenshire. Then at Christmas he asked an old friend from London, David Bowie, to join him for a couple of gigs in Falmouth. Bowie had recently had several months with the Lindsay Kemp troup, but at that point this was unaccustomed to travelling very far from his home turf in South London.

Gerry: *I'd done a number of gigs with David. We did the Festival Hall gig with Peel and Tyrannosaurus Rex and people like that. David was getting into his Lindsay Kemp phase and I used to run him around and take him down to see his mother in Bromley and do his sound for him. I knew him from the music industry. I wanted to be a pop singer too. I used to hang around the Giaconda coffee bar, in Denmark Street along with the likes of Lulu, Tom Jones, David, Hendrix.*

The first Summer I was there I worked with Roger Brokenshire, doing the halls. Then that winter I started working at The Flamingo, The Garden, The Blue Lagoon and Anaclatos in Falmouth. I left Anaclatos to open up a Middle Earth-type place in Falmouth at the Princess Pavilion and I had David Bowie on twice doing his mime thing.

And we had The Deviants with Mick Farren. It was a snowy winter. There was about 8ft of snow and The Deviants got all the way there from London. I drove back to Redruth with David afterwards and it was still throwing it down with snow. By then I had a little Morris van with little windscreen wipers. He stayed for a few days over Christmas, then on January 4th 1969, I put him back on the train at Redruth station saying 'I'll see you again soon', because I honestly thought I would.

In fact Gerry Gill stayed in Cornwall for several more years, often working with John Lumley-Saville and billed as Magician's Workshop and later as Gandalf's Garden. Jill Johnson returned to her rehearsals with The Famous Jug band and Sue Johnstone joined another group called 'Wizard'. Sue: *Pete Bawden booked Wizard in at PJ's a few times. I still have the receipts of my wages and I appear to have earned £1.10 shillings a gig! The line-up was myself, lead vocal, Trevor McKay, guitar and vocals and John Orange, guitars and vocals. John was a hugely talented guitarist who's real name was Jon Affleck and he was a shark fisherman at the time.*

1969: The year of The Smile

After spending Christmas in Cornwall, Les and Roger returned to a surprise at Sinclair Gardens. Les: *Over the Christmas period we lent the flat out to someone, and when we came back and walked in there were about 30 hippies sleeping there on every square inch of the place! One guy had O/D'ed the night before, and there was also, bizarrely, a huge stack of frozen cod that someone had lifted from the street outside a fish and chip shop...*

On 27th February Smile played at the Albert Hall: a charity concert that was photographed and filmed by Doug Puddifoot. The grainy black and white cine footage conveys a sense of three musicians that were casual in their appearance but confident in their ability. As well as Smile, The Crazy World of Arthur Brown appeared. Pete Edmonds: *We've still got one of Doug's photos from that night. I always kept it because it was the first time we ever did a really big gig. We were bottom of the bill but it was fantastic. Most of the artists were Island Records artists: people like Spooky Tooth and Free and Joe Cocker.*

John 'Acker' Snell, saxophonist with the Reaction, travelled to London especially to see Roger play that night. Together they had performed with The Reaction at some large venues, but none as grand as the Albert Hall: *I saw Smile at the Albert Hall. I stayed at Roger's flat with my wife who was my girlfriend at the time. Smile were louder than the headline acts. So loud it was difficult to listen to - and the sound balance didn't seem right - maybe because of the acoustics in the Albert Hall which are quite strange anyway...Roger was out all night after that gig - celebrating probably - though I caught up with him again the following morning. That weekend one of the Sunday glossy magazines - Observer probably - described Smile as the 'loudest band in the western world'.*

Doug also took photos of the band outside the Albert Hall on the steps that lead down to Imperial. Les: *Roger is wearing my fur coat in those photos of Smile. It's one I bought for a girlfriend then gave it to Roger because it fitted him. He was very skinny when he was young!*

Tim Staffell in Sunbury in 1969. Behind him is his collection of sci fi books. Photo Ian Lynch

In 1969 Roger Taylor's new band went on to play dates in Cornwall almost as regularly as his previous one had. Other biographies have vaguely referred to Devon or The West Country, but it was to Roger's own home town, Truro, that they travelled. Pete Edmonds was the person who initially drove them, having swapped his car for a bottle-green van: *I had an MG A. It was a lovely car. I can even tell you the registration number: 202 APB. I sold it for the van, which was a*

Thames, though later it was replaced by a Transit van, as the Thames was never really big enough. I did the driving and equipment. After a gig we split out the money afterwards. Not that there was much money - but what there was we shared.

The first Smile concert in Cornwall appears to have been at the Flamingo outside Redruth on 22nd March, when they were mistakenly billed, not for the last time, as 'The Smile'. That weekend Wendy Edmonds came down from London in the van with the band: *I went to the Flamingo and saw them there. There were no motorways then. The route was via the A30 and the A303. It was a nightmare. The roads were hellish, and there'd always be a jam at Honiton. It would take at least 8 hours. The only motorway then was the M1 which went as far as Leicester. Coming to Cornwall would have taken a whole day but, still, we had a good laugh once we'd got there.*

The A303 includes the ancient road that passes close to the Stonehenge monument. Pete: *I'd keep the van wherever I was living at the time, and I'd go round to everyone's house and pick them up. We wouldn't have really stopped off anywhere. We'd have just travelled during the day, though not usually the same day we were playing. And each time we came down we'd try to stay for a while and have had a few gigs booked to make the journey worthwhile.*

Smile's many trips to Cornwall provided Les Brown with an occasional cheap and entertaining journey home: *I didn't have a car in those days so I came down in the van with Smile. I did that 3 or 4 times at least. Or I'd just see them because I was down in the holidays anyway. In the van-trips people would be singing and trying things out all the time, and just throwing musical ideas backwards and forwards. I'm very unmusical so I didn't really appreciate it, but I have memories of Freddie doing operatic stuff in the van too.*

Richard Thompson also, later, helped with transportation. Les: *I got on well with Richard. One night we were travelling back to London with Roger, Brian and Tim in his Transit, and we'd bought a barrel of cider in Cornwall. There was this amazing electric storm as we were crossing Bodmin Moor. There was a huge flash of lightning and the whole of the moor was momentarily lit up - everything went completely blue - and I had to leap into the back to stop this big barrel of scrumpy from falling over...*

Smile's first advertised concert in Cornwall, 22nd March 1969.

In Cornwall Smile were less inclined than The Reaction had been to advertise their concerts, and their equipment was still quite rudimentary: Pete Edmonds: *I don't remember Smile putting up posters or doing much promotional-type stuff in Cornwall. We didn't have a mixing desk. We didn't even carry a PA as such. We would have used something in-house. We just brought the guitar, amplifiers and Roger's drums. They were mainly kept at Imperial at the time.*

On the weekend following the booking at The Flamingo, the band played the first of 14 gigs at PJ's, a club in Truro where Queen too would perform the following year. They were initially billed as having *'appeared at London's top clubs and recently broadcast on Radio 1's Top Gear',* a claim later refuted by John Peel the radio show's presenter. However it appears that the band was at least close to being given a session on the programme, and Richard Halliwell remembers Roger buttonholing Peel when the young DJ later visited The Garden in

Penzance. The occasion was on 14th August, an evening when the heavy progressive blues Edgar Broughton Band were playing. Richard: *Taylor and I went to see lots of bands at The Garden in Penzance. Jethro Tull, Eclection, Family, Van der Graff Generator…We also went to see Edgar Broughton, but perhaps more importantly to see John Peel whom Taylor had previously met and given demos to. He was anxious to get a Peel session for Smile. We definitely spent some time talking to Peel that night – and he bought us a drink. My recollection is that Peel remembered Taylor and they'd had some contact before.*

Tim Staffell described PJ's club in Truro as *'a smokey, upstairs UV sweatbox'* (RC). And though it might have been a 'sweatbox', it was a venue that Smile went on to play more than any other.

Pete Bawden was the founder of the club. He had come into the music business as a guitarist with his friend Manny Cockle, before playing with the Staggerlees, the band that, back in 1962, Roger and Dave Dowding watched win the Rock and Rhythm championship. The Staggerlees recorded several upbeat Beatles-like singles with Oriole, but in the end touring outside Cornwall proved too much. Pete: *The Staggerlees asked if I wanted to join them which I did for 2 or 3 years until we had a crash and that put paid to myself, the drummer, and the other guitar player. When we were in hospital I decided that was enough. We'd been travelling all over the UK earning no money at all. In fact day of the crash we did a one night stand in Halifax and had to deliver the van back to Plymouth and it was too much.*

Pete returned to playing the local circuit with Manny for a while, then set up 'Room at the Top' in Truro which opened on 29th September 1967: *That was the original disco that we had before PJ's. It was in High Cross opposite the Cathedral. I opened it with a partner, Dave Penprase, known as Dave Lee from the Staggerlees. We had to shut it down because it didn't have a rear fire escape. There were no bands, it was all disco then. It was very shortlived but it was hugely successful. There was nothing else to go to in Truro.*

In the middle of 1968, just over six months later, they went their separate ways, and in August Dave Penprase opened a club by the same name in Redruth. It would become a successful folk venue where Jill Johnson and the Famous Jug Band amongst others sang regularly.

Pete, though, stayed in Truro and found a larger venue further up Pydar Street. Roger Taylor recalls its precise location: *It was at Moresk on the junction of Pydar St on the right side (near the old T.A drill hall).*

The junction of Moresk Road and Pydar Street as it was in the late 50's. PJs is most likely to have been the breezeblock building partially visible on the far left, its eventual entrance obscured by the small shed visible in the photo. Most of the other buildings would have been demolished to make way for a road that was widened at least as far as the position of the black car. The shop visible on Pydar Street is Slater and Son's grocers: now a betting shop.

Bert Biscoe is now a city Councillor: *The PJ's building was was semi-derelict. The council had bought up the whole of that side of Pydar Street in order to carry out a comprehensive re-development, and it was all taking a long time so they rented the building out very cheaply.*
The club opened in time for Christmas on December the 13th 1968 and Pete called it PJ's taking its name from his own first initials. Coincidentally the day before it opened the West Briton had described a meeting of the musician's union at The Flamingo, in which a spokesman had warned of *'the national trend towards replacing groups in discoteques and ballrooms with recorded music'.* Using the moniker 'Emperor Gill', Gerry Gill had, ironically, by then started a regular stint running discos at The Flamingo.

PJ's, under Pete Bawden's stewardship remained a stronghold of live music, but, across Cornwall as a whole, the number of bands and live venues was slowly on the decline.

Previously thought by Pete to have been a drill hall or armoury associated with the Cornwall Light Infantry Offices in Pydar Street, the PJ's building had been affected by the demolition of many of the buildings nearby. Initiated by Jill Johnson's father and his colleagues, the Pydar Street redevelopment was underway and there was dust and rubble everywhere. Pete: *It was a complete mess. It was like a building site. But we got hold of some wood paneling: got hold of a ton of it. We made it quite nice inside actually, but it was still pretty much a dive. It was a rough place and it didn't get much better I have to say! It wasn't a plush club - but that was the appeal of it. I think we did a couple of nights midweek and Fri, Sat, Sun. Discos some nights but the emphasis was on live music. We had some pretty good music.*

Pete remembers its layout: *The entrance was on Moresk Road. Then you went in and turned left and up some stairs and the bands appeared upstairs, and the stage was the Pydar Street end. There were no windows. Upstairs there was seating around the edges. The 'bursting capacity' was, maybe, a couple of hundred people. There was a bar - after a fashion. But it was n't licensed by the way. Never licensed!*

The toilets were behind the stage upstairs. If you looked at the stage there was a booth on the right- hand side that the DJ sat in - a glass booth - and between the booth and the stage you walked through to go to the toilets. I don't recall any kind of dressing room so what you turned up in you played in.

There was a guy who was an art student who eventually went to South Wales. As you walked up the stairs at PJ's there was this black wall - we painted everything black and covered the windows up it was all artificial lights indoors. He used a pot of white paint and did a relief of Jimi Hendrix the size of the wall.

When they knocked the building down I remember driving through Truro and they'd knocked down half the building but this wall was still stood up, so there was just this vision of Jimi Hendrix remaining.

Connie Bawden, then Pete's wife, recalls other colourful designs on the walls by the unknown art student. These included a mural inspired by Tim Staffell's logo that confirmed Smile's status as PJ's honorary house band: *We had these panels that hung down in the middle of the coffee bar and one of them was painted with great big smiling teeth.*

Upstairs, in the dance hall area, primitive psychedelic lighting was more of a feature, as remembered by visitors. Connie: *There was this light machine that made it look like you had loads of dandruff all over you! Pete bought a magic lantern from an antique shop, and we used to put Epsom salts into it to get bubbles on the walls...*

Louis (now Mal) Rushton from Newquay was the singer in The Good Times, a band that changed their name to Safron late in 1969, and went on to win the Rock and Rhythm championship in 1970. Roger Taylor is known to have deputized for drummers from a number of other Cornish bands, and Good Times/Safron were one of them. Louis: *I remember all the girls loving Rodge: he was blond and slim, with swirling sticks. He was a good drummer but in those days people remember him for his style. He depped with our band a couple of times. I think he did a gig with us at RAF Culdrose once.*

Aerial photograph 1961 looking southwards: A) Site of contemporary multistory car park, B) The windowless building most likely to have been PJ's, C) Junction of Moresk Road and Pydar Street, D) Corner leading to Union Street (largely unchanged). In the foreground is a square of ancient alms houses (now demolished)

Good Times/Safron played at PJ's under both their names. Louis: *If you remember PJ's you weren't there! The gig was a great gig to get because there was always a helluva'n atmosphere. People used to flood in there and it was just brilliant. Pete Bawden wasn't a prima donna but he was so sociable. He was a great host, a great club owner and terrific with the bands.*

By the end of the decade Ginhouse from Bodmin had become another one of Cornwall's highly regarded outfits, having won the Rock and Rhythm Championship in 1969. They appeared at PJ's 4 or 5 times playing mainly covers of numbers by 'Crosby Stills Nash and Young', and 'Yes'. Guitarist Colin Brokenshire recalls visiting for the first time: *When we first went there we thought 'Blimee! What a place to come to!' It was just barren land then. It was like a derelict site really. I remember the building stuck out in the middle - with nothing much around it - as PJ's. It was like a football pitch with a club house stuck in the middle. None of town centre was there then. It was just barren land.*

Colin remembers it having an unusual, non-standard door: *When you first went in there, you couldn't see much inside because there was very low lighting! Everything was blacked out except the big front door. Whether it was two, like, open stage doors or one big door, I'm not sure. I wouldn't say PJs was massive - it was not a very big place. But it was a really good club. It was a good gig to get, and it had a good reputation with bands.*

As a sixteen year old, Linda Roach used to visit PJ's with a group of friends: *I remember seeing Roger's first band Cousin Jacks in the City Hall when I was about 10. My Uncle organized the children's games. Later I was part of a group of girls from the Girl's Grammar School who used to go to PJ's. I saw Smile there at least once. I remember the logo on the bass drum.*

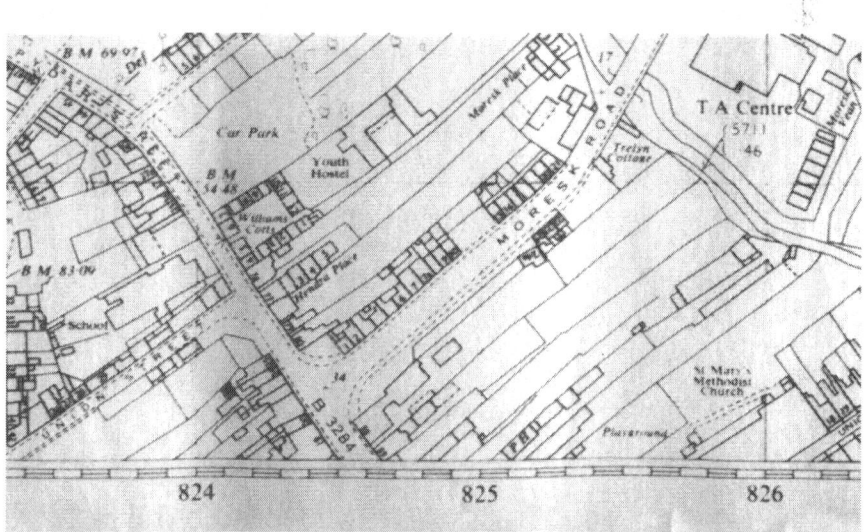

Moresk Road, Truro circa 1970. Mid redevelopment, the terrace of residential houses on the north side of the street remain, but the road has been widened on the south side, leaving the PJ's building, numbered 88, exposed at the junction with Pydar Street. Photo John Snell.

We would be escorted home by our parents. But one evening one of them decided to go inside and he was not impressed. He was a fireman and he thought it was a considerable fire-risk. There was only one exit and there were loose wires hanging down and so on and so he recommended a 'D7' which is when the fire-brigade have to investigate whether it's safe.

There was no official bar or license for a bar. But everyone used grass - especially out in the car park. Some of the Truro boys were famous for their prodigious use of drugs...

In 1969 Mike Grose, who was soon to become Queen's first bass player, had a short stint in London with guitarist Tony Coxon where he had coincidentally come to know Tim Staffell's father whilst working briefly in a factory that he ran. Mike and Tony were from St Austell, a town less than ten miles from Truro, surrounded by white hills of china clay. The clay was used in pharmaceutical products, and during the sixties the wash from the quarries turned the river that runs through the town a milky white colour.

Mike had a long involvement with the Cornish music scene, and as well as being the only person other than Roger Taylor to have played with The Reaction, Smile and Queen, during the sixties he also played with semi-pro Cornish bands The Jaguars, The Individuals, The Smokey Joes, Joseph, Jason's Mind, Bent Cement and Safron.

Mike switched to playing bass for The Individuals in 1965: *I was only 15, the other guys were 20 or so and they all wanted to be the lead guitarist. Luckily for me I came across from lead guitar.*

Jason's Mind and Bent Cement both played on the tiny stage at PJ's. Mike: *Bent Cement was a four piece: Tony Coxon on lead guitar, Paul Moon on drums, Phil Bassett, vocals and myself on bass. We had two stacks of 8x12 Marshalls, a huge WEM PA and we were seriously loud. We played at Meva (Mevagissey) Feast Week and managed to get music banned from the quay for many years!*

Guitarist Tony Coxon visited PJ's several times: *I remember the building being surrounded by wasteland. There was rough ground towards the right of the entrance as you approached the building. I can visualise scooters being parked there. I don't remember a pavement or road being near it. You had to actually walk across rough ground to get to it. There was no alcohol. We had to go to the pub between sets...*

It was dark with low ceilings and that little stage which I remember because I played 'Man of the World' by Fleetwood Mac on that stage which I was very pleased with.

Mike Grose decided to put some money into the PJ's venture. He denies ever owning it outright, but regarding eateries and nightlife in Truro at the time he recalls there being very little. In November, coinciding with a performance by a Cornish band that were Radio One regulars, The Onyx, Pete and Mike opened a coffee and griddle bar downstairs. Mike: *We used to cook burgers and that kind of thing. I opened it at 10.00 AM. Closed at 2.30. Then open again at 7.00 till closing, most days of the week. We worked long hours, and Pete and I took turns. Plus we had other staff. A young lady whose name I forget. I remember we agreed that she should clean the ladies loos. I used to do the cooking and make the coffee and tea and so on. We would go to the cash and carry and buy burgers and chips. The kids loved it!*

Downstairs there was a pool table on the left hand side and tic-tac-toe fruit machines. You'd put a sixpenny into them. The toilets were upstairs behind the stage somewhere. I used to put on pool tournaments to try and draw in the punters. I did all sorts actually.

Mike remembers a spot of trouble at the club: *One night we did have a gang down from St Austell. They were hooligans who stuck a pole through the door and charged it down, knocked it completely off its hinges in fact. But by that time we'd evacuated the club out the back door and down the fire escape, and disappeared. When I was in bands in Cornwall I was threatened with a knife on two occasions: once in Camborne and once in Falmouth. It did get nasty sometimes.*

Pete and Mike ended up employing a doorman. He was a friend of Mike's from St Austell called Trevor Mannell. Trevor reminisces: *I knew Roger Taylor when he still kept his drums in the back of his little convertible Triumph Herald. I worked at a garage in Tresillian and used to do a few jobs for him on that car. He used to come regularly to have his hair cut in my flat in St George's Road Truro, too, because I had a friend, Heather Turner, who was a hairdresser. I think she gave him blonde highlights as well. And I remember him saying to me after he'd joined Smile, that they had a concert at the Albert Hall and that they had something like 12 record companies after them.*

Marvelous Kid at PJs in 1970. The piano was one found in Truro for Freddie Mercury. Photo Tony Coxon.

Trevor was at PJ's one night when someone upstairs was causing a disturbance and had to be ejected. As a result, though still a teenager, he was offered a job working on the door. It became his vocation, and his company 'Stout Security' now employs doormen across Cornwall. Trevor: *I remember the night that a motorbike gang in all their leathers roared up, parked their bikes outside the club and came in. They were The Scorpions, from St Austell and there were more than twenty of them. And I had to keep the peace!*

Bill Tonkin was playing drums in a band called Cellophane Cloud that night: *Whilst playing a gig at P.J.s in Truro I remember the manager frantically waving at us to keep playing, we were puzzled until we noticed an army of blokes at the top of the stairs kicking , punching and throwing bodies back down: apparently the St Austell Grease (bikers) had turned up for a ruck.*

Trevor: *Generally, though, it was a friendly, relaxed club and everyone knew each other. I met my wife at PJ's and I also got to know Pat and*

Sue Johnstone. I've got photos of Pat and Sue and Mike Grose at our wedding.

Trevor saw Smile at The Flamingo and PJ's: *Later on there were a lot of psychedelic posters upstairs in PJ's and ultraviolet lighting which was still quite a new thing at the time. PJ's was a unique venue, and Smile gigs were always well attended. There were lots of good bands at PJ's but Smile were definitely one of the best. Though I don't remember the performances I remember helping Brian May and the band carry their gear up the narrow stairs there.*

Pete Bawden booked roughly one live act a week, and he drew on Mike Grose's first-hand knowledge of local bands to help him do this. As well as Onyx, Ginhouse, Good Times/Safron and Marvelous Kid the bookings of Cornish bands included the likes of Made in England, Mr Lucifer and Constable Zippo's Band, all of whom played PJ's more than once.

Roger Taylor also took an interest in the bookings, and helped Pete secure more prestigious 'progressive blues' groups from outside Cornwall like Mighty Baby, Third Ear Band, Warm Dust and Empty Vessels (later Tanglewood, then Wishbone Ash). Pete: *Roger was the sort of guy who if he met someone as interested in music as he was, was absolutely passionate. We used to talk about which bands to book into the club and he was always full of enthusiasm. He was different from the rest. Very dedicated to the music and he never varied.*

Tony Coxon's Marvelous Kid made their debut at PJ's in June 1970. Tony: *Paul Moon and I formed Marvelous Kid with Steve Betts who later was keyboardist with The Eurythmics. Then Spike Hooper joined us. Mike Grose would have been our bass player but at the time he was busy with Queen.*

Tony's photos of the highly regarded Marvelous Kid playing at PJ's give a clear indication of the size of the venue. Tony: *I'm positive that through the door with the coloured ribbons is where we put the gear. It had a little dressing area and a toilet, and we would have put the guitar and drums cases there. But the flash on the camera is misleading. Actually that room was always dark and so you wouldn't have seen the decoration on the walls. There were no windows. It was probably a fire-risk.*

None of the bands that played at PJ's played there as often as Smile did, however. In the West Briton there are adverts for 9 gigs in PJ's that year, including one on Boxing Day, where they were billed as appearing with 'friends' or 'special guest artistes' (which could, conceivably have been Freddie Mercury's then band, Wreckage). In 1969 six of the gigs were weekenders: typically Friday and Saturday double bookings. They had won lots of admirers, and after their first gigs of 1969 there were requests for more appearances. Underneath an ad for professional Cornish psych-rock band The Onyx, Pete wrote *'and for all those who kindly asked Smile will be back... on July 19th'*.

Tony Coxon: *I remember seeing Smile play there on that little stage. I was in awe of Brian's playing. It was the first time I'd seen them and I was very impressed. I think they played 'Sitting On Top of the World': the blues standard that Cream recorded. I remember the impression they made on me – a really full sound and great melodic guitar. It was impressive stuff, but being a guitarist it was Brian's playing I recall the most.*

By 1969 Pete Bawden's friend Manny Cockle was involved with a different group after brother Peter, the bass player in his own band, had drowned in the sea near St Agnes. Manny was another admirer: *I saw Smile at least once in PJ's. They did a rendition of Aquarius and it stopped me in my tracks. It was off the clock. I stood there with my mouth hanging open. I couldn't believe the sound they were making. There was a lot of falsetto going on that night. But you could tell they were going places: they were head and shoulders above everyone else.*

As well as covers, Smile played their own songs at PJ's, as Penny North of Jayfolk recalls: *I did go to PJ's, but I think it was during my time at college, so only during the holidays. I used to go with people like Sue and Pat Johnstone and Les Brown, and remember Smile playing there - in particular Brian's song about a polar bear, which I loved! Haven't heard it since then!*

Although ex-Reaction members Mike Dudley and Geoff Daniel were also at College, in the holidays they too returned to Cornwall and saw Smile play. Mike: *I watched them a few times, at PJ's in particular where they were extremely good, and where there was often a distinct smell of pot!*

Marvelous Kid playing in PJs. Behind Paul Moon the drummer is moulding visible on the wooden-panelled walls as originally fitted by Pete Bawden and helpers. Photo: Tony Coxon

On the weekend of September 13th and 14th 1969 Mr Lucifer, a band that had moved to Cornwall from Cambridge, shared the bill with Smile. Will Wright was their drummer: *We did a double header with Smile at PJ's. I knew Roger Taylor because we had a mutual friend in Rik Evans. Roger had only recently gone up to College. We agreed that Smile would headline one night and so we headlined the other. Mr Lucifer then were doing Cream and Hendrix and were very R'n'B influenced. We were similar to Smile in some respects.*

I remember we were playing there one day with Smile when all of a sudden 40 or 50 bikers walked in the door and came upstairs. The audience sort of parted to let them in. And they stood and looked at us for a while. We thought let's keep playing, and we bashed through a couple of rock and roll numbers: some Steppenwolf and Eddie Cochrane, and they turned around and just walked out again.
Les Brown has his own memories of that weekend: *Paddy Sargeant from Mr Lucifer I remember. He was a shortish chap with very big hair. I got to know them simply because the bands played together that weekend. Mr Lucifer was a rock band like Smile. I have great memories of that evening at PJ's: the first half anyway! There was a really good*

atmosphere going around. Sue Johnstone out of the Jayfolk was there as well. I very rarely dance but I was dancing like a maniac that night!

The Smile gigs with Mr Lucifer did receive some publicity. Denise Craddock later lived with Roger and Freddie Mercury in Barnes, and often saw Smile play in London: *I have a photo of me pointing to a Smile poster in Perranporth. I was down on a geography field trip. The poster looks like it was in the window of a shut-down newsagents.*

Denise Craddock pointing to Smile posters in the window of a tobacconist's in Perranporth. Photo Denise Craddock.

Posters and adverts were not the only literature produced by the club. Pat Johnstone learnt some of the skills she used later with the Queen fan club whilst working at PJ's: *I did a little in-house newsletter when I worked at PJ's. It was a listings thing, advertising everything that was happening in the Truro area. Like a free newspaper. I also did cold-calling and spoke to advertisers.*

The members of Smile, particularly Tim, also designed their own publicity material. Roger had the phrase *'Don't forget to Smile'* written on his drumkit. It became a strapline used to good effect both in Pete's adverts and in posters printed for the band at Ealing College – possibly by Freddie.

Brian May had a reputation, as a young man, for forgetfulness. Geoff Daniel: *The 'Smile' visits to Cornwall were mostly at PJ's. At one Brian May gave me his wallet for safe keeping. We went to the pub and forgot. I went home to St Austell only to be woken by a frantic phone call at 3 AM from an anxious Brian!*

But Brian was also unusually talented. Famously, as a teenager, he worked with his father to construct the guitar that he played and still plays, more than forty years later, with Queen. Designed and made from scratch using handtools and household materials, including the wood from an old fireplace, it is a truly remarkable feat of engineering. Those in Cornwall saw the guitar as yet further proof that Smile was no run-of-the-mill band. Pete Bawden: *Brian was a stunning musician. I remember him showing me his home-made guitar the Red Special, in PJ's. I said to him 'you did this?' I just couldn't believe it. He said 'Yes, I made this, and then I made that' and he demonstrated all the different settings and features it had. It was incredible.*

His ability as a guitar player together with Roger's dedication and commitment put them poles apart from the other musicians that were around at the time. We all played, we all had little amateur careers but it was a bit half-hearted really. There weren't many people who stood out as being really, really good. And I'm not just saying this with the benefit of hindsight, it was apparent then.

It is clearly evident that Pete Bawden loved Smile, and his respect for their ability was reflected in the superlatives he always used when placing their adverts in the West Briton.

Adverts for nine concerts by Smile in PJ's in 1969

Apart from PJ's and the Flamingo, there is some mystery regarding exactly where else Smile performed in Cornwall. There is an advert for a gig on the 5th of April 1969 when they played alongside London-jazz-rock outfit 'Eclection' at the Winter Gardens, and Tim Staffell, when interviewed in the 90's (LJ), told of Smile performances at beach parties, Fowey Carnival (Regatta) and St Ives.

Graham Hankins of The Reactions remembers a hotel: *When Roger came down to Cornwall with Smile he often used to contact me. So I saw them a few times at PJ's, and also at a hotel somewhere, in Porthtowan or Portreath in a big function room. In fact that night I didn't pay admission: Roger signed me in for free. The main thing I remember about Smile was the way they looked: long hair and pantaloons, Brian especially. To me they seemed quite 'far out' really.*

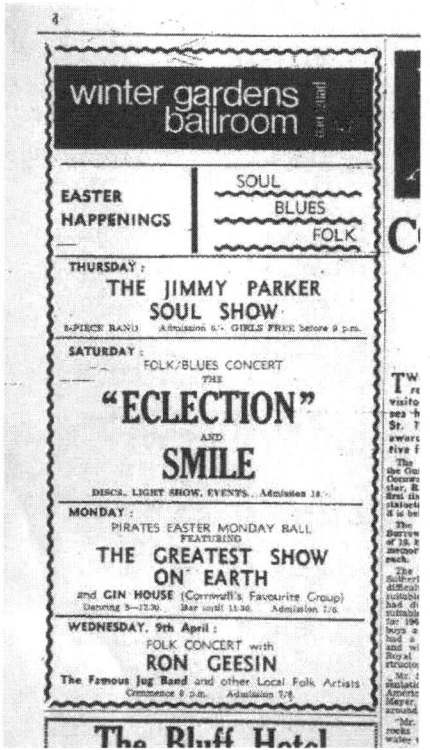

Peter Gill-Carey, who came out of hospital only a few months before Smile formed, recalls another gig where Roger may have been on the door: *The only time I saw Roger play after the accident on Goss Moor was when Roger and Brian May came down as Smile and they played in a Church Hall in Truro – I think St Paul's. I can't remember if they'd got the hall and were taking money at the door - like we did at the Guildhall in St Ives, but I think they may have been. Brian and Roger are the ones I remember, with the singer, Tim Staffell.*

Pete Edmonds: *PJ's was the main place. But then we did some other places around Cornwall. We played in Wadebridge. It was a church hall, or a town hall. It was a long space: not a club anyway, more of a hall. Somebody else would have been on the door taking the money that night. I used to just set the equipment up. And we played somewhere in Falmouth. In fact I think we played the Art College there.*

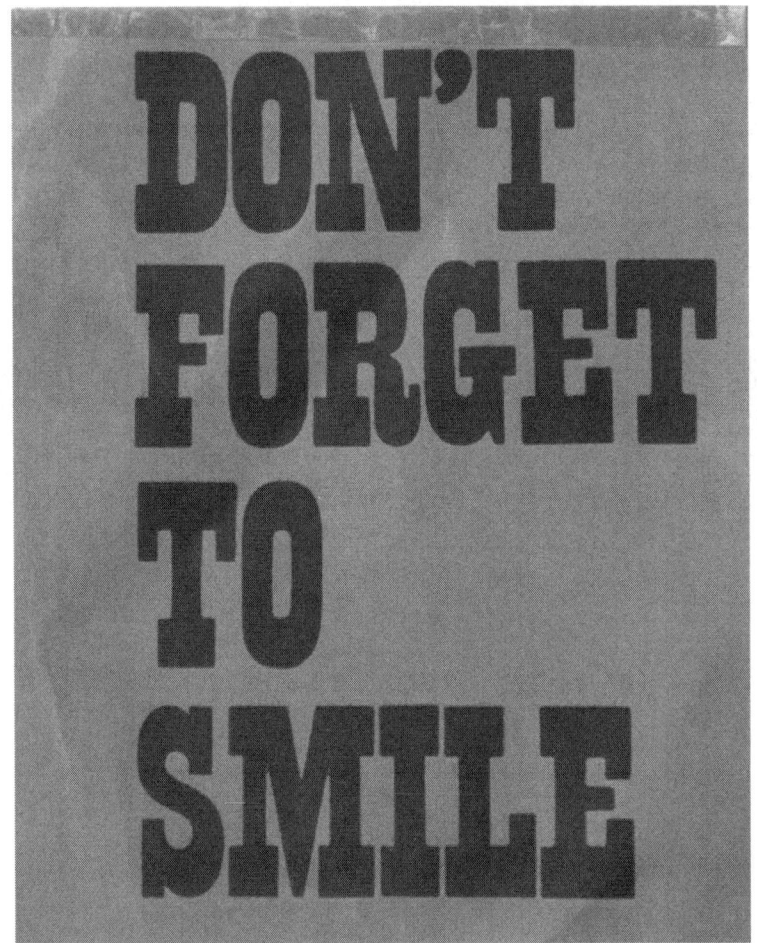

Smile poster possibly designed by Freddie Mercury. Lettering is black on a red background.
Collection Martin Skala www.queenconcerts.com

But Wadebridge I remember particularly because there was a fight there. The first Queen album was produced by John Anthony. He was quite a 'bad boy': long hair and everything else and he pissed off the local guys because he was chatting up the girls. It got a bit ugly and we had to do a runner out of the gig to the van. They followed us down the road with Roger leaning out of the window shouting at them and goading them on.

John Anthony, who, as well as producing the album Queen 1, also produced the Smile single in Summer 1969, has described using a mic stand to defend himself that evening (TRL). The gig is likely to have been in the Town Hall in Wadebridge, as there are no other comparable halls in the town.

Gerry Gill - as well as DJing - was often employed as an MC: *I introduced Smile and Queen onto the stage a few times. St Austell YMCA comes to mind. That was one Smile gig I think. Bands like Onyx, Wishful Thinking, Safron, Coconut Grove also played there. It was in the middle of the town; one that started at 7 thru to 10.15 on a Monday night. I got to know Roger pretty well because we had a mutual friend in Rik Evans.*

It is n't just the Cornwall gigs that have not been reliably recorded. There was, for example, a concert organised at Marjons teacher training college on the King's Road by Roger's friend Richard Halliwell. *When I was at Marjons I was 'ents sec' for a while, and I booked them for the Summer Ball there, but they didn't go down very well because they were too loud and heavy. People complained because it wasn't dance music it was 'stand and watch' music.*

Another of Roger's friends from Cornwall, Penny North, also found the band opportunities to perform: *As Smile, I got them a gig at my College's summer ball at Ball's Park College Hertford, and they went down really well, earning them a return fixture. I got them the gig with the then social sec, a girl whose name I have forgotten. It must have been in the summer of my second year. That would have been with Roger, Brian and Tim. She was very impressed with them, and recommended them to be booked again. By this time it was 1970 and they had reformed as Queen.*

Constable Zippo's Electric Commode Band, to give them their full title, was a five-piece that played at PJ's, and were based in East Cornwall. Nigel Chappell, who later worked as Queen's accountant, was their bassist: *I remember you had to walk across rubble to get to PJ's...It had a low stage, only about 6 inches high. PJ's was a very good club for the time, though. They had some really cutting-edge bands.*

The Smile gig at the tiny Perceval Institute in North Cornwall. 'Earth' had been recorded during June 1969 and, at the time, it was their latest and only record.

Through playing at PJ's Nigel got to know Mike Grose and in fact still has a Fender Precision bass that he bought from him. He also met Pat and Sue Johnstone, and as a result ended up later sharing a flat with them in Victoria, West London. And Nigel recalls another previously undocumented Smile gig. This time Constable Zippo's played as support.

Nigel: *I didn't see Smile at PJ's but I did come across an early version of Queen at a little village hall. It was in 'St something'. I remember it was a bit of a hike to get there, and dusk was falling when we arrived. We were supposed to be supporting another band. Turned out the band was Brian May, Roger and Freddie. Freddie certainly sang at this gig. I can definitely remember that. He may not have sang all through the set, but I do remember him singing. And for the time they were a really spectacular band. All of us in Constable Zippo thought 'bloody hell what's happening here?' We couldn't believe what we were hearing. I certainly remember Brian May's amazing guitar-work that evening.*

There is an advert that allows this Cornish gig, at least, to be accurately pin-pointed to the small rural village of St Minver near Polzeath in North Cornwall, where it took place on 25th July. St Minver is a hamlet of less than 20 houses, and The Perceval Institute has a maximum capacity of around 100 people. It is still used for coffee mornings and, once a month for musical recitals, but none quite so loud as Smile would have been in 1969.

The Perceval Institute, St Minver (2010)

The trio had played the previous weekend at PJ's, and, being the middle of the Summer, it is likely that they had stayed in Cornwall for the whole week at least. But is it possible that Freddie Mercury, then still Freddie Bulsara, sang on stage with them? Given his enormous enthusiasm for the group it seems that he must have done, at least in an informal way. This would have been more likely in Cornwall where there were lots of relatively low-key gigs and audiences were less likely to notice, or care, if the performance wasn't perfect. It should also be said Nigel Chappell is n't the only one to remember Freddie singing with Smile in Cornwall. Sue Johnstone: *I'm sure Freddie sang in PJ's when Tim was there too.*

Jackie Gunn and Jim Jenkins describe Freddie as being a very frequent if not constant member of the Smile entourage. Wendy Edmonds: *We used to see Smile play at Imperial College - some of them were lunchtime gigs. I saw them rehearsing there too in one of the lecture halls. Freddie used to come along to Smile gigs and hang around and play the piano - that kind of thing. He would just tag along.*

Brian May: *Freddie was a friend of Tim Staffell's and came along to our gigs, and offered suggestions in a way that couldn't be refused! At that time he hadn't really done any singing, and we didn't even know he could...*ITOW

The day after the St Minver gig was Roger's birthday and it was the first of three consecutive years when Brian and Freddie would celebrate it with him in Cornwall. Freddie is known to have been one of the gang stranded in Cornwall without transport that July after Pete Edmond's green van had broken down in Andover. In the end they all took the train from Truro station, loading all their bulky musical equipment into the carriage despite the protestations of the guard AIB.

On their trips to Cornwall Roger, Tim, Brian and the others stayed overnight in a variety of locations, and most of the visits would be sociable and fun. Richard Thompson, drummer with 1984, also helped with the transport and came to Cornwall with them a few times: *I didn't keep a diary then, so most dates are very hazy. I do remember watching the Moon landings at Roger's Mum's house in 1969. They must have had a gig that night too. We used to go to the beaches as well but we didn't surf! I mainly stayed at Les Brown's parent's house in Truro. He was at Imperial with Brian, but I lost touch when he went to Paris to work. We came down almost every other weekend in those days as petrol was cheap.*

During the Summer holiday Les was already in Cornwall:
One night they said they were coming down but there was a problem with the van and they were delayed. Then when I woke up in the morning there they were. We lived in Crescent Road, near Jill Johnson's place, and there was a corner shop there. And all these guys said 'Hey we've been sleeping in the van all night' so we said 'oh you poor sods' and we went over to the shop and bought bacon and eggs for about 17 people and fed them all around our kitchen table. It was Smile and Freddie and people like John Anthony I remember being there that morning.

Sue Johnstone was a regular at PJ's, and she also helped put members of Smile up. *I was a part of those days and will always remember the moon landing and all of us watching it at Roger's house, plus the great nights at PJ's. As more and more people came down with them we'd help Roger put some of them up. Brian and Freddie stayed with my father, sister and I on one occasion in Highertown, where we had just moved, and we had a great time partying together: my Dad and Freddie on the piano and Brian on guitar…*

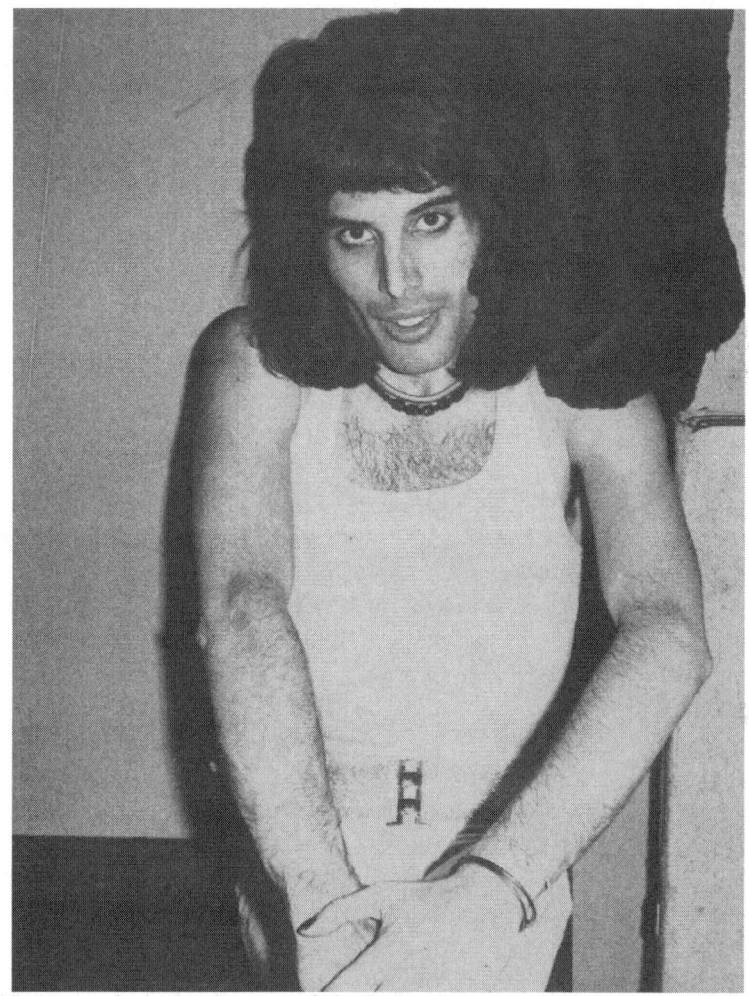

Freddie Mercury in the dressing room of The Garden, Penzance, 1974 (photo Karen Silverlock)

Penny North was another member of Jayfolk who helped provide accommodation: *I first encountered Roger one evening outside the Blue Lagoon in Newquay, when I wished his band luck with the forthcoming*

Rock Championship in the City Hall. He told me they didn't need luck as they had talent! I got to know him better after that through Jill Johnson, and we kept in touch after I went to College in Hertford. One occasion when Smile was playing a gig in Cornwall, I cadged a lift down with them for the weekend, and Tim and Freddie stayed at my home in Grampound. I can still picture them sitting in the kitchen with their long hair and fur jackets, chatting to my grandmother, who, until then, had no time for the 'hairy youth', like those who 'made a racket on Top of the Pops'... She was surprised and delighted to realise that they were actually very intelligent young men, and 'so interesting to talk to'! At the time that they stayed with me, Freddie was just a mate coming along for the ride, and maybe helping out in the background. I remember feeling quite surprised when I first learned that he was to be the lead singer for Queen.

Penny describes the subsequent overnight journey back to London again: *I think it was just Roger, Brian, Freddie and Tim with Pete Roadie, as we called him, driving. I recall we borrowed two caravan mattresses from my Dad, to put in the back to make the return journey more comfortable. Those mattresses remained in the Barnes flat that Smile lived in later, and they came in very handy when parties were held and people stayed over. I do know my poor parents never got those mattresses back! I don't remember much else about the journey, except stopping for breakfast at a transport cafe. But there was, of course, some spontaneous singing as we went along, too.*

Pete Bawden also gave members of the band board and lodgings. Brian stayed with him and his wife Connie on more than one occasion in their house on 'Sandy Lane', St Austell. Connie Bawden: *When we lived in St Austell Roger and the others would come up for dinner, then stay with us: sleeping on the floor in the front room.* Pete: *Brian May was into astronomy. Still is. Once when he stayed with us in St Austell he got a thick block of board and put hundreds and hundreds of pins in it and traced a web of cotton around the pins and made a whole thing about the planets, and it was amazing. It was beautiful and I thought if only I'd hung on to that!*

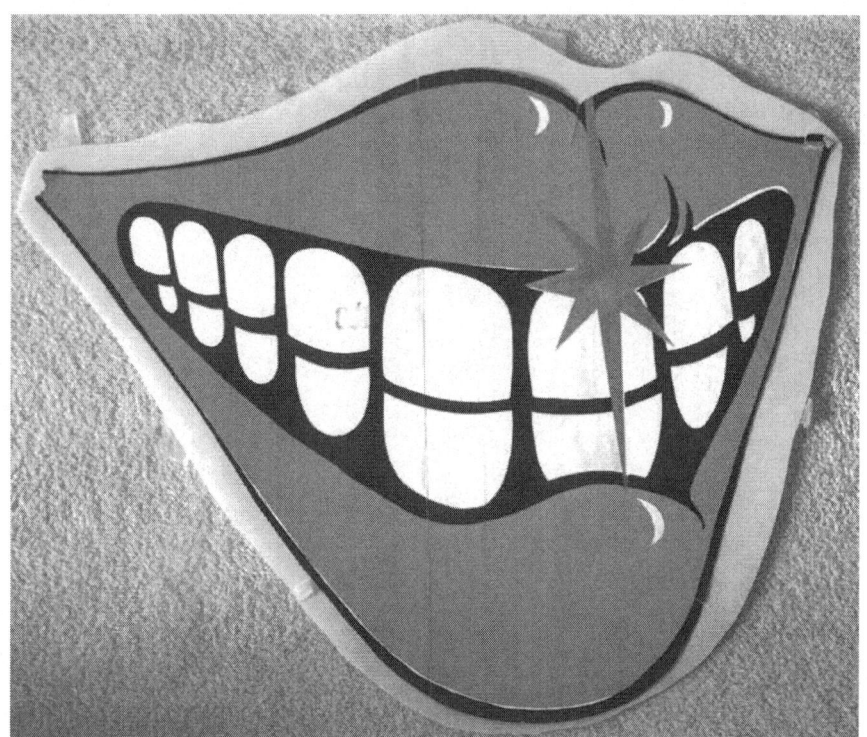
A brightly coloured 'Smile' print designed for Roger Taylor's bass drum: photographed on the floor attached to the remains of a drumskin. Photo www.queenconcerts.com

The Smile entourage also visited an address in Falmouth. Residents of 11, Penarth Road - Ian Lynch and his brother - had known Roger Taylor since his days with The Reaction. Ian: *There was one weekend after Smile played in Truro City Hall, when Tim Staffell stayed behind after the others had gone back to London. He stayed with us in Falmouth for what seemed like months. I think Tim was sleeping on a sofa in my front room for a few weeks at least, so my parents, who were normally very relaxed, kept saying 'when's he going back?' I remember playing guitar with him in the house, and he sang me his own songs, like 'Earth' - just him and a guitar. We went to our local, The Four Winds, most nights and I remember him pulling the barmaid.*

Ian and Tim became friends, and they subsequently travelled back to London and stayed at Tim's parent's house in Sunbury-on-Thames.

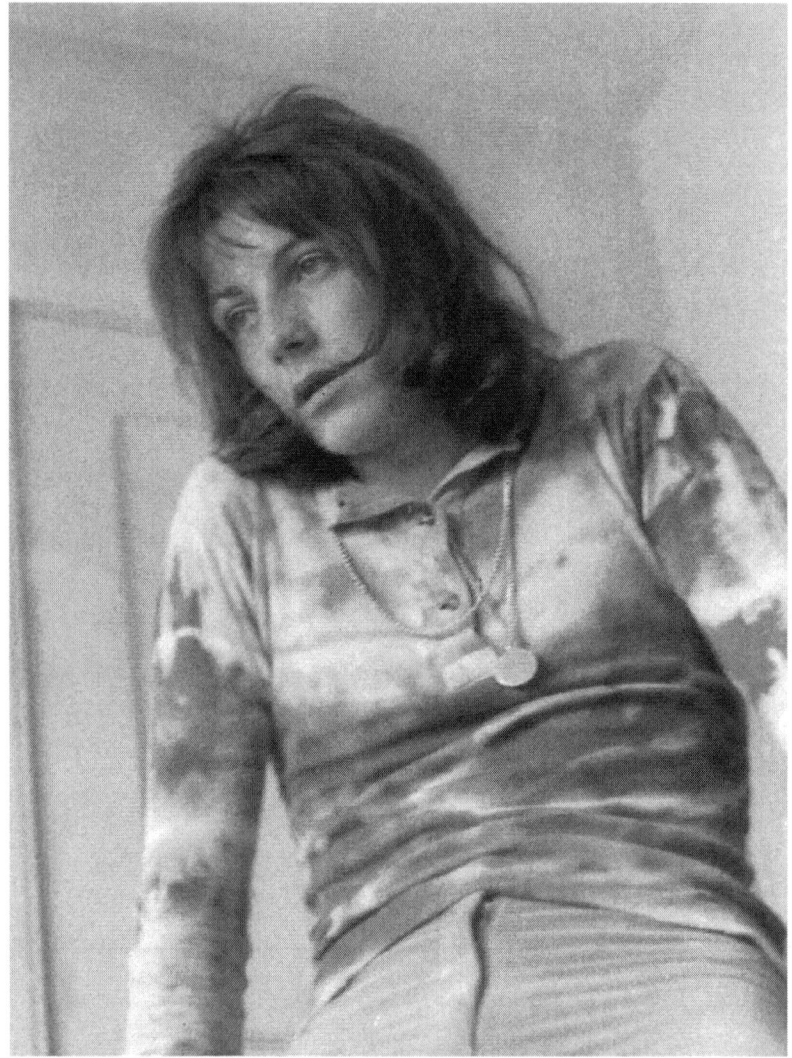
Tim Staffell in his bedroom in Sunbury, 1969. Photo Ian Lynch.

Whilst there, Ian took an informal, but evocative, set of photographs of Tim wearing a tie-dyed vest.

When Smile were down in Cornwall it was, however, Roger's house in Park View that was the busiest. Pete Edmonds: *We mainly stayed with Roger's Mum. It was a bungalow in a quiet little cul-de-sac. We stayed with Sue and Pat Johnstone too. We went to a few pubs in Truro, but I* can't remember their names. We would sometimes spend a couple of weeks down in Cornwall at a time. We were students and didn't have anything much else on in the holidays.

Mike Dudley, Roger's closest collaborator during his Reaction days remembers meeting Brian May, the man who had taken his place in Roger's musical affections: *I met Brian on several occasions when they came to Cornwall. He tried to show me how to play the lead in 'Hey Joe' at one time. 40 years later I've worked out how to do it! I met him in several places, but that particular occasion was at Roger's house in Truro.*

Apart from the fact they gave Roger a chance to visit home, it's not entirely clear why trips to Cornwall were so attractive to Smile and their friends. Pete Edmonds: *The thing about PJ's I remember was the stairs going up to the main hall. It was a dark, dingey place. But it was good atmosphere. We liked playing there. Smile didn't get that many gigs in London. So it was an opportunity to play live and get experience. And the gigs in Truro were popular.*

Mike Grose: *As I found out when I was in London, it's not easy to get gigs up there, and they often expect you to play for nothing. It was just better for Roger to use his contacts in Cornwall to get decent paid gigs down here.*

Sue Johnstone: *I remember the band at PJ's with Tim. Tim was a great singer. Smile and their crew came down and we all sort of traipsed round together. And we did go to the pub. They may have visited The City Inn on one occasion, because we were living in that part of Truro, but the Navy Arms was the main one. I went there with Smile and Queen on many occasions.*

One afternoon John 'Acker' Snell found himself stuck in Playing Place, about a mile out of Truro, with the three members of Smile: *I went with Roger Taylor when they decided to go for a drive and see a bit of Cornwall. We only got as far as Playing Place because their sparkling new Transit van got a puncture! So we pulled into the garage and spent a fruitless hour or two trying to change the tyre. Tim Staffell and Brian were there.*

They ended up turning the van around and driving back to Truro. Luckily Keith Harding, Roger's neighbour was on hand to help out. Keith: *Roger was down with his friends from London and their van - a Transit - had a puncture. He was pretty hopeless when it came to anything mechanical and anyway they didn't have any tools so I helped them changed the tyre. The tyre had a left hand-thread which is what threw them...*

Tim Staffell: *Those weekends in Cornwall were highlights of our time with Smile because everyone used to make so much fuss of us. It became a great social thing with lots of drinking sessions* (MH). *We would set off in the van and head west with anticipation. These were semi-pro days so the social nature of the activity was as important as the music. Many people - myself included - regarded membership of a band as a particularly effective social device, especially where attracting females was concerned! Roger was a strongly hetero-sexual adolescent and was the one who was most popular with the ladies! He was the best-looking member of Smile and had a more accessible personality. I used to think it has something to do with him being a provincial lad...*(LJ)

In May 1969 the three-piece were signed to Mercury Records, and later that summer they recorded two songs that were released as a single. 'Earth' by Tim was on the A-side and 'Step on me', by Brian, on the reverse. Both are pleasing and characterful songs, the same blend of pop and heavy rock that Queen perfected later.

I might be at a table and suddenly I'll catch
a fleeting vision of her crystal seas
or I might be standing in a crowded dockyard far away
underneath the sun I've never seen
For I have seen many worlds for what its worth
but I'll never see again the planet Earth, my Earth.
From 'Earth' words and music by Tim Staffell

The single was engineered by John Anthony and recorded at the prestigious Trident Studios, where Queen would return a couple of years later. The record was released in the USA but not UK, and its subsequent failure, whilst not surprising under the circumstances, was a source of disappointment to the band.
Back in Cornwall, Sue Johnstone recollects a special evening and a unique but strangely apt performance by a group of friends who all had good singing voices: *Once when Smile came to Cornwall we went to St*

The Smile single as released in the US in 1969. (SIS)

Agnes with Brian, Roger and Tim. We went to the Driftwood pub and then walked along the cliffs there. I'm sure Freddie was there too. And we found a cave down on the beach and sang inside it, and did this brilliant 5 or 6 part harmony of 'Earth' which was Tim's song. Then we walked up on the headland and the whole place was completely covered in glow worms. It was amazing. The sky was so clear and every star was out, and of course Brian, because of his expertise in astronomy, could name them all. He named all the individual stars and constellations...

Jill Johnson visited Roger in London in 1968 and '69, after which time their relationship ended: *I stayed in the Shepherd's Bush flat 2 or 3 times. It seemed there were always a lot of people staying there! I think there were four main residents of whom Roger was one. I saw Smile play twice in London, at a couple of clubs. I thought they were a great band and I loved the music. As musicians they were all very accomplished, and Tim Staffell's voice was amazing - better than Freddie's I always thought. I saw them once in Truro at PJ's - but then Roger and I split up and that was it.*

In a frank magazine interview, published later in the 70's, Roger Taylor was prompted to recall his relationship with Jill Johnson: a relationship that started on the banks of the River Kenwyn, in the idyllic surroundings of Dave Dowding's farm in Little Canaan: *My first real love was a girl called Jill. A mate and I went to a club and there was a folk group playing with a girl singer in it. My friend was older and had a car and we gave her a lift. As it turned out we all went to a nearby fair. Then, when I ran into her again, we ended up together for four years.*

She was small and wore short skirts, which were 'in' at the time. We had lots of rows but I think that's a reason why I liked her so much. She had a very strong mind and she knew what she wanted. I can't stand dumb girls - I like girls who can take care of themselves. Things fizzled out for us at college: she joined another folk group, and went out with the guitarist, and that was the end of it. She was quiet in some ways, now that I think about it, but she had a lot of power in her. SIS

For much of her time in 1969 Jill was tied up with the other folk group, namely, The Famous Jug Band. Their first album which was recorded that year includes one standout track 'A Leaf Must Fall', written by Clive Palmer. Clive recognizes Jill's outstanding contribution: *She made it a classic, and the voice is so clear. I wrote the song in the caravan at the Folk Cottage in ten minutes. It's based on a Chinese poem.*

The caravan in question had been recently vacated by singer songwriter, Ralph McTell. The Famous Jug Band played on the college circuit in venues across the UK in 1969, accompanied at times by guitarist Wizz Jones, and in June they were featured in the Melody Maker. Jill had been on television, made an album and had now appeared in the national music press. Jill: *Roger and I had a friendly bet on who would make a record first, and who would be on TV first. I won!*

Classic example of winning the battle but losing the war! Roger was always supportive. I don't think he or his friends were envious of me. Roger was single-minded and determined, and he always knew that he would be famous.

What! A jug band from Cornwall? FJB in Melody Maker June 21st 1969. Cutting collection Jill Johnson.

The photo of FJB in the Melody Maker was when we were in London doing gigs and promotion for the first album which came out in July '69. We spent a lot of time in London during the year (it was a good base for touring), initially staying with people, and then had flats there as well as in Cornwall. Clive left us - in the lurch - after a dispute at a gig in Coventry and just before the album was released, so Wizz Jones joined us for a little while. It didn't work out though, so we ended up with just Henry, Pete and I.

During 1969 Roger, and to a lesser extent the other residents of Sinclair Gardens, had made the acquaintance of Pat McConnell and Denise Craddock, two students at Maria Assumpta Teacher Training College living within stone's throw of their flat in 36, Sinclair Road. Pat and Denise had been at secondary school together. Denise: *I don't remember meeting Jill Johnson in London. But I do know she was the girl who broke Roger's heart. I remember him being really cut up over her...*

Pat McConnell and Denise Craddock outside 36, Sinclair Road. Summer 1969. The number on the door is just visible. Photo: Denise Craddock

It was Pat, not Helen McConnell, myself and a girl called Ann Shepherd who lived in that flat. Helen McConnell was down for the Summer. Pat was her sister so she came and stayed from time to time but never rented the flat.

We always used to go to The Kensington Pub: that's how our paths crossed with Queen's initially. You'd go for the last drink of the day, as you did when you're a penniless student. The Kensington had a small corner room which was L-shaped, and a longer room where they had a lot of Jazz events on Sundays afternoons and on the odd evening in the week. We knew who they were because we had seen them perform as Smile at Imperial College.

Imperial had relatively few female undergraduates, and as a result the Catholic girls from nearby Maria Assumpta were always welcome. Denise has fond memories of the girls' trips to Imperial College Union to see the band that later became Queen: *The Imperial College buildings are huge and amazing. At night the lights would reflect on the wet road, and I remember we'd swing round the parking meters. It was a really magical time. We were very lucky.*

Another regular at the Kensington was John Harris. Denise: *John was studying at Imperial. I think he was studying maths and flunked out after a year or two. We all used to go to a disco in the common room of Queen Elizabeth College up by Kensington library.*

Freddie Bulsara, born in 1946 on the island of Zanzibar in the Indian Ocean, had sung with a band called 'The Hectics' at a private school in India. He moved to the UK in 1964, and, as a teenager, lived in Feltham and studied fashion and then graphics at Ealing Art College. At the point of leaving Ealing Freddie had not sang with a band in Britain, but rectified this when in August 1969 he joined Ibex.

Hailing from Liverpool, Freddie first met them at The Kensington, on the night of Pat McConnell's birthday celebration, recorded in Denise's diary as Thursday 31st July. Denise: *Ibex were friends of Pat's. Ken Testi who was going out with Pat's sister, Helen, was their manager and he brought them down that Summer. They originally came down to see 'Blind Faith' with Eric Clapton in Hyde Park (June 7th 1969).*

Later that fateful evening Smile, Ibex and their entourage are known to have decamped from the pub to 36 Sinclair Road, where Ken Testi recalls witnessing Brian May's guitar playing for the first time. Then, having persuaded Ibex to accept him as their fourth member, on 23rd August Freddie Bulsara performed with them for the first time at a gig in Bolton.

The balcony at 36, Sinclair Road. Summer 1969. L to R Ken Testi (manager of Ibex and Queen), Pat McConnell, Mike Bersin (guitarist of Ibex) and unknown. Photo Denise Craddock.

With no immediate prospect of receiving a regular wage, Freddie subsequently opened a stall in Kensington Market, a venture in which, Smile and dentistry commitments allowing, Roger joined him. Alan Mair was already there: *Kensington Market had three floors. The basement and ground floor were all clothes shops. On the first floor it was nearly all antiques. It was lucrative. There were unbelievable amounts of money being taken in the market because there was nothing else like it. The big stalls on the ground floor could take £10,000 a week. Jimi Choo shoes started there, but had a different name then. People would come into the ground floor and didn't come upstairs at first. With the other people on the first floor we felt like the outcasts* from the rest of the market until our floor also started to become popular.

For a few weeks I went there to ask the manager if there were any stalls coming up, and eventually he gave me one that was the first shop unit upstairs, inside what would have been the antiques market. Then it was in a passageway known as Death Aisle because no-one survived if up there if you were selling or making clothes. But the antiques got pushed out by other stalls after I moved in.

Alan recalls the interior: *There were wide double stairs in the middle of the market - a good ten feet wide. So you went up them and the passageway was round to the right, about 6 feet wide, and it would have had about ten shop units on either side. The floor had these large black and white tiles, like kitchen tiles. It was quite dark, with no natural light, and the shop owners would have had their own music playing. The units were all slightly different sizes. Mine was one of the larger ones and it cost £15 a week, about twice the size of Roger and Freddie's. All the stalls were about 10 ft deep, so Roger and Freddie's would have been 10ft square. Each stall had proper stud partition walls that you could lean against. I was definitely there before Roger and Freddie, because I was on my own at that stage thinking 'who's going to come here to buy clothes?'*

Eventually Alan was joined by other like-minded stall-owners, and when Freddie and Roger arrived they are known to have sold some of Freddie's artwork: including drawings for his dissertation which took Jimi Hendrix as its theme. Alan: *Opposite me was a lady called Amanda who made clothes, and then next to her came Freddie and Roger. Their stall was art and antiques to begin with, including some of Freddie's paintings and drawings, and clothes only later. They sold a range of men and women's clothes. It wasn't 'specialist' clothing, it was mainly second-hand clothes that they'd picked up from charity shops. Mary Austin may well have helped them find things for the stall. She was in the market a lot and became a friend as well.*

Kensington Market (1976) Photo: Klaus Hiltscher/Affendaddy

Freddie at that time was always well-groomed, but Roger was more 'hippy-looking'. He would, maybe, wear an Indian shirt with no collar and five or six buttons along with some beads. There were quite a lot of drugs in the market. Not so much the staff, but there'd be people doing drugs in the toilets, and sitting stoned on the stairs. But Roger and Freddie were both pretty clean-living and 'undruggy'. Everyone was very friendly and it was a very creative environment. There was no rivalry as such. In '69/70 if people had something unique you respected them for it.

Roger and Freddie also mixed second-hand with new designer clothes. Wendy Edmonds was at the London College of Fashion: *I made clothes for Roger and Freddie when they had the stall together. I would cut up curtains to make panelled velvet jackets and bags and things like that.*

Denise remembers Wendy and Freddie sharing a passion for fashion: *Wendy Edmonds used to look amazing in Ozzie Clarke thin-waist dresses. I was very envious of her!*

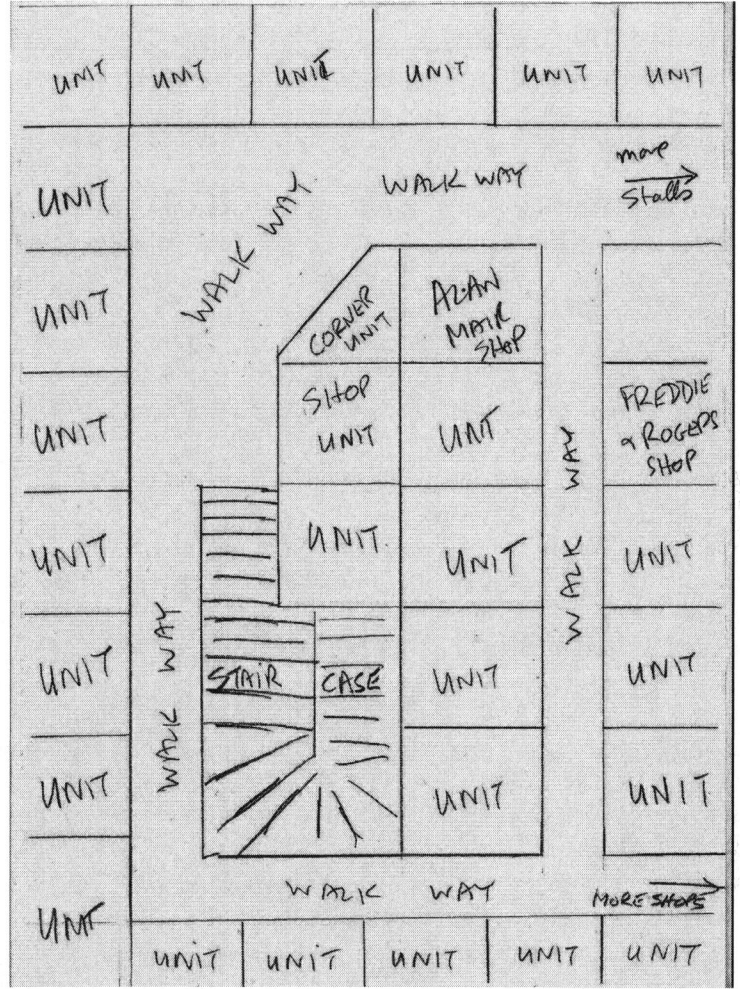

Map of the second floor of Kensington Market as it was in 1970 by Alan Mair

Brian May was not overly impressed by the market: *Freddie always looked like a star and acted like a star even though he was penniless. Roger and Freddie were in on the beginnings of what became Glam Rock with that stall, though some of it was incredibly tatty. When we started sharing a flat Fred would bring home these great bags of stuff, pull out some horrible strip of cloth and say 'Look at this beautiful garment! This is going to fetch a fortune!'* ITOW

The market was, however, a perfect meeting place. By then Richard Halliwell from Truro School was at Marjons Teacher Training College in nearby Kensington: *Roger had the dreaded stall in the Market. I bought a nearly full length ginger fur coat from them, and somewhere I have a polaroid of me wearing it standing next to Fred in the market.*

Denise: *When Roger was a student he had very flexible hours...some days he'd have lectures and some days not, and they were n't always there at the market all the time. The market was a happening kind of place; a tapestry of all kinds of creative people. It was a place to call into to have a chat, and catch up, and move on. My college was round the corner in Kensington Square. There was a little cafe stall and there was all kinds: from jewelry to clothes to painting to furniture...*

At the market Roger would also bump into John Lumley-Savile. As John Sykes, John had been a founder member of The Smokey Joes from Portscatho near Truro. John: *I was working in the basement in Kensington Market and Roger and Freddie were upstairs on the top floor. Roger was in Smile and I was in The Neat Change: a band that had a regular slot at The Marquee. I remember once giving Roger a lift home, and listening to some demo tapes, but it was n't really my bag.*

At the end of the academic year Les and Roger gave up the tenancy on Sinclair Gardens. Denise describes subsequently finding the flat to which Roger moved, and in which Queen formed: *There is a picture of Freddie sitting on a couch with a poster behind him that was taken in Batoum Gardens. There was a whole different group there: Peggy, Anne McCormick, Celine Daley (girlfriend of Mike Bersin of Ibex) who sold a letter that Freddie had written to her. That was their flat. After Batoum Gardens we stayed in 19, Coningham Road with Pat and Freddie. Ken Testi and Ibex were there too for at least a month.*

Whilst still living at Coningham Road Freddie, as well writing songs with guitarist Mike Bersin, decided Ibex should change their name to 'Wreckage' probably on the basis that it made the band sound more like a heavy rock group. Though he got his way an argument ensued and two days later, Miff, the drummer left, to be replaced by Richard Thompson.

Denise: *Coningham Road was a bit of a doss house, so Pat and myself started looking for a new place and Roger was also searching for a flat.*

In those days you didn't really have a mixed flat but we decided to join forces. That's how we ended up at number 40, Ferry Road, Barnes. It was John Cussens who actually found the flat. John was training to be a dentist with Roger. Initially it was John, Richard Anderson (another dentist) myself, Freddie, Pat and Roger who lived there, but then John Cussens moved out and I think John Harris moved in.

From Hammersmith, Ferry Road is a twenty minute walk - at least half a mile - across the cast iron splendor of Hammersmith Bridge. Apart from jumbo-jets flying overhead, the road is quiet and lined with trees and large, detached houses.

Denise Craddock's diary records the date they moved in as Friday 10th October, though Roger had inspected it a couple of weeks earlier: *I remember before we moved in, Fred and I sat in amazed excitement as Roger told us about the flat: floodlit patio, 23" TV, phone, piano and fully equipped kitchen. We thought it sounded fantastic! Freddie bought six giant sparklers for each of us to light on the first night we were there. It was typical of him that he wanted to make an occasion of it.*

The landlady lived upstairs. She was eccentric. She was called Miss Scott-Allen. God knows how she survived. She didn't interfere too much, but occasionally complained about the noise. We would send John Cussens to her with the rent, because he was very respectable and well-presented! I used to go and fetch her medicine from the chemist. I think she got a bit worried at the end. One day she came out and took all our photos. Perhaps she was worried that we would do a midnight flit! Actually we polished the place so it shone when we left it.

One of her friends was that aristocratic gentleman Lord Longford: a tall bald-headed gentleman with tiny round specs, who was involved with the government at the time. It was a well-to-do area. We had Silvia Syms, the actress, living on one side of us. Some of the biographies refer to Ferry road as a dosshouse - but it absolutely wasn't! It was quite a delightful spot. It had criss-cross leaded windows and rambling roses around the door...

Pete Edmonds, who stayed there for a while, concurs: *It was a big detached house, and quite a lot of us lived or stayed there. It was a pleasant house in a pleasant neighbourhood.*

40, Ferry Road, Barnes (2010). Queen lived on the ground floor. Freddie and Roger's room looked out on the road.

For most of the year at Ferry Road Freddie and Roger shared the large bedroom at the front of the house. Denise: *Ferry Road was very chintzy and well-decorated so we didn't put up posters in the communal areas. Fred and Roger when they had that front room put up posters in their room like the view of Earth from the Moon, though, and probably Hendrix posters and that kind of thing.*

When we first moved in Pat and I had that room, but at one point we swapped round. It was quieter the other end of the house. Except one morning at about 8 o'clock when Roger came through saying 'wake up you slags it's 12 o'clock!'. We were manically scootering around until we realised the time was completely different. We were all having to get up at unearthly hours in order to get in for 9 o'clock lectures. After a late night in the lounge that was not always easy!

Being more spacious than flats in the middle of London, it was ideal for student sleep-overs. The Johnstone sisters, after their mother had passed away, had remained living in Cornwall with their father but visited London regularly. Sue: *Once Roger got involved with Smile, we would hitchhike up, Pat and I, to see them play. We'd take a ride on a lorry all the way to London and, rather than PJ's, actually I think I met Brian and the others for the first time up there. We used to often go to Imperial College Union, where I saw T-Rex. The Ferry Road flat was a big flat. It had a large living room with a conservatory and a nice garden. There were mattresses all over the floor, and we would just dive onto one when we got there and 'crash'.*

Some of those same mattresses had found their way up from ex-Jayfolk Penny North's home just outside Truro. Penny herself recalls visiting Ferry Road too: *My fondest memories at College are from my second year when I used to catch the Green Line bus through to Barnes at weekends, when Roger, Freddie and Tim, along with Denise and Patti, shared a house there. I used to take things like coffee and cereal with me, as there was rarely very much in the larder there! I do remember being slightly late one Friday, and the others had left for a gig or party that we were all going to. Roger had waited for me. In the sitting room he had positioned a chair between two large stereo speakers, where he was listening to Jimi Hendrix. Sitting in the chair you could experience the guitar riffs shooting through your ears from one speaker to the other.*

Denise: *Penny North - lovely lady - stayed, and Pat and Sue. Yes I remember. People would just sleep in the sitting room. There were couches and cushions, and other things that could be laid out. You could keep the bodies and the havoc at one end, because the house went off on a long corridor with bedrooms off.*

It was £25 a month I think, which sounds nothing now but we had to scratch that together as students, and we were not well off. Freddie was especially struggling to make ends meet. He had very few clothes and his shoes had holes in them. Their tops would be immaculate and white, but the soles would have holes all the way through!

The fridge never had any food in it. More often than not we'd go to The Stockpot in Earl's Court. That was the best venue for a serious eating session. It used to have exotic things like an American Salad, which involved having half a tinned peach on top of your salad! We didn't really go to pubs in Barnes or even go for walks in Barnes. There was so much going on in the flat, and you had people like 'Pete Roadie' arriving with big vans to take you to much more interesting places! I went to all the gigs with Smile in London. I also went to Hertfordshire where Penny organised a gig.

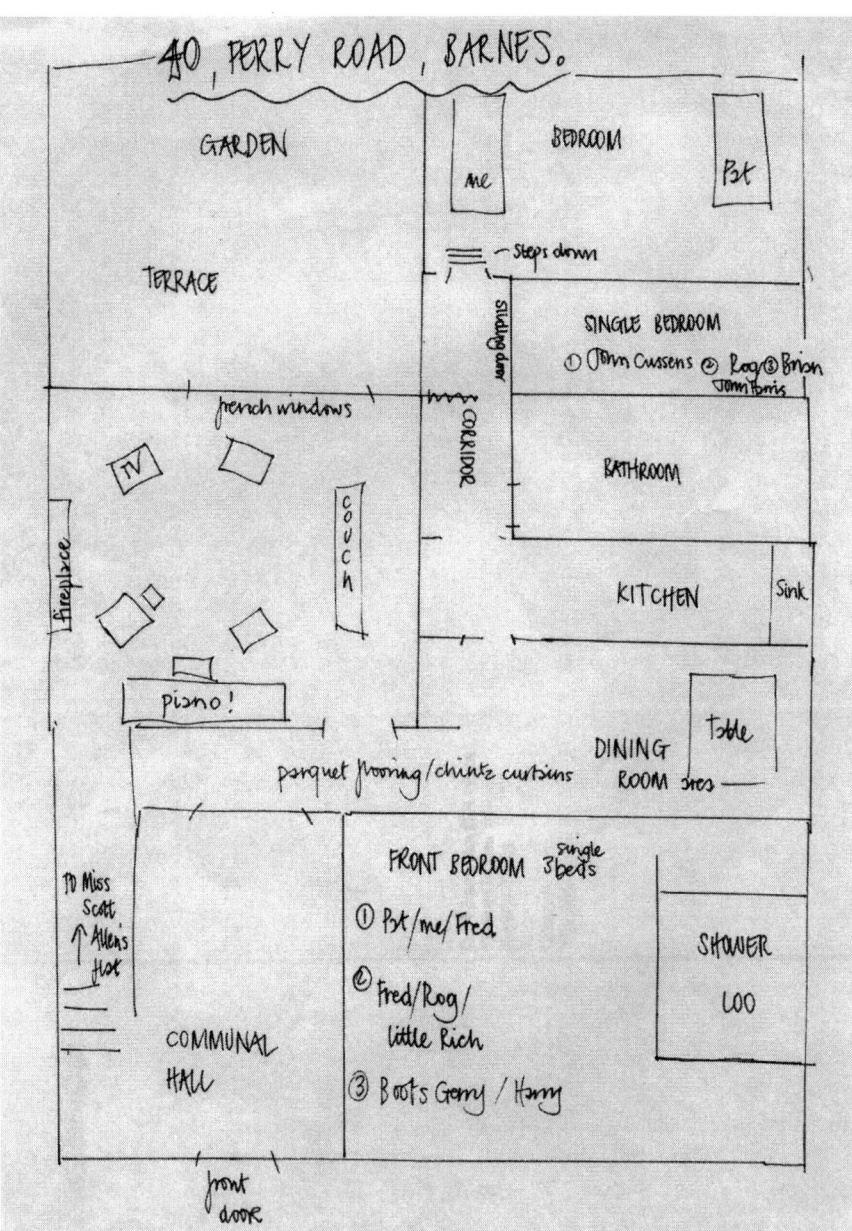

Plan of the ground floor of 40 Ferry Road, Barnes drawn by Denise Craddock in 2011. The different inhabitants of the main (front) bedroom are detailed in chronological order. Mike Grose and Brian May also used the front bedroom.

As well as overflowing with bodies, the flat was used to house the band's equipment. Denise: *They still owe me a set of luggage, because they used my cases for keeping their cables, and microphones and things in! John Harris needed a case for putting all the electrical stuff into. I had an expanding case that got adopted and that was the end of that!*

They did not generally practice with electric instruments at Barnes, but the band-members certainly wrote songs there. One Smile song written at the flat later appeared on Queen's first album: *There was an upright piano in the lounge, and they would sit together and sing along. I remember the band writing songs but not really practicing there as such. Songwriting involved sitting around knocking ideas about, trying out different tunes and words. That's how I got the piece of paper with the original lyrics to 'Doing Alright' on it. I wrote in my diary Roger and Brian had been running through it, and Tim had also been scribbling some of the words...*

Three of the most highly prized pieces of early Queen memorabilia were preserved in this way by Denise: *I had a pinboard in my room - the room I shared with Pat. I used to do collages, and cut things out of magazines. I found this file with 3 pieces of paper in it – which were all on this pinboard. One was a postcard from Freddie, another was a gig list for Ibex, and the other was the words for Doing Alright. Collage was big in the 60's. Freddie used to do the same - with Sunday Times magazines: cutting out pictures of Afro-haired ladies, beautiful sepia photos - and making up collages.*

Constantly short of money, Freddie was looking for work as a graphics artist or illustrator. Denise: *I don't remember Freddie drawing that much at Barnes, but he had a spell when he was trying to get a job illustrating children's books, and on the back of the Doing Alright lyrics were all kinds of doodles. I'd doodled some names, and Freddie had doodled some pictures of biplanes. But he didn't have too much success. It was for a firm in Chancery Lane - Austin somebody. I don't think he swung it - but he'd got a new set of felt tips. Getting the pens was a big event and a big investment!*

> Yesterday, my life was in ruins,
> Now today, I know what I'm doing,
> I've got a feeling, I should be proving whats right.
>
> Where will I be, this time tomorrow,
> Smothered in joy, or sinking in sorrow,
> Any day, I should be feeling allright.
>
> Feeling alright.
>
> I should be waiting for the s...
> Anyway I gott to run
> I'll never see the sky again
> I'll never be the guy I was.

Lyrics to 'Doing Alright' (then Feeling Alright) a song that appeared later on Queen 1. Although undoubtedly written at the flat in Barnes, there is some dispute as to whose handwriting is visible. The blob in the right hand side is a multicoloured abstract doodle in felt-tips by Freddie Mercury. Photo Denise Croaddock.

Freddie's parents were nearby in Feltham: *Freddie went home once a year on his birthday. That's the only time I registered him going home. He probably did go at other times but he made a point of going home on his birthday. But when you're young and footloose and fancy-free you don't go home that often.*

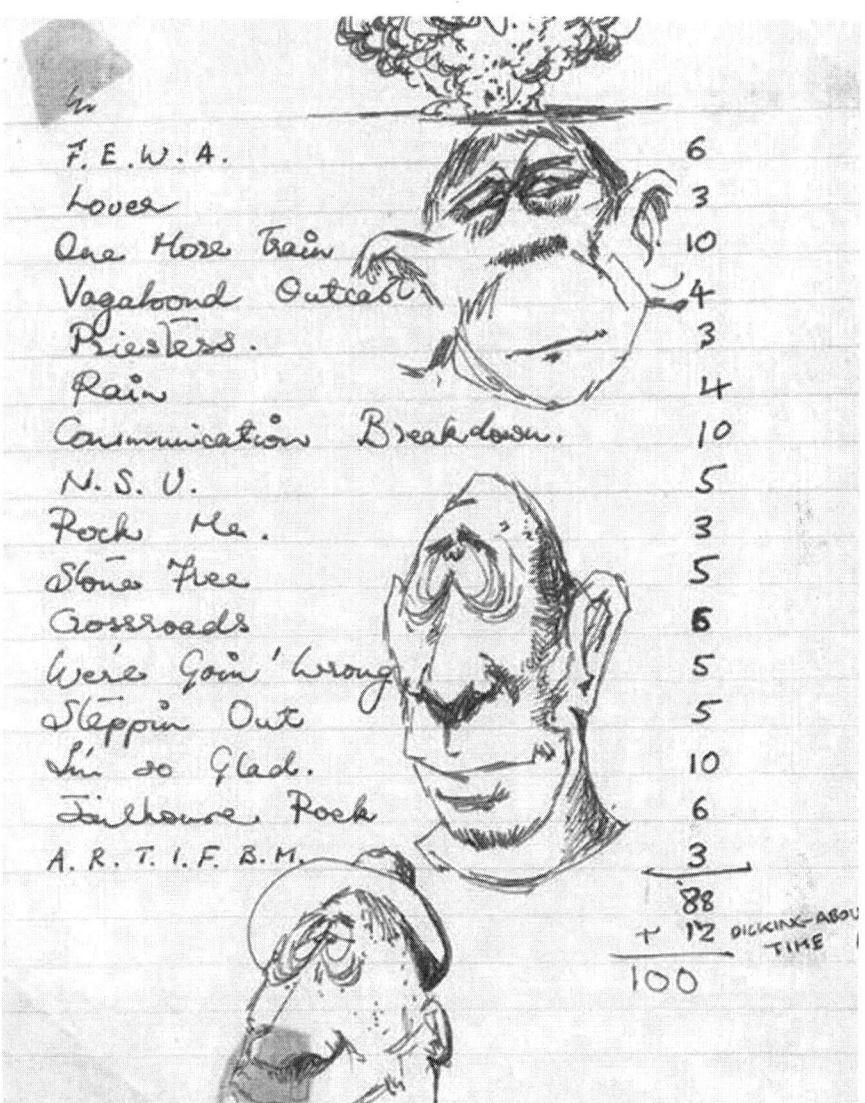

Ibex set-list in Freddie's handwriting. Many of the songs are original. Photo Denise Craddock.

Penny North describes another of Freddie's art projects: *I remember he and Tim had a mural-type project that they were working on together at the house - it was hanging on the wall while they worked at it, and there were plenty of debates and arguments about it too! One of my abiding memories of Freddie at that time was the way that he used to look at himself in the mirror, push and pull at his long hair and lament 'Oh why am I so ugly?*

In autumn 1969 Wreckage (previously Ibex) followed Freddie to the Ferry Road flat in Barnes, where one night recordings were made of the band rehearsing a song called 'Green'. But they split up before the end of the year when their guitarist, Mike Bersin, who had not intended to stay in London for long, returned to Merseyside.

The remaining Ferry Road inhabitants went to see The Who on the 14th of December. The rock opera 'Tommy', which had been released earlier in the year, was a record often played at the flat. Wendy Edmonds: *I remember going to see The Who perform Tommy at The Coliseum, London with all the band - and Pat and Sue as they were massive Who fans.*

During 1969 Brian and Roger had found new girlfriends. They were two women they had met also from Maria Assumpta by the name of Chrissie Mullen and Josephine Morris respectively. Denise: *Jo Morris had a flat in Earl's Court on West Cromwell Road. She was another Maria Assumpta student two years below me. Same as Veronica Tetzlaf, John Deacon's wife. We would have met up at gigs: I don't remember her coming to Ferry Road very often.*

Meanwhile in Cornwall, the West Briton carried special reports *'from the barricades'* of Northern Ireland on Cornish soldiers in the First Battalion Light Infantry.

1970: 'Queen' or 'Build your own boat'?

At the end of December 1969 Roger gave up his dental studies. Mike Dudley of The Reaction was surprised by this turn of events: *When I met Roger in the holidays, I remember he seemed very pleased with the idea of dentistry as an occupation. He would talk in an amused fashion about walking around in a white coat, with people calling him doctor! And he'd describe dissecting bodies and how they'd hide the eyes and the bits of these bodies that they'd chop up! He packed up the dentistry because of the car accident and the court case that ensued, and because he 'needed to disappear off the face of the earth'. Or at least that's what he told me.*

In fact there was another more mundane, and understandable explanation. Distracted by his music from a course for which he cared little, Roger had simply not passed the necessary exams. After receiving the news on the 12th December the household at Ferry Road went ahead with a Christmas party they had planned for that night anyway (DD). Denise Craddock: *He dropped out of dentistry. We were in Barnes, and I remember one night they all came back - John Cussens celebrating because he'd got a star first or whatever, and Roger looking glum because he hadn't, together with Richard Anderson, who we called Little Richard (we had to differentiate between him and Richard Thompson). I remember that night when they all got their results, and it was very variable. It was an awful situation. Do we celebrate? May be we shouldn't...*

Barnes was never very convenient for his studies, though. We were the wrong side of Hammersmith Bridge. You had to get a bus to get to Hammersmith tube - or walk - it was not ideal...especially for Roger having to get to Whitechapel. How much time he actually spent there, though I'm not sure...I seem to remember him sitting in an armchair with a large book open at some page and coming back three hours later and he'd still be on the same page...

Roger, later, described his experience of dentistry in very stark terms: *I hated the work and I hated the people. I was at my all-time low...*SIS

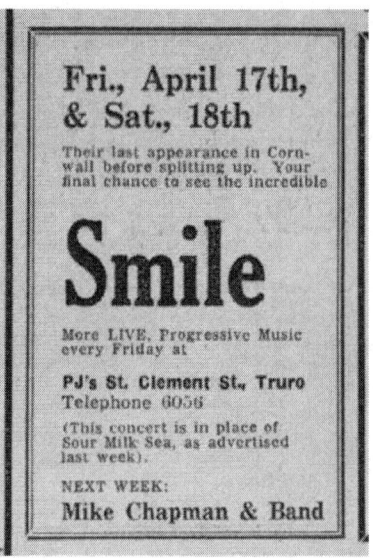

Adverts in The West Briton for five Smile dates at PJ's in 1970. The undated ad is for 7th and 8th of March. There are two separate ads for April 17th & 18th.

Ongoing court proceedings following the crash on Goss Moor were another source of anxiety for him. They had continued into the following decade, as it became clear that his friend Peter Gill-Carey would never completely recover from his injuries. John Snell: *Civil action to assign responsibility culminated in a court hearing in Bodmin long after the group had ended, whereby everyone who could be traced who was present on the night of the event - or who were involved with the ownership or maintenance of the van - were called as witnesses. It was around 1970 or after, when the long term extent of Peter's injuries had been determined. We all had to spend most of the day in court.*

Smile's first engagement of 1970 was, once again PJ's in Truro: a single performance on 17th of January. The band was to return twice more in the spring to play double bookings at weekends, which were interspersed with gigs in London.

Back in London, on January 23rd, Roger Taylor went to celebrated folk venue Les Cousins in Soho with Penny North and John Harris to see Jill Johnson sing with the Famous Jug Band. DD.

The first of two West Briton adverts for Queen's first concert in Truro City Hall.

Jill: *I believe we played at Les Cousins in Soho a couple of times: once during our first tour with FJB. It was very dark and smoky, with a small stage. It was the place everyone went to see everyone else! I think Wizz and perhaps Whispering Mick (Mick Bennett from COB) were with us at the time. I remember Roger coming as well. He also came when we played in some other places, like The Half Moon in Putney, and the Marquee.*

Then on February 12th an early advert was placed in the West Briton by Roger's mother for the concert in June that is now acknowledged to have been Queen's first. *British Red Cross Society, Truro Detachment have invited SMILE to play on Saturday June 27th, 1970. We invite YOU to come and DANCE. Further announcement next month.* It is unusual for an advert to have been placed this early - after all, the concert was still four months away.

FEBRUARY (47-318) **1970**

16 Monday

Breakfast at 11.30. Wait in lounge sewing my skirt then lunch and off to Truro. Penny & I in her van, John & Rog in the mini. Good fun, we gave them quite a licking! Up to Pat & Sue's, we all got in the vans and came down to Porthtowan. Terrific night, moonlight bright. Stood on cliff edge watching sea coming in straight at me. Cooked a meal the rest prepared it. Well appreciated thank goodness! Sat around singing, laughing, making patterns with Joss in the dark, laughs over Rog & the light bulb. Walk down to the pub at 10.15. Talk to John & Sue serious then climb up in a tree. Sally free & easy — esp for Cait. Always get what you want, Stones Let it Bleed L.P. excellent. P.M. hearing Mick

A holiday in Porthtowan recounted in Denise Craddock's diary

Only a couple of months before splitting up, Smile returned to the studio. Having recorded their single at Trident Studios in 1969, in mid-February 1970 they recorded Blag, Doing Alright, Polar Bear and April Lady at Kingsway Studios in Holborn. The producer Fritz Freyer is known to have had more than one meeting with the band at Ferry Road late in January. (DD)

Immediately following this, the Johnstone sisters - still living in Cornwall - received visitors themselves in the form of Ferry Road residents Denise Craddock, John Harris and Roger Taylor. Penny North travelled to Cornwall with them and visited her family whilst Roger, John and Denise stayed in a coastal village just west of Perranporth. The little holiday was recorded for posterity both on a postcard, and in Denise's diary: *I went down to Cornwall with Roger and John Harris. We stayed in Roger's Auntie's chalet in Porthtowan. It was on the left hand side of the beach: a wooden chalet and one of the last ones on the end of the cliff. It was a bit cold. Lots of blankets and greatcoats and we all got into bed to keep warm. It was February. It wasn't the right time of year really. It was all walking along beaches and dashing in the sea and dashing out again very quickly!*

After the demise of Ibex/Wreckage Freddie attended at least two auditions for new bands in December and January before joining Sour Milk Sea on 23rd February, after seeing an advert in Melody Maker (DD). Sour Milk Sea (pictured with Freddie opposite) had a rehearsal base in Dorking and was comprised of members that were younger than Freddie. For a while the 17 year old lead guitarist of Sour Milk Sea, who was the son of an Oxford don, joined the throng at 40, Ferry Road. Called Chris Dummett (now Chris Chesney), the close relationship he formed with Freddie caused a rift within the group that led to their breakup only weeks later. It seems Freddie's own need for creative expression was part of the problem.

Chris: *Freddie had a passing facility on piano, although we never wrote around that when I knew him. He used to play a cod 'jazz piano'. But he also had a Telecaster electric guitar and could strum chords with no problem. So he'd use the guitar and we'd write songs by sitting together in the flat and trading ideas.*

The first thing he did was graft his own lyrics onto Sour Milk Sea's songs. I think I'd written most of them. I really didn't care - thinking that Freddie was taking me on artistically - but I think the other members of Sour Milk Sea felt this to be presumptuous and an intrusion.

Some of Freddie's songs had been penned whilst working with Ibex/Wreckage the previous year: *The songs we worked on were 'FEWA' - an acronym of 'feelings ended, worn away' – 'Lover' and some others. We were young. Lyrics were mostly (including mine) written on a barely conscious level: collections of words which sounded plausible and carried a melody which fitted with a riff. As for the fairies and ogres and the fantasy imagery that appeared on the first couple of Queen albums - I think this, on Freddie's part, was in imitation of Robert Plant of Led Zeppelin. All that clap-trap about Golum and the evil one - Freddie was a great admirer at the time. There were other songs he'd written which we played. I contributed to these by adding great big pompous instrumental passages...*

Though full of enthusiasm, Freddie lacked confidence in his songwriting which is surprising given that, within a few years, he would compose some of the most powerful and enduring pop music of the 20th century. Whilst living in Ferry Road Chris and Freddie were in awe of Smile, and the Smile records that were played there: *Smile had acetates (test pressings which wore out quickly) of some demos. These were far more professional sounding than anything Sour Milk Sea had managed, though we had been into the studio (Bell St, Surbition, and another one I think in Denmark St.). 'Earth' and 'April Lady' I remember were very impressive. 'Earth' like 'Lover', had a science fiction theme. Then there was 'Doing Alright' sung by Roger which later found its way onto Queen I, but resung by Freddie. I always marvelled at Roger's voice which sounded like Rod Stewart. I think he very consciously modelled himself on that.*

Whilst most of the Sour Milk Sea songs have since been lost, it can be said that Chris indirectly contributed to the first Queen album: *Brian did apologise magnanimously to me for nicking a riff of mine which ended up in the Queen song 'Liar'.*

Chris feels Freddie helped steer Queen away from 60's blues-inspired groups, towards something more original. And though he rarely talked about it, it is likely that Freddie's upbringing in India helped shape his eclectic tastes: *Freddie always had a great pop sensibility and instinct - which I was only too willing to learn from. I for one had come from a culture of Blues - where every middle class white kid from Cheltenham (eg Brian Jones) wanted to be John Lee Hooker. Freddie was older than me and I think his role model was more Cliff Richard. In 1969 there was a dilemma going on: how to break free from the cocoon of blues-inspired music into 'progressive' rock. But to me Queen really were a thing apart from that.*

In mid-April 1970 an advert for the last Smile concert in Cornwall appeared in the West Briton. In small print it says '*this is in place of Sour Milk Sea as advertised last week*'. Placed by Pete Bawden, as all the PJ's adverts were, it gives important clues as to the exact timing of the breakup of the two bands. As it turned out they were breakups that were both necessary to the formation of Queen.

Chris: *The ads are really poignant, because they are a reminder that at the time we split, Sour Milk Sea were booked all over the place and might have been on the verge of making a bigger impact early in 1970. I know we had a Roundhouse gig with 'Implosion' that was cancelled - thwarting a long-held ambition of mine to play that venue. I've seen another ad for us supporting Rory Gallagher's 'Taste' which we also didn't do owing to the break-up. I've no idea how this booking at PJ's came about, but it must have been organised by Freddie...*

Sour Milk Sea broke up amidst much acrimony. Smile's breakup was less painful, though more perplexing. It is known that by spring 1970 Tim wanted out of Smile. According to Denise Craddock's diary, Smile had announced their intention to split by the beginning of March. Denise: *6/3/70. I have a quote from my diary on that day. It was possibly after a Smile gig: 'Weird evening at the College of Estate Management as Smile is folding now. John Harris was in a mood - having a tantrum'...*

Jackie Gunn and Jim Jenkins said that Tim had had enough of *'slogging around the college circuit and wanted something more'*, but he told Mark Hodgkinson that it was more musical differences that were the issue. He was becoming less interested in heavy rock than the others: *'I was not enjoying the direction in which we were moving. I'd heard James Brown and thought 'God'!'*

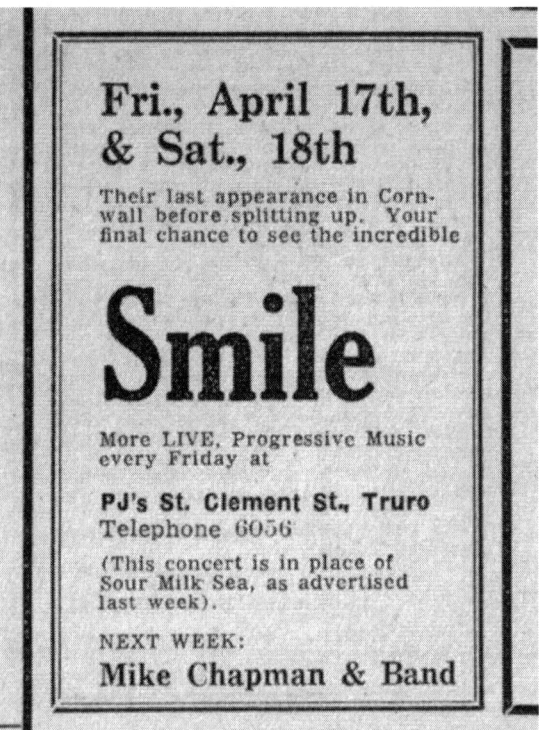

One of two adverts in the West Briton marking the last appearance of Smile in Cornwall, April 1970

Only days before the April PJ's gig Tim had been for an audition with 'Humpy Bong'. Some have speculated that for the April gigs at PJ's he may have stayed in London and given up vocal duties to Freddie, which seems highly plausible given that Freddie had planned to perform with his own band.

Pat Johnstone is one of a number who believe that Freddie sang with Smile in Cornwall: *The best performance that I ever saw by the Queen boys was when they played at PJ's and Freddie leapt on the floor and began to take the place of Tim as the lead singer. He thrashed himself about as beautifully as Freddie always did. But it was an amazing performance because none of us had seen it before. That was the first time I'd seen him perform.*

I do remember that performance. It was stunning. PJ's had a small stage. But he leapt up from the dance floor and joined in with the band. It was very different from Smile - Freddie was really something else but you don't expect it to go on to become as big as it did.

They were between Smile and Queen. Tim had gone, and they were stuck, and Freddie said 'I'll do it'. And he leapt on stage and did the most magnificent performance. It wasn't planned. They were still Smile, and once Freddie had done this performance they realised they had something special, and so they became Queen as he began to take over. He then became their driving force.

We all went 'Oh my God he's fantastic'. Me and Sue were both there and Pete Edmonds leapt on the floor and did the most fantastic dance, and we all went crazy! We were all gyrating about. We couldn't help ourselves! It was a wonderful night and it was really inspired by Freddie.

He was an amazing character from the word go. We were all amazed at how talented he was. He was a one-off in the music industry. We loved his performance that night and all embraced it.

Pat admits she may be describing another weekend, perhaps in March or August, as Mike Grose remembers the events in April slightly differently: *Talking of the Navy Arms on Fairmantle Street where Jayfolk sang: you've reminded me that I went for a drink there with Tim Staffell. I offered to buy him a beer. He said that he didn't drink beer - but I got him a pint and he drank it in 3 or 4 seconds, then had another. He had four pints like that! I think he normally drank shorts. In fact that was the same weekend he left Smile and went back to London. I liked Tim. I got on well with him. But Roger and Tim used to bicker quite a lot. It was schoolboy stuff really. But Tim fell out with Roger during the weekend of that Smile gig at PJ's and I stepped in.*

Mike recalls that they shared the singing, and that Freddie did not sing on the night that he played bass with Smile. Mike also didn't rehearse with them beforehand: *We didn't have time. It all happened so quick. Tim left and went back to London and PJ said to me 'Christ Mike you'll just have to play'. So I dug out my gear. We were really stuck. We ended up playing things we all knew already. Things like R'n'B standards and Led Zeppelin numbers. At that time they were advertised on the poster as an international touring band.*

The second of two West Briton adverts for Queen's first concert at the City Hall in Truro. Jeff Spence was the stage name for DJ Roy Sheen.

Whether or not Freddie sang with Smile, he certainly wanted to and found it hard watching from the wings. Initially, though, Smile had ignored his solicitations. Tim: *We didn't take Freddie that seriously as a singer first, as it took a few years for him to develop the quality and assurance he showed when he was into his stride'.*

Mike Grose: *Tim had a much better range than Freddie and was stronger in the higher registers. Roger of course had a helluva falsetto voice. But Freddie's singing improved a lot. I was very fond of Freddie.*

But when I first knew them Freddie used to plead with them to be in the band. The others just didn't take him seriously.

Denise Craddock: *Freddie would always go to Smile practices and say 'you should be doing this', or 'I can sing that', and referring to Smile as 'our group'. His singing was there but it had a long way to go to be refined. The guy that he replaced, Tim, had a voice and a half. He had such a wonderful voice, it was a blow to Brian and Roger when he decided to go. Freddie needed time to evolve. But the moves and techniques and so on were there from the beginning.*

Sue Johnstone: *Freddie was always on the sidelines of Smile. At that time you have to remember it was quite difficult because they were at the stage of having to decide whether to finish their courses or take the jump and go for their music. Tim was an artist as well and had a huge talent. And Freddie was so determined to be part of the band, in the end he just stormed his way in...*

Roger Taylor: *Freddie had a natural musicality. It was a real gift, but he had a very strange vibrato when we first met, which some people found rather distressing. But he applied himself and forged his own persona: he invented himself.* MOJO

Roger and Brian were left disappointed by Tim's departure. Roger: *Smile ground to a halt. We didn't have a manager, we didn't have anything. We were lost in the wilderness and also still students at the time. It ground to a halt and Tim lost interest.* SIS

Freddie, when he joined, brought enthusiasm and an exciting new visual focus to the band. Brian: *Smile completely broke up, and we gave up - and Freddie was the driving force for getting us back together. He told us we could do it, and said he didn't want to play useless gigs where no-one listened, and that we would have to rehearse and get a stage act together. He was very keen for it to be an actual act and we started again, taking a couple of songs from Smile and a couple of songs from groups he'd been in.* ITOW

Pat Johnstone: *Roger was doing dentistry but he knew that wasn't going to be his career, Freddie Bulsara made him realise that that music was what he really wanted to do. Freddie really brought out the showbiz part of Roger's personality. They all responded to that in*

Freddie. Freddie showed them how to be stars. There was nothing in Freddie that was afraid. It was 'Stay with me, or don't stay with me but this is where I'm going'. Freddie believed they were going to the biggest band ever.

The three musicians hadn't yet agreed on the Queen name, but they knew they needed a bass-player, and because Mike Grose had already proven himself in Cornwall, he was the man they turned to. After receiving a phone call from Roger, Mike drove himself and his bass up to West London in his Thames van.

Mike: *I played in the gig at PJ's, then a week or so later they rang me up to ask me to join them. PJ's had a demolition order on it in six months time, so I thought I might just as well go. I met them at West Cromwell Road. There was Roger and Brian, and Freddie Mercury who was still Freddie Bulsara at the time, and we all shook hands and that was it. And I presumed we were still called Smile at the time, though nobody ever discussed it.*

They explained to me that Freddie was now in the band - that they'd known him for ages, and in fact that he'd wanted to be in the band for ages. I liked Tim's voice more than Freddie's. Tim was good, bloody good. Freddie used to sing flat. When he got to high notes he would pull the microphone away from his mouth so you wouldn't quite hear him. But Brian used to talk to me about Freddie, and I think it was Brian who really believed in him at that stage.

I spent about a week at Roger's place in West Cromwell Road in Earl's Court where he was living with his girlfriend and a couple of others, then moved to Ferry Road.

Mike remembers his time in Barnes vividly: *It was a nice house - built in the 30's, I think. We had the ground floor of the house. The landlady lived upstairs and she had a crush on Brian. We used to tease him about that! There was also a guy called Jerry who I think used to know Roger. I remember me, Brian, Jerry, and a Scottish guy whose name escapes me, all sleeping on mattresses on the floor in one room.*

The two girls lived in another bedroom – though actually we didn't see that much of them. We shared the kitchen. Everything in the fridge there went green once after the Scots guy disappeared and took the electricity money and rent with him. Jerry used to clean up the kitchen whilst high on speed. Later he had a collapsed lung, and I remember bumping into him at the Tregye outside Truro - and playing music with him actually - he was a singer.

The others all used cannabis. Everyone used a bit - but nothing much else. Brian's Mum lived fairly nearby so he could live a rock and roll lifestyle and still be able take his clothes back to her to wash! As well as the band members I remember people like Tim Staffell, who by then was in 'Humpy Bong' and soundman John Harris at Ferry Road.

Denise Craddock: *Jerry we called 'Boots' Jerry. Tall, long, lean and he used to wear very high boots, dungarees and wild shirts. And there was also Harry. Harry and Boots were around together towards the end of the let and, yes, Brian used to come and stay regularly.*

Mike: *A month or two went by, and we were in the garden just learning a number and they came up with the name of Queen - which of course was Freddie's idea. They said to me: 'what do you think?' I know it seems ridiculous today - but 40 years ago if you called yourself Queen it was a bit risky really. I said 'well if we didn't get arrested or anything at least people will remember us'! At that time nobody knew that Freddie was gay. He used to sleep with two girls...*

The Johnstone sisters had continued to visit Ferry Road in 1970. Sue: *We would hitch a lift back to Cornwall from the start of the M4, and on one of these occasions Freddie walked us to the bus stop and said 'what do you think of the name 'Queen'?' We thought it was hilarious because he was always so camp. And we just laughed and thought of the gay connotation immediately, but he tried to make it more acceptable by persuading us that it was 'regal'. At that point he'd already started working on the crest and the logo. He'd thought about the whole concept from the start. He had a great marketing mind, and that's probably what swayed the others. And he usually got his way.*

They were all very clever boys and knew what they wanted out of it but Freddie just bowled you over. He was fantastically sweet and kind, and so over the top it was hilarious. He was one of the nicest, kindest people I've met: absolutely georgeous. And he didn't change with time, he just got more of his own way!

Truro City Hall. The 'Annexe' where Cousin Jacks and The Reaction played was behind the pillars to the left. Queen played their debut concert on the main stage in 1970, and twice in 1971.

Denise: *He announced his idea for the name, and tried it out on everybody he met. Most of us just raised our eyebrows and went 'mmm, yes, yes' to humour him...just like when he'd say 'I'm going to be a superstar my Dear' and we'd go 'Oh yes Fred of course you are...'. Somehow he persuaded Roger and Brian. God knows how he did that. But he was very convinced and convincing, and when he got an idea there was no stopping him. Yet on the other hand he could also be the shyest, kindest, gentlest person you'd ever want to meet.*

They were all very intent, and driven on making something happen for them. They were knocking on doors endlessly trying to find a way through - but he was the one who had the big picture of what he wanted to create. He did fashion at Ealing and at the flat he used to doodle sketches of women in exotic dresses, but then he got the opportunity to fully exercise his creativity through the group. He was heavily influenced by Free and Led Zep but he ended up making it his own thing.

Deciding on the name is one of the most important decisions any band makes. Despite Freddie's charm and ability to get his way, Roger as well as Brian still took some persuading. Roger: *It (the name) was a reflection of the social world we were in at the time when he and I were working together in Kensington Market. In those days there was a pretty eccentric crowd there, people in sobreros, and a lot of them were gay and a lot of them pretended to be, and it just seemed to fit in.* ITOW

Brian and I weren't that sure, but Fred was so convinced and he was very powerful, and very driven and sure about things when he made his mind up. Like changing his own name. And he said 'it's got two e's, and it's short, and it's regal dear, it's regal darlings'. And we didn't particularly want to be regal, but we stuck with him because we believed what he believed. So Queen it was, and of course, it had those slightly ambiguous overtones as well R2.

The new band intended to concentrate on its own material. Mike Grose recalls rehearsing tracks from the first album, as well as Father to Son from Queen II and Stone Cold Crazy from Sheer Heart Attack. Mike: *When I went up there first it was too cold to be in the garden so we played in the front room. I remember playing the song 'Father to Son' a lot. Brian couldn't make up his mind on some songs... And he kept changing the arrangement then wondering why I wasn't fitting in with him! I also remember rehearsing Stone Cold Crazy, definitely, from Sheer Heart Attack as well as others that ended up on Queen 1.*

There was a lot of song writing when I was there. When we played it was mostly their own songs. Obviously the dominant writers were Freddie and Brian. Freddie would just come along and sit in the garden and he would tell you what he wanted, and would say sing a tune, or he'd have the lyrics, and we used to piece it together. Simple as that. He might have come with chords or an arrangement on the odd occasion. There was only the three of us, and Roger would be there tapping away on a box or whatever.

Mike Grose spent a lot of time in Barnes, but he also got to hang out with Freddie in fashionable Kensington: *Brian was at Imperial quite a lot of the time during the day, but I used to go and visit Kenny Market to see the other two. They were busy there but never made any money!*

I remember going drinking with Freddie on the King's Road. He used to like going to the flash bars there - and he would just love posing! He would wear these little white satin jackets and drink vodka and tonic. He used to tell me that I shouldn't drink beer because I'd ruin my waistline!

As well as music rehearsals Mike recalls some of the other preparations Freddie made on behalf of the new band: *Freddie and I went shopping for stage gear - I think on the King's Road - and he got me into these black velvet trousers that were so tight I could hardly walk! Then later I was in this tube station wearing them and they split as I sat down so I was there with my arse hanging out!! It was really funny - we were both in stitches about it. I wasn't fat, but I was compared with the others. Freddie was muscley but slim hipped, Roger was very slim, and Brian then was like a walking matchstick!*

Queen's first ever concert was planned for the City Hall, Truro on 27th June 1970. It was the benefit concert organized by Roger's mother, and booked originally for Smile. She recalled Freddie explaining the new band's name at her bungalow on Hurland Road: *'He just kept saying how regal it sounded'* she said. TEY

Pat and Sue Johnstone provided accommodation for half of Queen on that historic weekend. Pat: *Brian and John Harris and Freddie certainly stayed with us in Rosedale up past the City Inn when they played their first gig at the City Hall. They stayed in our attic room and Freddie would stand on his head with his legs crossed doing yoga against the wall. He had long hair and would use our heating tongs to curl his hair in the way he wanted. And my Dad was completely taken aback and initially thought they were all a bit weird.*

We hadn't been in the house for long and there was a garden at the back that my father had wanted to get sorted, but had never got round to it because he was working so much. And so the boys said, 'Well, let's do it for him'. And that weekend they dug the whole garden up and they planted everything he wanted planting, and did the lawn and the flowerbeds and everything else. They were lovely and they adored my Dad. We had a really nice time that day and Sue and I were making them bacon sandwiches and so on. And when he came home from work my Dad was so emotional and grateful. He said 'thankyou boys, that's so lovely of you thankyou very much I'm very touched'.

Pat suggests that the band were still in the throes of deciding on their name. Having jettisoned 'Smile', Freddie and Roger had decided on Queen, but Brian was still considering other options: *In the tiny little living room there was a bookshelf and there was a book there called 'Build your own boat' because that's what my Dad fancied doing. It was a kind of escapism for him. Brian was sitting in the armchair, looking at the bookshelf and he saw it and said 'Let's call the band that' and Freddie was like 'no way, we're Queen'. But Brian really caught onto it 'It'll be great - it'll be a great name for us'.*

Sue Johnstone is not sure whether she went to the band's debut concert, but she remembers Freddie's early performances with Queen. As promised, he gave them another dimension: *He would get up on the stage and strut his stuff like he'd been doing it all his life. He was well prepared. He didn't just get up and sing, he got up and performed from day one. I loved Tim's voice, but he wasn't the same as Freddie as a performer.*

Roger Taylor does recall the gig: *I do remember it slightly. We got fifty quid between us which seemed huge. We thought we were rich! It was Freddie's first actual proper performance with us. My mother was quite shocked. And he didn't really have the technique that he developed later on. He sounded like a very powerful sheep! We had about two lights and whatever they had there. But there was very little. It was very 'bare bones' in those days.* R2

Mike: *I know we had £50 for it. But there wasn't enough there to pay us I don't think, as it was a very small crowd. It was advertised as Smile but by then we were Queen.*

The new band are known to have opened their set with Stone Cold Crazy, an early example of speed-metal later covered by Metallica, which Freddie originally performed with Ibex/Wreckage. The rest of the set was a mixture of original songs and covers.

The early Queen gigs included rock and roll standards by Elvis and Little Richard. Brian: *Our stage act was a show, more rock and roll oriented than the first album. If you go on stage and people don't know your material you can get boring if you do your own stuff all the time.* ITOW

Mike: *The performance at the City Hall was a bit scrappy. Nothing was ever written down - it was all based on memory. Doing, say, Led Zep songs was easy. We just played it like it was on the record. But with our own songs it was different because the arrangements kept changing.*

Hall for Cornwall (previously Truro City Hall) (2010). Photo kernowbeat.co.uk. Although the interior has completely changed since 1970 the façade has not.

Freddie always had strong views about the look of the band, and, unlike Smile who were less visually appealing, stage clothes were part of the Queen concept from the outset. Despite splitting his first pair, Mike still wore tight velvet trousers: *We were all dressed in black. We wore black crushed velvet trousers and black t-shirts and stack-heeled boots. It was definitely that all black look that they had for a couple of years.*

Jim Jenkins: *Fred told me about that gig. He wanted them to look good and to wear stage costumes. He got them to wear velvet trousers because he didn't want them to just wear jeans. They'd have looked the same as they did in the photos of the Imperial gig.*

Whilst at Ferry Road, John Harris had helped make Freddie's emerging vision for the band become reality. Denise: *John Harris used to knock up leather wrist bands by the dozen back at Barnes, and they became quite a feature; the wrist accoutrements. He did it as something to do to fill in time. He'd always gone in for belts and leather fringes. Fred used to also regularly raid our jewelry boxes and borrow blouses and that kind of thing...*

Brian May had been persuaded by the need to project an image: *When we were starting off it was fashionable to go on in your jeans, and be dirty, and play without ever looking at the audience. We (Queen) were a reaction to that.* TMY

Importantly, it was the first time Freddie had rehearsed and then performed properly with Roger and Brian. Jim: *Roger said that Freddie didn't shut up when they were travelling home after that gig. He was buzzing. Absolutely buzzing. The £50 covered their expenses. In fact Roger remembered that gig really well, and he remembered the numbers they played. They opened with Stone Cold Crazy. They'd already started work on that. Then they did Son and Daughter. John Harris went to that show and in fact he would have made a recording of it.*

Although he does n't remember the journey, Mike Grose thinks he drove the band back to London. *Freddie put a lot into that first concert at the City Hall. I remember he jumped about all over the place, prancing about, a bit like Mick Jagger - but Freddie-style.*
I didn't pay rent in London, but Queen used my van which was a 15 hundred-weight Thames in lieu of rent. I used to leave it at Barnes and we definitely used it to transport stuff between Barnes and Imperial - and I think to also travel down to Cornwall in.

It was after the first gig at Truro City Hall that Freddie started to use the second name 'Mercury' instead of Bulsara. The name-change enabled a man who was quiet and diffident off-stage, to reinvent himself as a performer. Brian May has said subsequently that the idea had come from a song that Freddie had recently started working on. Called 'My Fairy King', the title of this breathtaking track from Queen's first album refers to Edmund Spenser's epic poem, but the lyrics borrow phrases from Robert Browning's The Pied Piper:

Someone, someone just drained the colour from my wings
Broken my fairy circle ring
And shamed the king in all his pride
Changed the wings and wronged the tides
Oh Mother Mercury
Look what they've done to me
I cannot run I cannot hide.
My Fairy King (Freddie Mercury - from Queen 1)

It seems that through a process of poetic free-assocation Freddie had identified the Mother Mercury of the song as his own mother, or to be precise, as the mother of his new alter-ego, the extrovert singer with Queen. In the process he was also finding a powerful and unique voice as a song-writer. Brian: *Freddie was a virtually self-taught pianist, and he was making vast strides at the time* ...ITOW

Mary Austin was to become Freddie's life-partner, and the person who later nursed him through his final illness. She worked in the BIBA shop in Kensington which was very close to the market. Alan Mair: *All the time I worked with Freddie I never thought he might be gay. He was effeminate, yes, but because Mary was around we all assumed she was his girlfriend. I think he had a physical relationship with her at that time. He would refer to her as his girlfriend, and they were cuddly and affectionate, and so we had no reason to question it. I didn't think of the gay connotation of the Queen name either. I thought it was more about simply making a bold statement. I visited Freddie in his house in Kensington a couple of times in the early eighties. Mary inherited it and lives there now. She was a real sweetheart of a girl. She was practical, earthy and no nonsense. She was very beautiful, with a lovely way about her.*

Mary first met Freddie during the summer that Queen were playing their first gigs. She recalls, at the time, standing by the fireplace in Barnes, where Freddie was still discussing with Brian the merits of the new band's name. According to Mary, Freddie had already decided on 'Queen' but Brian was still lobbying for 'Build Your Own Boat', the name that he had come up with in Truro. DMW

Denise: *When Freddie was at Ferry Road he went out with someone called Eve, then with Rosemary Pearson, then after that it was Mary...*

Queen played their second concert at Imperial College New Block on 18th July, 1970 in one of the college lecture theatres. Mike Grose: *I don't really remember a proper gig there. There might have been 20 or 30 of Brian's mates there but that's all. I remember on three or four separate occasions using that room to play our set to music business people as there were a few who would turn up to listen to us. At Imperial College we only ever played in this one lecture theatre - it was the kind of lecture theatre that had seats going up on a slope. It wasn't that big. But we also practiced there at least once or twice a week, and John Harris was usually there, as I remember once having a contretemps with him.*

Ian Lynch, from Falmouth, visited Kensington Market regularly in 1970 and once stayed in Freddie's flat in Victoria Road. He also went to the concert. Ian: *It was a small lecture theatre with tiered seats for only 50 or 60 people maximum. I remember they were using one of the first transistorised PA systems that night rather than a valve system. And at that gig they announced that Freddie was joining and Tim was leaving. Tim wasn't there that night, but I don't think it was a bad-natured split.*

Off stage Freddie had revealed to John Anthony, who also saw them at Imperial, where some of his ideas had come from: *Freddie showed me copies of 'Queen', the fashion magazine. He said 'This is what we're about...but not just the name...the pictures, the articles, the whole thing. This is how we want our record to sound'* MOJO.

Mike: *Regarding agents I remember us visiting two brothers who were music agents of some sort. They both had Ferrari Daytonas parked outside the office. They offered us a crappy deal. I can't remember who they were now.*

Doug Puddifoot took photos of the band in and around the Imperial campus. One of the better known images was taken in front of an electricity substation on the college site. Mike Grose still has an unusual, and possibly unique, print of this photo superimposed on a negative image of a young woman's face. If the photo is reinverted, her portrait can be seen quite clearly. Doug Puddifoot: *The photo is of Sue Johnstone, and surprisingly, I have managed to find a copy of the original. As I recall it was taken in Jillian's garden in Truro. I don't think there was any particular reason to use it with the photo of Queen, just that I had the photo, I liked it, and they made an interesting image combined together. I know the photo of Sue pre-dates Queen, because I remember making a large print, twenty inches by thirty inches, which was on the wall as a poster at Sinclair Gardens for a while, and someone stuck the 'Smile' logo (a set of grinning teeth) on it. The photo of Queen was taken when they were having a rehearsal session at Imperial College. During a break we took some shots around the college. I think it might have been that day that Freddie told me they* were going to called themselves 'Queen'. I think before that it had been 'Sheer Heart Attack' - Roger's idea.

Mike Grose played with Queen when they came back to perform at PJ's on 25th July. Mixed in amongst the gymkhana and fete notices in the West Briton paper is the advert for this concert which is the first time the band's name had appeared in the printed media. Pete Bawden sought to appeal to the fan-base that Smile already had in Cornwall by adding 'formerly Smile' in small letters.

The 1970 West Briton advert for Queen at PJ's: the first time Queen's name appeared in the printed media.

Pete Bawden: *I remember meeting with Freddie in PJs – I can picture where we were sitting: downstairs in the cafe area – and they were saying they were called Queen and I remember saying 'that's weird. People can say they're off to see the Queen'. And they said 'no not <u>the</u> Queen, just Queen''.*

Dave Dowding, Roger's first musical partner, saw the band walking around Truro: *My younger brother, Will, remembers Queen coming to*

PJ's, and going out trying to find a piano for Freddie to play. I can see it now. Walking down here (bottom of Lemon Street) I remember Roger walking in front of me with these long haired guys and saying 'Hi'. I didn't think anything more about it. But I didn't really follow them at that time. The next time I met him to say hello was at a Spring Fayre at Truro School. Derek Burrell had asked Roger to open it as guest of honour, which was ironic as Roger and Derek didn't really have any kind of relationship at school.

Marvellous Kid played at PJ's the following week and the piano in question, having been manhandled up the narrow stairs, is clearly visible behind Tony Coxon in the photo that was taken that evening (p.177).

Roger was 21 on the 26th of July and celebrated with a modest party at his parent's house in Hurland Road. Wendy Edmonds didn't always travel to Cornwall with Smile but did on that occasion, though Pete was ill with tuberculosis: *It wasn't a particularly wild party. Roger wasn't a big star then. It was mainly his friends from Cornwall that were invited. Pat and Sue would have been there, and the band. I'm positive Richard Thompson was also there, and his sister Clare. His Mum gave us all tea and cake!*

Mike Grose decided not to return to London with the rest of Queen. He'd opted to leave the band, and there were various factors that influenced his decision, including boredom: *I was used to working all the time. In Cornwall I used to have a day job and play in the evenings as well. And when I joined them I had sod all to do! That's why I left. I had mostly empty days. I'd been around the band long enough to realise that Queen might not make it even though I thought they were a great band. I truly mean that. I thought they had the potential to be great. I was then 22. It was 5 years before they broke through properly. You're 27 and that's a helluva part of your life gone. Also Roger was adamant about doing his degree and finishing it so that he could secure his future. They all took that view. And I thought: wait a minute - where does that leave me? That was another thing that put me off staying with Queen.*

In fact Mike was readying to take up the reins of his father's haulage business in St Austell, where the company had important contracts with English China Clay. After Queen's PJ's gig he stayed in Cornwall and helped Pete with a concert by Free in the City Hall on August 6th. Their big hit 'Alright now' had recently reached No 2 in the charts and the event was a sell out. Mike played in one of the support acts.

Tim Staffell was with them that weekend because the next day he is advertised as playing at PJ's with Mike and Nigel Uren in a band called No Joke! Tim had just appeared with his new band Humpy-Bong on Top of the Pops. Mike: *'No Joke'? That was Peter's idea. We wouldn't have chosen that name! It was probably chosen in one of Peter's giggly moments. He would have needed a band or something to play that Friday.*

Queen found a replacement for Mike Grose in the form of Barry Mitchell. Barry had been recommended to Roger by a friend of his that was on holiday in Cornwall that summer.

Barry's first concert with Queen was on the 23rd August at Imperial College. Denise Craddock was there, and made notes in her diary: *'Fred looked excellent in shiny trousers, velvet top, snake bracelet, boots and silver hair. Brian's guitar work excellent and Barry's bass beautiful. Big crowd of supporters'*.(DD)

The contract for the concert at the College of Estate Management, St Albans Grove, Kensington. Signed by Brian May, the fee was £20, for a 1 hour, 15 minute performance. The document was rescued from the archives of Moore Sloane and Co by Nigel Chappell.

Alan Mair, from the market, recalls one of the Queen concerts later in the Autumn: *The College of Estate Management was a stone's throw from the market. You came out of the market and turned left, and left again and there was a pub called The Greyhound, and you went past it and left again.*

Because it was so near, everyone from Kensington Market saw the gig, but it was really pretty bad. Roger and Brian were obviously already very accomplished but it was Freddie that was the problem. In the early days he had a bit of a habit of singing sharp. He would be too enthusiastic, and he would push his voice slightly sharp. And he was also quite awkward on stage. He would throw his head back and step forward but it would be slightly out of time. The Hall was very echoey too, it wasn't packed and it would have had minimum advertising. The audience could have been 3 or 4 times bigger.

I remember we all went to the pub, The Greyhound, after the gig, which is what we always did on a Saturday night. We were there, saying "What are we going to tell Freddie guys? As he's so excited about it and it wasn't very good."

Most of us went to the Greyhound on a Saturday night: Ken Ruskin, another guy who worked for me, Pat and Sue Johnstone who were diagonally opposite me, in another section of the market that opened once ours got busier. One of them worked for a friend called Chris Moss. The other members of Queen went to The Greyhound too. I remember Santana being there. Hurricane Higgins used to go there actually and they had a couple of snooker tables, and Freddie would join in with snooker. We played doubles sometimes, but it wasn't really his thing, and Roger and Brian were even less into snooker.

Freddie wasn't yet working for me at that point, but he started to look after my stall in the mornings, which was when I was in my workshop making the shoes, and he would look after both his and my stalls for a while, and I paid him to do that.

The contract for the College of Estate Management gig has recently come to light. Queen's 'office' at the time was nothing other than Brian May's dark, basement room on Queensgate Terrace. Denise: *He was still staying with his parents for some of the time I first knew him - but*

The Greyhound pub in 2010. It is situated diagonally opposite the Maria Assumpta building in Kensington Square.

later he had a flat in Queensgate. His room there was tiny. It was like a corridor, a long dark corridor in a basement. Quite strange.

After the successful Smile concert at Ball's Park College the previous year, Penny North of The Jayfolk secured a return fixture for Queen on November 14th 1970, but it was another less than perfect performance. Penny: *Unfortunately the band had huge problems with their PA system on this next occasion, and the gig was a bit of a disaster as a result. The line-up for The Winter Ball did include a very nervous Freddie. And I remember some of my friends being disappointed with the gig - not all I'd trumped them up to be! I had to really battle with the college social secretary to get them any kind of money for the gig. He felt they should not be paid at all, but they were still impoverished students at the time! However, I'm sure they came back later in the year and performed for free, and this event was a huge success (1971/72 I think). I've often wondered whether the students at the college at the time equated that 'disastrous' evening with what Queen eventually came to be!*

Because they had played at the college as Smile, the name change, not for the first time, caused some confusion. Mike Cole was the social secretary at Balls Park College: *It was not until the band turned up and we saw the drum kit with 'Queen' painted on it that we quizzed them - we at first thought that this was a substitute band and not the one we had booked. They then informed us that they had recently appeared at the Cavern Club - they then tried to squeeze a bit more money out of us on the basis that they were now more famous having played on the same stage as the Beatles!*

Pat Johnstone decided to move from Truro back to London again: *I realised I had to get a life for myself. I came home one night and I said to my Dad 'I'm going to London tomorrow. I'm going up to see Roger Taylor to see if he can help me find somewhere to live'. My father said 'I understand. I won't stop you'.*

By the time I got to London I had £5 left and I went to the market and found Roger and Freddie and said 'Help me!' When I first came up Freddie had a little dark place and I stayed there on the sofa for a while. And for a while I was hopping around from place to place living with each of them. Freddie and Roger got me a job at the market which meant I could stay with either one of them and sleep on a sofa and pay them some rent.

The wife of Richard Branson, who was a model, was working at the Market whilst I was there. So too was the partner of Jon Anderson of Yes. I worked for a guy that had a stall that was full of theatrical costumes – he'd go along to the Palladium and they would dump a load of costumes of him - and he once sold a single chain-mail boot to Frank Zappa! He was like: 'Where's the other one guy?'... 'I don't have another one'... 'Oh that's really cool man'!

In September Jimi Hendrix died. He had probably been the single most important influence on all the members of Queen, and Roger and Freddie are known to have closed their shop in the market as a mark of respect. Pat recalls having once met Hendrix in the street, probably when Smile were recording in the Trident studios in Soho: *I was walking down the road with Roger when the band were recording in a studio somewhere and Jimi Hendrix jumped out of a taxi, I think on Wardour Street. It was like seeing the most exotic bird. He had a jacket and trousers and boots and a hat and beads and feathers. I thought 'that's the most beautiful guy'. Roger went up to him and said 'Hello' and he said 'Hi' and he kissed me on the cheek!*

Kensington Market in the mid-70s. Photo Jim Jenkins.

Later I remember sitting in a pub behind Kensington High Street - not sure if it was The Greyhound - and we were staring across the road and Roger said 'that's where Hendrix died'. We didn't know what to say.

After a while Roger found a new place to live, and Pat moved in too. *It was a little cul-de-sac off the Fulham road, opposite the Chelsea FC merchandising company. Chelsea FC was at the back of the house. It was Roger and his girlfriend Jo, John Harris and me. John Anthony was there every evening but he didn't live there. I had a room to myself. Freddie was there for a while but went to live with Mary, and Brian was with Chrissy. Tim Staffell I remember visiting.*

It was great place to stay and we all mucked in together. But whenever there was a football match we either stayed away or we wouldn't go out because as Roger said 'Little guys like me with long blonde hair are asking for trouble when the football fans come out'.

I used to go and get what they call 'cabbage' which is offshoots of labels and designer gear. I had a full length leather coat with a hood and Robert Plant came to the market one day and got me to try and drop the price. He did take me out to dinner afterwards, but I was never into guys with frizzy hair!

Most of the bedrooms were on the ground floor and up, and you went downstairs to the basement and that was basically the living area and it was light and big and huge with big sofas and a kitchen and patio doors onto a tiny bit of concrete. But it was a good place and we all lived like a family. Everybody looked after everybody. And I was still in looking-after mode so did lots of cooking. John Anthony would bring people round to talk to the band and I didn't get involved in the discussions but I would cook them a meal and so on.

The only girlfriend I remember being there was Jo. Led Zeppelin was the band we mainly listened to most at that house. Plus Rory Gallagher's Taste, and Jeff Beck, too.

After in stint in London herself, Sue Johnstone's best friend Jill Johnson had returned to Cornwall. She was still busy with The Famous Jug Band who, without Clive Palmer now, recorded their second album, Chameleon, and were resident for much of the year at Room at the Top, Redruth. Despite the fact that the folk boom was on its last legs, the club attracted some highly respected musicians like The Strawbs, Long John Baldry, Noel Murphy, The Amazing Blondell, Davy Graham and Michael Chapman.

Clive Palmer had gone on to form C.O.B., a group made up of musicians who had played at the Folk Cottage. C.O.B. made two highly regarded and collectable, acid-folk albums in the early 70's.

1971 John Deacon and 'The Cornwall Tour'

Barry Mitchell left Queen early in 1971, apparently for financial reasons, to be replaced for two gigs by Doug Bogie who, at the time, was a mere 17 years old. Then, in March 1971, the Leicestershire-born John Deacon became Queen's fourth and final bassist after a lucky meeting at a disco at the Maria Assumpta Teacher Training College, the all-women's college in Kensington Square.

Denise Craddock: *Maria Assumpta was run by nuns. I don't think they put any kind of musical events on - apart from occasional discos. It was very conservative, and girls from Grammar Schools used to find themselves in Central London - that was the aim of the game - with all these amazing colleges nearby that did amazing musical things.*

Roger, John and Brian had all had girlfriends at the College. *Jo, Veronica and Christine Mullen were in the year below me and Pat at Maria Assumpta. Les Brown's wife, Chris, shared a bedsit below me with Brian's first wife Chrissie Mullen. When I went into a single bedsit in West Kensington after Barnes, they came and lived in the ground floor bedsit below. Before Chrissie, Brian went out with 'Little Mary' during the Smile period.*

Quiet, measured and also academic, John Deacon was reputedly in the audience at the College of Estate Management concert. In interviews in subsequent years John, who was only 19 at the time he joined the band, has said that for a long time he felt like an outsider. Brian, Roger and Freddie already had, it seems, an intense working relationship that was difficult to break into.

The Maria Assumpta building glimpsed from the far side of Kensington Square

The first half of 1971 was taken up with rehearsals. John, who was studying Electronics at London University, familiarized himself with the band's songs whilst they all worked on new material. They played two gigs in London that Summer, and Roger, allegedly missing his student grant, enrolled to study Biology at North East London Polytechnic, whilst also giving up his involvement with the stall in Kensington Market.

Meanwhile in Truro, the redevelopment of the Pydar Street area was encountering opposition. Bert Biscoe: *Arnold Hodge, who was the mayor of Truro at one point, told me that there was a scrapyard up behind PJ's and there was a bloke who lived in the middle of it whose wife had just died. The council wanted him out because they wanted to get on with their development and he was refusing to leave. There was a seige and this guy had a shotgun. It got very fraught, and Arnold was asked to talk him out.*

There had been advertised gigs as normal for PJ's in January 1971, but possibly because Pete Bawden was pulling out, adverts in March had a different look and a less prominent logo. In April and May the club even changed its name, briefly to The Camelot Club. The last ad was for Marvellous Kid on May 12th. Shortly afterwards the site was finally bought up by the developers, who offered a rather far-fetched sweetener to Mike and Pete:

Mike Grose: *When Tesco were planning to take the site the developers offered to build us an underground nightclub. The plan was I would take that, and Pete would have one in St Austell.* But it wasn't to be. Reluctantly accepting PJ's fate, Pete started to put more of his energies into his new booking agency, 'Eclipse' which was based upstairs at 9, Duke Street, Truro.

In London, Roo Fairbairn, ex-Truro School boy, visited Kensington market. Roo: *I got Freddie to make me a pair of knee-length fringed lace-up moccasin boots. Wish I still had them!!*

In 1971 Roo was living in Les Brown's new flat. Roo: *The flat was near 'The Jolly Brewer' at 8, Halford Road. Everyone used to congregate at the pub on Sunday. I was at King's and Imperial doing Volcanology and lived in this flat with Les Brown, Paul someone, Sue Bagguley, Sue Henry, and Sue Jaffa.*

Group photo taken in 1971 in the back yard of 8, Halford Road. Back row: Les Brown, Brian May, Tony Regan, John Copeland Front row: Trevor McGair, Chris Farnell, Chrissie Mullen, Chrys McGair, Judy Regan, Denise Craddock, Lionel Ousdine. The five couples would all marry within a couple of year s of the photo being taken. Photo courtesy Denise Craddock.

Les had lived with Roger Taylor in Shepherd's Bush: *We were only in Sinclair Gardens for a year (68-69 academic year). I then moved on to somewhere godawful in West Kensington, and then onto Halford Road, in Fulham. Paul was Paul Kelsey: Pete Kelsey's brother. All the girls (the Sue's) were teacher-training at Maria Assumpta College, in the year above Brian May's first wife Chrissie and the same year as John Deacon's wife Veronica.*

The network of friends extended widely. Sue Johnstone: *I knew Les Brown from Truro very well. He was my first boyfriend. He was exceptionally bright and spoke seven languages.*

In June 1971 the Halford Road flat was the location for a fancy dress party that the members of the network, including Queen, attended. The party will be forever immortalized in photographs that were printed in a collage on the back of the first Queen album. Roo: *It was Les Brown's 21st and we used Yes' amps. Steve Howe, the lead guitarist with Yes, had triple leads out of his guitar that went to three amps. 100 watts per channel on each channel and we invited the whole of Fulham. I think Yes came too. I was dressed as Dracula. I had long finger nails made out of a Crisp 'n' Dry bottle which were Araldited to my fingernails. Brian May was a penguin. Roger was the Mad Hatter, and Freddie was a kind of cavalier*

Les Brown: *We asked people to wear the most outrageous fancy dress possible and then made a last-minute decision to start the party in the pub, which was resolutely non-trendy: old dears huddled over Mackeson's in the corner, brickies downing pints at the bar, that sort of thing. Hamish (my brother) was in long hair and a slinky silver lamé dress donated for the evening by my girlfriend. I was a witch doctor, wearing an old beige shirt as a loincloth, full body makeup, bottles of chicken giblets and other assorted nasties suspended on a belt around my waist, and chicken bones stuck in my hair. Roo had an immaculate Dracula costume, and he went into the local chip shop, and ordered cod and chips and had a blood capsule in his mouth, and bit into his cod and spewed blood everywhere! Brian had the most amazing penguin mask that actually worked: when he spoke the beak opened and closed! Doug Puddifoot took most of the photos.*

In July Freddie closed the market stall and Queen returned to Cornwall for more than a month, during which time they played 11 dates. Pete

Ad for gig on 17th July, 1971, West Briton

Bawden and Eclipse helped organise both the Driftwood Spars and City Hall dates that year, though most of the others would have been organised by Roger either from London, or opportunistically whilst already in Cornwall.

In what was only John Deacon's third concert with Queen, the first gig on the 1971 Cornwall tour was on 17th July at The Garden, Penzance. It was a venue on the promenade previously known as the Winter Gardens, where The Reaction had played in the 60's. Entry was 25p.

This was followed by one of two concerts at Hayle Rugby Club, the first being on July 19th. The advert optimistically described Queen as *'publicising their new LP soon for release'*. A rugby club might seem an unlikely venue for an ambitious band from London, but the clubhouse had been very recently built (1969), and with a stage, lighting and a capacity of around 300 people, it quickly became a rival venue to those that were more established in Cornwall.

Hayle RFC clubhouse in 2010: unchanged since 1971. The stage is visible at the far end of the hall.

John Deacon's diary explains a little more as Jim Jenkins recalls: *The Hayle Rugby one was a charity gig for Camborne Boxing Club, and regarding the first gig in Penzance in 1971 the diary says they were support to Caravan.*

The 24th of July saw Queen play in Wadebridge for the Young Farmer's Club. This would have been the Town Hall in Wadebridge, but there are no known adverts or memorabilia.

Later, on the 29th of July, Queen returned to The Garden, Penzance, to play as support to a jazz-rock fusion band with a couple of albums already under their belts. Called 'Warm Dust' they were a six-piece that, somehow, had managed to fit on the tiny stage at PJ's the previous year and later would return to play at Dave Penprase's Room at the Top. Their soulful singer Les Walker recalls: *In 1971 we stayed at the surf-village outside Penzance. I think we'd heard of Queen and were disappointed to find out that they weren't all gay, because - given the name - that's what we'd expected!! I remember Freddie's slight speech impediment. But I also remember thinking they were good. Very good.*

On the 31st they were back at the City Hall in Truro, where they were billed as appearing with 'Dream Machine Disco'. Connie Bawden remembers this first City Hall gig of 1971 better than husband Pete, because on the night he was called away. Connie: *It was a bit of a fiasco. Pete got a phone call: the entertainment hadn't turned up at the Tregye Hotel so he had to take all his disco equipment out of the City*

Hall and go there instead. So in the end it was just me and the band and no disco.

Freddie had joined by then. Queen were n't famous, but they were a sell out. They already had a following in Truro then. When half-time came they traipsed across to the Navy Arms and it was like death in the City Hall, because there was no music as we'd planned. Then they came back from the pub and Brian's guitar string broke so it took about another half an hour to get that sorted!

The Navy Arms used to be quite the place. We often went to the Navy. Pat and Sue Johnstone were there that night, and I remember Queen going off with them.

On August 9th at St Agnes' Driftwood Spars - a small hotel known to locals as the Driftwood - the landlord decided the band were too loud, and repeatedly asked them to turn down their amps. At the end of the gig an argument ensued. Pete was at its centre as he tried to secure the band their payment: *Queen went to the Driftwood Spars and that's the first time I can really remember Freddie on stage. They performed a fantastic set and the guy who ran the Driftwood Spars, Robin Oxland-something, at the end of the gig said 'That's rubbish I'm not paying*

them'. And I said 'I think you are'. And it all got a bit nasty actually. And it was a pittance of an amount. I'd never heard anything so bad. But they were brilliant. It was the first time I'd seen them play as one unit without Freddie sounding like he was just kind of joining in.*

Afterwards their van was, reputedly, chased out of the village by youths in a battered car.

August 9th 1971: Queen playing at The Driftwood Spars. Ads courtesy The West Briton.

The Driftwood Spars is built into the side of the cliff, next to the road that leads down to St Agnes beach. Richard Halliwell, enthusiastic about live music since the days of The Reaction, was there and remembers exactly where the concert was. *There was an area that was part of the main bar. At the front of the hotel, close to the road. I remember they were beginning to play their own songs, and Freddie and John Deacon had come in.*

The Driftwood Spars (2010) looking towards the low stage.

Members of 'Hairy Magpie' describe Roger sitting in with them during their performance at The Driftwood a few days earlier, when it is likely he visited the bar to ensure arrangements and publicity were in place for Queen's visit. The other members of Queen have always teased Roger about the advert - probably placed by Pete Bawden - which refers to him as The Legendary Drummer of Cornwall.

Other confirmed dates were the NCO mess at Culdrose RAF base. How or why this might have been organised is unclear, but Freddie remembered it clearly when interviewed by Jim Jenkins in the 80's.
Jim: *Culdrose NCO mess. Freddie remembered that. He said during all these gigs in Cornwall he was building his confidence up.*
On the 17th of August Queen played for the last time at Truro City Hall. This time they were support to East of Eden: a jazz-rock fusion band that by 1971 had released two albums and had had a top ten single.

Sound and lighting that night was provided by Magician's Workshop, comprising Gerry Gill and John Lumley-Savile. Gerry had already worked with Smile: *I did that gig at the City Hall with Queen. It was a good crowd. I was handling the sounds, MCing and playing rock tracks of the day in the interval and beforehand. As I recall I was to one side on the stage.*

John, meanwhile, knew Roger from Kensington Market and whilst in London playing with The Neat Change he picked up the latest lighting techniques inspired by musicians like Zoot Money and clubs like UFO and Middle Earth. Though he does not specifically recall the Queen concert that August, he remembers regular spots in 1971 at the Driftwood Spars and The Winter Gardens Penzance where they used some of the same techniques.

Roger Taylor has said that his mother was n't keen to have the whole band and their convoy sleeping on her front-room floor in Hurland Road in 1971 - it was getting over-crowded with roadies, girlfriends and hangers-on - so they rented a small three bedroom cottage just outside Truro, in the picturesque village of Devoran.

A postcard written in Devoran by Freddie Mercury is one of Denise Craddock's mementoes from the period. Bearing an Arthurian-themed map of Cornwall and a Truro postmark, it was written to Denise who was flat-minding in London. It hints at Queen's domestic arrangements in the Cornish cottage:

Dear Denise,

Thought I'd drop a line to keep you happy and take your mind off the two pests for a short while. We're staying in this cottage in Devoran and there are a few kitties rushing around outside - so it's not too bad. By the way I've got to rush 'cause there's only one pen and I've got it, and Brian's at my throat...Will be back Sunday by which time you will have gone. Rueben will look after things I hope.

All the Best Freddie...Excuse Haste.

At the time Freddie's modest £10-a-week bedsit in London was shared with Mary Austin. It was in Victoria Road, on the edge of Hyde Park, a few hundred yards from the Market. Mary: *We had so little money then that we could only afford one pair of curtains and we hung them in the bedroom. We shared the kitchen and bathroom with another couple.*
DMW

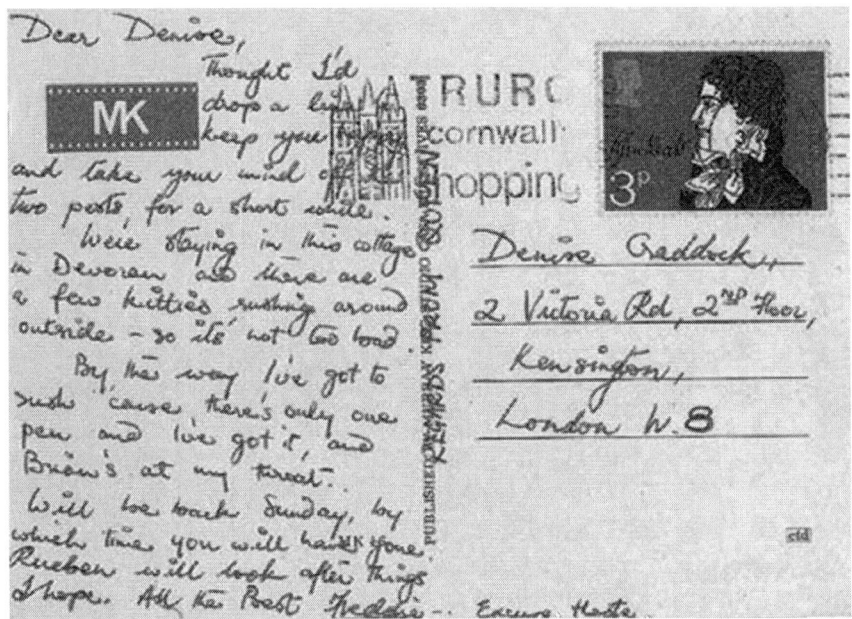

Postcard written by Freddie and sent to his flat in Kensington in 1971. Collection Denise Craddock.

Denise: *It's possible Mary came to Cornwall with Queen that Summer. I was looking after Tom and Jerry in Freddie's second-floor flat. These cats used to come alive at 11 o'clock in the evening and just go wild. So after a week with the cats I was more than happy to be handing over to somebody else! They couldn't get out and would sit on the window sill looking longingly towards Kensington Gardens. The cats were Freddie's love at the time.*

One of the other smaller photos on the back of the first Queen album is an image of Freddie standing in the open countryside, in what looks like the estuary of the Devoran River. The band would have gone walking along the river that leads to Restronguet during their holiday there, and would also have visited Flo's Bar, one of Roger's favourite pubs. Although a far cry from the extravagant no-expenses-spared stadium tours they would experience later, the Cornwall tour gave Queen their first taste of an extended period on the road together, and would have helped cement their friendships - especially with new boy John Deacon.

John Deacon: *It (the Cornwall tour) was good because we got to know each other really well and it settled us as a group...*

That summer Queen spent time at the Bawdens' house in Truro, where Connie Bawden also got to know the band well: *Queen used to come round to our house all the time, in August 1971 when James my youngest was first born. They used to come over most mornings and just hang around...*

We'd moved from St Austell to live in Tresawls Avenue on the way to Treliske Hospital and James, my youngest, was a newborn baby. Freddie used to often hold him: if only I'd got a picture!

I remember Freddie or Roger having a girlfriend called Jo. Freddie got more theatrical as they got bigger and more famous. He played it up and must have thought 'I'm good at this' and became more flamboyant. I remember then he always wore immaculate white satin trousers.

The last gig on the 'tour' of Cornwall in 1971 saw Roger once again teaming up with friend Rik Evans who was helping to organize a rock festival. It was held in the grounds of Tregye Country Club in Carnon Downs, a couple of miles from Truro.

The handbill, which is thought to be one of the first bearing Queen's name, offered food, freaks and lovely things alongside a photo of a naked flautist. Whilst Roger had performed outside with the Reaction and Beat Unlimited on many occasions, this was to be Queen's first open-air gig.

Rik Evans: *We had Crazy World of Arthur Brown at the top of the bill, and Hawkwind second. The Dusty Bennett Band was another. It was a one-man band: he played all the instruments and had a minor hit in the 60's.*

It was an all day festival that started at lunchtime and went on to midnight. It was in the walled garden at Tregye which was a country club at the time, and we cleared the garden with a bunch of volunteers and friends. It was totally overgrown. We rigged canvas over the whole thing and built a stage down at the bottom. We slung poles up and draped canvas over them. Don't know what would have happened if it had rained. It would probably have filled with water and fallen in! It was beautiful weather, though, I remember it.

I know Roger was desperate to play that one and he pleaded with me to put them (Queen) on the bill. He probably wouldn't say this now 'oh no I didn't plead with you' but he did! I got them on second from the bottom and we probably paid them 7/6.

Les Brown was one of Rik's assistants that day: *I put the stage up for the Tregye Festival. At one point I was under the stage pulling something out with a crowbar and I banged my head. It bled like hell, and Rik was really worried and rushed me off to hospital but then when he found out I was OK it was like' right get back to work!'...*

It was a bugger putting the canvas up. The stage was at the bottom of the slope so it was a bit like an amphitheatre. It was a very steep bank and not very comfortable but the day was good fun. I worked for Rick for 3 or 4 years over the summer when I was down in the holidays.

The event received plenty of free pre-publicity with some memorable headlines in the West Briton: '*A hamlet mobilises for pop invasion*'. The main organizer, Mike O'Toole, found himself having to work hard to reassure local authorities. Mike, under the moniker of Mojo Entertainment, had organised a number of events in the East Midlands and Graphite, one of the bands who had already worked with him, were booked to play at the festival. Graphite was a progressive blues band that formed in 1968 at Reading University. In 1971 they were busy gigging on the College circuit and were marginally more established than Queen. The guitarist, Dave Hook recalls: *The dressing room was a great big room in the Tregye Hotel - one of the big lounges - and all the bands taking part shared it. It was an all day gig so we all spent the day either hanging out in this room, or we'd be down watching the other bands. I'd met Arthur Brown and Hawkwind before and actually Arthur had been at Reading as an under-graduate so we had lots in common. Arthur was the same off stage as he was on it: larger than life. And in the dressing room he would do these amazing singing exercises. Scales and so on. He had a great voice.*

MOJO MANAGEMENT,
37, Harcourt Street,
Newark on Trent,
Notts.   Telephone No. 71389

AN AGREEMENT made the ...3rd... day of ...JUNE... 19 71
BETWEEN ...MIKE O'TOOLE......... hereinafter called
The Management of the one part, and ROGER...TAYLOR....
hereinafter called The Artiste of the other part.
WITNESSETH that the Management hereby engages the Artiste(s)
and the Artiste(s) accepts an engagement to present ....
.....QUEEN..........(or in his usual entertainment) at the
dance hall/theatre and from the dates for the periods and at
the salaries stated in the schedule hereto.

SCHEDULE
The Artiste(s) agrees to appear for 1 x 90 MIN AFTERNOON
performance(s) at TREGYE HOTEL, CARNON DOWNS, TRURO
on 21st AUGUST.......19 71 for a salary of £25............
on the gross advance and door takings. The Management agrees
a minimum of £25 .

ADDITIONAL CLAUSES
1. The Artiste(s) agrees to arrive at the venue by 11:00 A.M.
   ~~p.m.~~ and to perform 1 x 90 MIN.........................
2. The Management agrees to provide suitable and adequate
   dressing room facilities.
3. Payment: CASH ON NIGHT.

SIGNATURE....Rog Taylor........ADDRESS 302 Westbourne Grove........
                                       London, W.11..........

Contract for Tregye Festival. Collection Dave Stone.

I don't really remember much about Queen's set. Which is extraordinary given how successful they later came, and how amazing they were live. Though I did watch them, I think they seemed rather ordinary. I remember thinking they were just another heavy rock band and there were loads of them around then.

But I do remember them off stage. In the dressing room Queen had a real presence: a real aura. They weren't casual like the rest of us hippies. They seemed more arty and stylish. And they had hangers on, which perhaps helped give them that bit of aura too. I can't remember exactly what they were wearing but they reminded me a bit of Roxy Music, who I met later. It was that kind of style. And I remember thinking when I saw Roxy that this was the end of the hippy era.

Gerry Gill was the MC for the Tregye Festival. Gerry: *I was there doing a disco at Tregye and Mike O'Toole came in and said he wanted to run an outdoor festival and he booked me as MC. So on the day I was on the side-stage, making sure that the stage management was getting it together and we weren't overrunning. I was trying to add a bit of personality, putting some good sounds out in the gaps and introducing the bands as they were ready.*

Flyer for the Tregye Festival: collection Dave Stone

Some have described Roger Taylor's drumkit sliding backwards on the makeshift stage during the gig, but it did n't seem to affect the way the band's performance was received: *The first band I introduced was Queen and they'd changed their line-up since I'd known them as Smile. They had a new singer and they looked like a little Led Zeppelin. And they were brilliant. Far too good for the opening act. I thought Hawkwind were probably the best band that day, though. They created the best effect, and Arthur, who was drunk as a skunk, couldn't really follow them. But Queen started the day's proceedings at about 12.30 and they were really on the ball.*

Rik remembers Freddie's performance in particular: *If you listen to the first album the style was already there. And Freddie's influence was enormous. He was not quite so flamboyant but he certainly had style. It was obvious. You see some people who you think will make it at a plod. But he was a natural for a man who was relatively shy, but when he got on stage: wow it all came out.*

Dave Hook: *It was a lovely sunny day and the audience were very polite and clapped appreciatively. But that was the norm then in the days before all the hype that outdoor concerts and festivals seem to have now. It was a young crowd, almost all in the 16 - 25 age group.*

Rik Evans *What's amazing about music is that Queen would have done lots of the songs from their first album which became a good seller once it was released. And of course no-one was at all interested, and were probably talking through the set and so on. Once a band starts to get some fame everyone says 'I must listen to that'. But it's the same music and same act as when they're playing the stadia.*

Graphite played after Queen, having been billed above them, and their performance was recorded and released much later as a CD, which also featured photographs in Dave Hook's archive. The atmosphere at Tregye was described as 'mellow'. Dave: *We released two albums retrospectively through Audio Archives in the 90's. One of them was the Tregye gig that was recorded by Gerry Gill. The usual hippy thing then was to ask the audience if anyone could put the band up that night, and I think it was Gerry who put us up after the gig.*

Graphite onstage during the Tregye Festival. Photo Dave Hook

Was Queen's set recorded too? Yes, but not by Gerry. Jim Jenkins: *John Deacon has recordings of the Tregye gig. John has loads of them! John Harris the soundman recorded them all, including the first ever Queen gig in Truro.*

Jim met John Harris on a number of occasions, and is confident that John was one of the 'hangers-on' that Dave Hook noticed that day. *Harris loved Queen. He absolutely loved them. And he knew they were going to be big. He would take a lead from the mixing desk to make the recordings.*

By the time headliners Arthur Brown and Kingdom Come appeared it was dark. Rik Evans: *Arthur Brown was on at the end of the evening. And part of his act was being crucified on a cross that he dragged down through the audience, and the roadies would erect it on the stage. All through the day the roadies kept coming up to me saying to me 'can you raise the canvas higher?' and we kept hauling the canvas and trying to get it higher. But Arthur was on so much medication, illegal probably, that he could n't even stand up by the time it came to his gig late at night.*

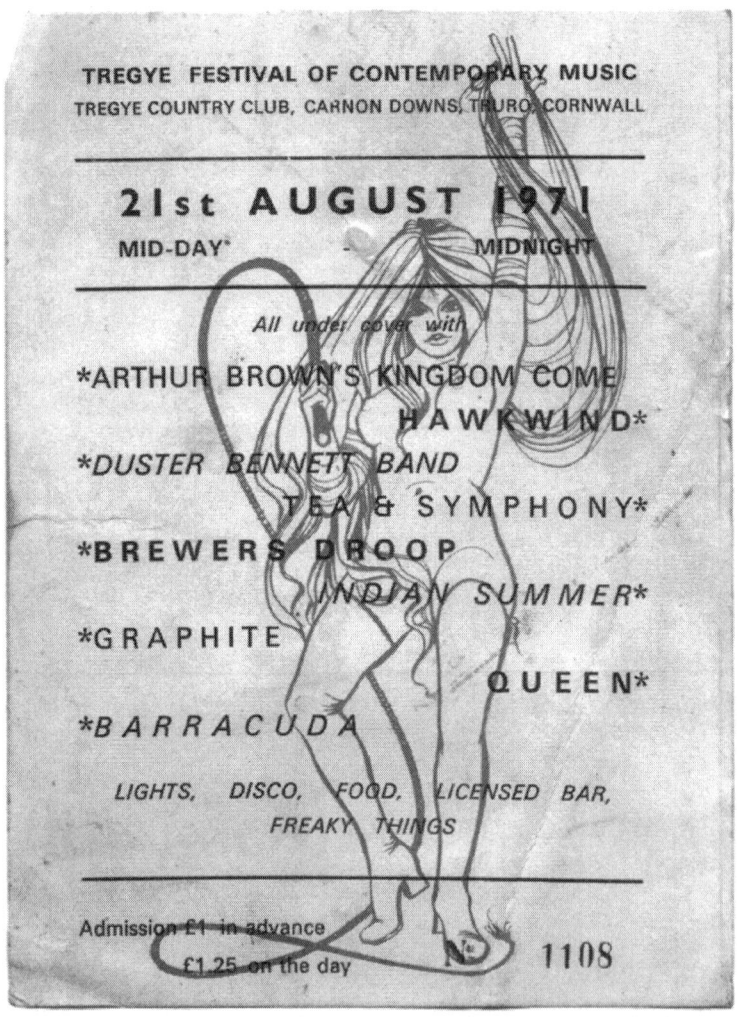

Ticket for the Tregye Festival (collection Bert Biscoe). The whip-wielding woman is printed in red ink.

The outlandish singer, with half a beard and hair cut short on one side of his head, had, allegedly spent most of the day at the bar inside the hotel trying to deny his true identity. Paul Brown has relatives in Cornwall who brought their children to the festival, and was keyboardist with Arthur Brown's band that night. He confirms that remaining unrecognised had been part of an elaborate ruse repeated only a few weeks later at the Glastonbury festival: *The thing about the music was that we played the Kingdom Come album 'Galactic Zoo Dossier' so that all the songs seamlessly merged into one another. The act started with a 12 foot high crucifix on the stage. Arthur was hidden in the audience, where he would pretend to be an old man, and we would drag him out. He'd be wearing a costume which at that time featured half a pinstriped suit and half a hippy outfit with half a beard. He'd be lifted onto the cross and he'd jump off to sing the first note. Quite often we'd do it in almost complete darkness but I think Tregye was quite light. We had a hamper full of costumes. They stank because they were never washed! My favourite then was a gold lame suit. I used to wear a silver fireman suit too sometimes!*

Paul had bumped into Roger Taylor before 1971: *I remember speaking to Roger on a few occasions, especially in Kensington Market. We were on the same circuit and would exchange stories: the College circuit that had the same 20 bands on. People like Van der Graaf generator were on it too. Of course they (Queen) outgrew that circuit eventually, but actually they were still really struggling then.*

Tregye is in the countryside two or three miles from the centre of Truro. Sue Johnstone: *I was at the Tregye gig but the thing I remember most about it was a whole lot of us walking home afterwards - and it was a long walk - in pitch darkness. A great big crowd of us used to go around together: several girls and all the boys from Truro.*

Tregye Festival flyer (reverse) printed in red ink. Mojo Management organised the event. (collection www.queenconcerts.com)

It was the last time Queen would play live in the Truro area, and afterwards they returned to London. By autumn 1971, Alan Mair's shop in the market was specializing in hand-crafted boots only, and Roger and Freddie's shop unit had closed. Alan: *I asked Freddie if he wanted a part-time job looking after my shop. He accepted but said that he wouldn't be staying for too long as he and Roger had their group and hoped to sign a deal soon. In fact he stayed until about a month after Seven Seas of Rye came out in 1974.*

Lots of musicians used to visit the shop. We sold boots to The Rolling Stones, Santana, and Iron Maiden. I had a workshop making leather trousers, but then I changed the workshop and had 4 or 5 people just making the handmade boots. The boots were quite chunky and square - cowboy style - and they all have a gold stamp inside. There's a Santana double album gatefold and they're on a great big long double couch and they've all got Alan Mair boots.

During 1971 David Bowie was preparing to launch Ziggy Stardust on an unsuspecting public, and was a regular visitor to a club called 'The Sombrero' on Kensington High Street near the market. Alan knew David because his band from Scotland, The Beatstalkers, had shared the same manager, Ken Pitt. In 1968 and 1969, around the time that Bowie had come to Falmouth with Gerry Gill, he wrote three songs for The Beatstalkers that were recorded and released as singles: *David came to the shop with Angie. I asked if he was looking for a pair of boots. He said 'No, I don't have any money'. I said 'But you've just had a big hit single'. He said 'yeh but you dont know how f***ed up the music industry is'. I said 'don't worry about the money. Freddie here*

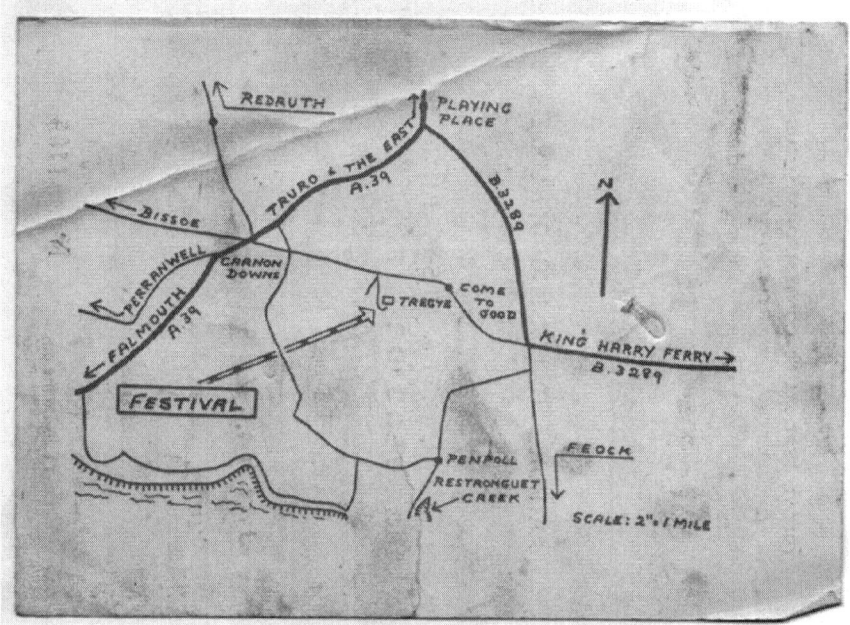

Reverse side of ticket for Tregye Festival (collection Bert Biscoe). The map is printed in red ink.

will sort you out with a pair'. Who would have thought it? Freddie Mercury, shop assistant, fitting out David Bowie with a pair of boots he couldn't afford…And David also wanted my wife, who was a model, to help fix up Angie with a modeling agency.

Alan describes Freddie as having been a smart and trustworthy employee, though his time-keeping left something to be desired:

Freddie was always immaculate. His clothes were well tailored and fitting. The only thing that was at all extravagant about him was his black nail varnish. He didn't wear much jewellery. He was well-groomed. In fact from behind people would think he was a girl because his hair was long and in such good condition. They would say 'excuse me miss'.

Amanda, whose stall was opposite mine, once said to me: 'I feel like I'm telling tales but I think you might be losing sales, because Freddie comes in late quite often'. The market would open at 10 and he would come in at 11 or so, and I think he was just having a bit of a lie in. But actually, I didn't mind, because the boots were still selling. Plus he was a decent guy and I knew I could trust him. He didn't talk about music, and was very modest and self-effacing. Freddie carried on working for me for at least another year.

Pete Bawden visited the market at around that time: *After PJ's finished, I was involved with promoting bands for a bit longer in Cornwall then I joined EMI and was up in London. I remember bumping into Freddie in Kensington Market. I was going up one side of the stairs as he was going down. I heard someone call me: 'Peter!' and it was Freddie. We had a coffee. He always came across as so friendly, and so approachable as a person.*

The gigs that Smile played at Imperial had helped them forge some friendships in the business, and in autumn 1971 one of their contacts, Terry Yeadon, offered Queen time at De Lane Lea, a new recording studio then setting up in Wembley. The studio owners needed a band that could help them by testing and demonstrating the equipment and Queen were grateful for what they took as an opportunity to make their first serious demo tape. The recordings, produced by Louie Austin, comprised five songs, and included a version of '*The Night Comes Down*' that was good enough to be used unchanged on the debut album.

Before the end of the year Queen played three more concerts. One of them was at a swimming baths in Epsom, where once again they shared the bill with Arthur Brown's Kingdom Come.

Sue Johnstone moved to London late in 1971, to join her sister Pat. Sue: *Everybody had left Cornwall and I felt like I'd been left there on my own. Roger used to come down regularly and visit and would say*

Roger Taylor backstage at The Garden, Penzance 1974

'you've got to come up, you've got to come up, we'll get you a job and we'll do this and do that'. Pat was living with members of the band in a house in Fulham. Then when I decided to take the plunge Pat found us a flat in Earl's Court.

Pat: *When I moved out of the Fulham flat, Roger's cat - called Ziggy - had just had kittens and he gave me one. Then I found another flat but the landlord kicked me out, and put all my things in a skip, because there was a 'no pets' rule. So I ended up with this bedsit in Earl's Court Road.*

Brian, bless him, came round and helped me to stick up posters to make the place look funky and more welcoming so that when my father arrived he wouldn't look too closely at how naff it really was! Brian was so lovely and he was able to reassure my father. The guys then were at their best when it came to all being friends and caring for each other and looking after each other. It was a lovely time.

Sue: *Pete Bawden and my Dad drove me up to London in my dad's Mini Clubman. On my first day there, Roger took me to Kensington Market and introduced me to everyone, and I got myself a job in the employment agency literally above Kensington Market. I started just doing Saturdays and weekends at the market, then met two wonderful ladies, Hazel and Gaby, who sold 1930's and 40's clothes, and I started working full-time with them.*

At the time we all used to hang out together, Roger, Brian, Freddie and their girlfriends and we went to various parties and gigs. I remember some weird gigs up at the Roundhouse, for example. Once we went to see a Japanese percussionist called Stomu Yamashta, which was great but I remember it mainly because I fell off the pavement and did my back in...

1972 and after

Queen played live only five times during 1972, and one of those dates was a gig at Bedford College attended, reputedly, by only six people.

For almost a decade the bungalow at 1, Hurland Road had seen Roger and the members of all four of his groups pass through it, but by the end of April 1972 Roger's parents had divorced and Win, his mother, had sold it. She moved instead to a new house on Treyew Road, near the flat Rik Evans was living in at the time.

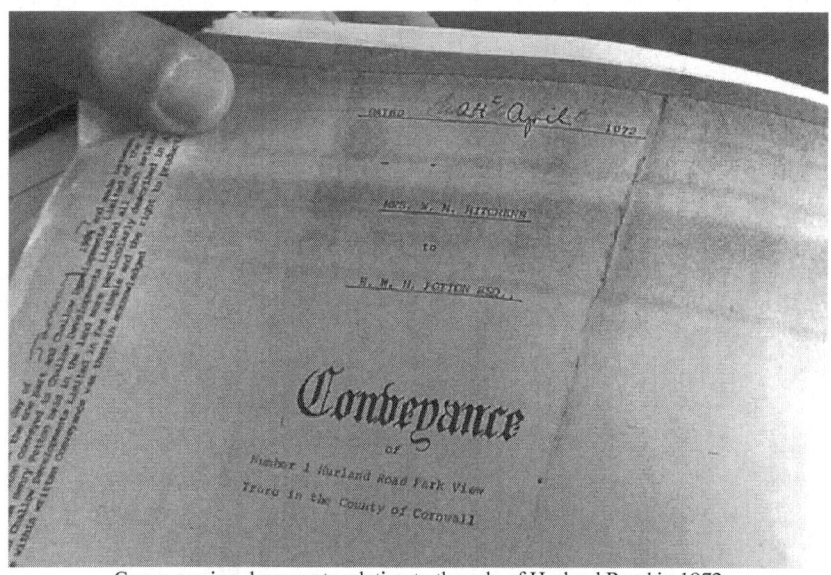
Conveyancing documents relating to the sale of Hurland Road in 1972

Rik: *Roger used to come round a lot to see us when my wife and I were living up in Treyew Road when we were first married, and he brought us the demo tape when they were first trying to get signed. We sat there listening to it. I remember saying 'great band Roger but not sure about the singer'! He didn't take a blind bit of notice luckily! The Donnington Hotel is now in the building where we used to live, and where Roger played us his demo. The left-hand one is where we had the flat. Steeleye Span slept on our floor there at Treyew Road too.*

Pete Bawden also remembers Roger in Truro babysitting his children at around this time.

By 1972 Wendy Edmonds, Pete Edmonds' wife, had started working at Kensington Market. Wendy: *When Freddie worked with Alan Mair Boots, I worked with Anne Harding on a stall. Freddie got me the job. Roger was back at college then.*

It was at around this time that Freddie started experimenting with a more deliberately constructed on-stage look. Wendy: *Freddie knew how to sew. He was pretty good, so for example, he'd at least sew on sequins himself. Then I made him these wrap-around tops to wear on stage. He was very specific about what he wanted and he'd ask me to copy things. So he had these little women's ballet tops, crossover things, and he'd give me the stretch velvet and say 'can you copy this?'*

A couple of years later Wendy, who had trained as a fashion designer, was asked by Freddie to make his most famous outfit: the 'Mercury Suit' that he wore on the Bohemian Rhapsody video: *Freddie wanted to look like the God Mercury. He went and bought the fabric from Borovick's in Broadwick Street in London. You could buy stage fabrics there. It was a stretch satin, skin tight, with a low v-neck and a zip. The sleeves were long and tight, and I made a little padded wing on the cuff. And the wings on the heels were Velcroed on so they were detachable. They were quilted, like a bird's wing and attached with Velcro on the front. He had the ideas and we worked on them together.*

Then I made him a little white waistcoat which you can also see him wearing in the Bohemian Rhapsody video. I also made a black suit which was very similar with a low neck at the front, with a spine down the back. He wanted it to look more evil as it symbolized the Black Queen. I made several of them and 3 or 4 of the white ones, but one of them shrunk and I had to unpick it. Around that time Zandra Rhodes made Brian's lovely cape thing.

I went to Freddie's flat in Victoria Road for fittings with my son Luther who was then only 15 months old. Freddie always just wanted them really tight! It was great fun doing the costumes. They had my label in 'Wendy de Smet' inside. I've still got the original newspaper pattern.

Queen performing in Liverpool in the evening after shooting the video for Bohemian Rhapsody in Elstree Studios. November 14th 1975. Freddie is wearing the 'Mercury Suit' with winged ankles and cuffs, made for him by Wendy Edmonds. Photo: Les St Clair

Freddie also worked on other aspects of the band's image. During Summer 1972 he finished his designs for the Queen logo: an ornate heraldic crest featuring the band members' signs of the zodiac, all structured around a giant Q.

Queen's new demo tapes were being touted around the big record companies, initially by their friend from Ibex, Ken Testi, who helped organise meetings of band members with record company executives. Roger Taylor was apparently the most enthusiastic at that stage and *'was always ready to drop a lecture for virtually anything'*. Later the struggle was taken up by a professional management company called Trident Audio Productions with whom Queen signed a significant and binding contract in May. John Anthony had recommended them to owners Norman and Barry Sheffield and Jack Nelson, an American, became their manager.

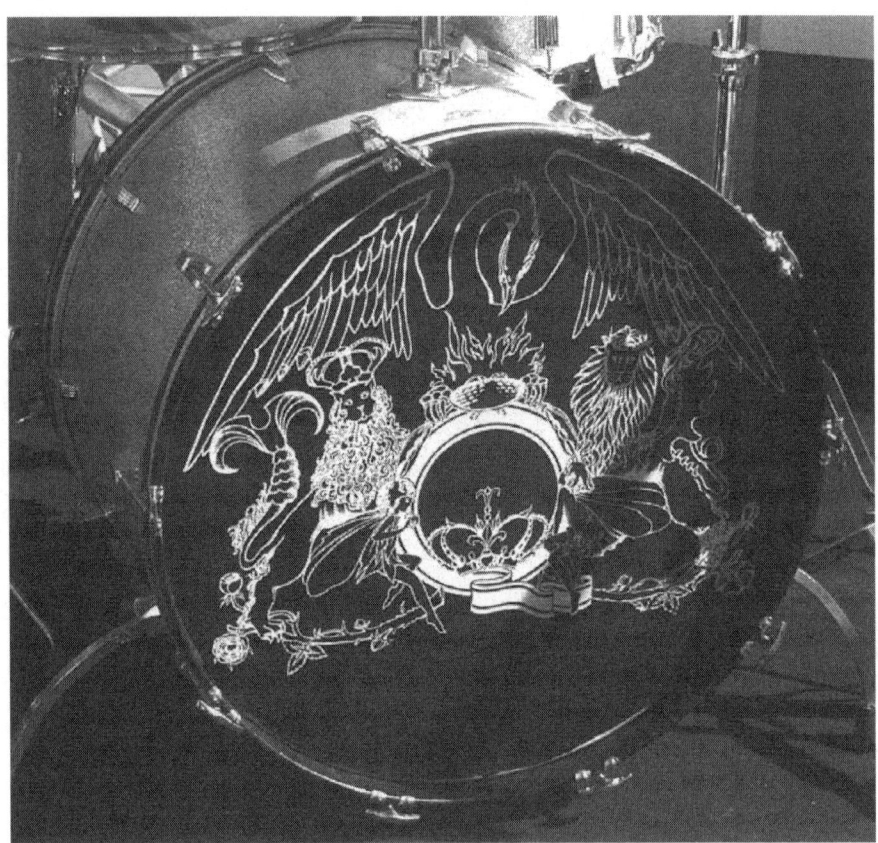
Queens crest circa 1975 as it appeared on Roger's Ludwig bass-drum. (SIS)

The band was generating interest but nothing more substantial than this, and so Trident arranged for Queen to use their own highly regarded recording studio, which at the time was booked out to the likes of Bowie, Elton John and The Beach Boys. An arrangement was reached whereby, again, Queen would use it in-between other bookings, priority being given to the more established artists. This meant that the first album was not ready until November 1972, and even then the piecemeal manner of its recording meant that it needed remixing.

After being turned down by numerous record company executives, Queen's Trident tapes were heard by Roy Featherstone of EMI at the beginning of 1973. In February they recorded a four-song session for Radio One's Sound of the Seventies, and by March they were signed to EMI, with Elektra having responsibility for their US distribution.

Another view of the white 'Mercury Suit' in Liverpool, 1975. Photo: Les St Clair

Doug Puddifoot who, since the sixties, had taken numerous photos of both Smile and Queen was called upon to help with the design of their debut album sleeve.

Doug Puddifoot: *The band originally wanted to use a photo I had taken of them in Freddie's flat, treated to look like a Lumière print for the cover. Working in the early 1900's the Lumiere Brothers had produced some of the first colour slides. Their process involved taking a glass photographic plate, and covering it with grains of potato starch which have been dyed red, green and blue. The effect is to produce a course, multi-coloured grain, with fairly muted colours. Anyway after much experimentation the method I settled on was to cover a sheet of black card with a mixture of red, green, and blue metallic glitter powder, photograph this, then use it as a mask negative over the original negative when printing.*

The band's tatty bohemian image at the time was well captured in the artfully blurred photo. Glam rock, as epitomised by Queen's peers Marc Bolan, David Bowie and Roxy Music, always featured a provocative element of cross-dressing. Wendy Edmonds: *Initially Queen's look was just black satin trousers and little black tops. No much colour there. Then later on they wore women's blouses and women's little fur jackets that they got from Kensington Market. In fact they wore them all the time. On stage and off. Kensington was quite a fashionable place then. They wore women's clothes with satin trousers and made them look great.*

Doug Puddifoot's first image wasn't used for the album, but a different version resurfaced later as a publicity shot distributed to fans via Pat and Sue.

Brian May had always been interested in photography. Doug: *A short while after, I was told that they had had a different idea for the album. They chose a photo I'd taken in the Marquee the previous year. Brian, I think, had been doing some experiments in college with polarising filters. If you put sheet cling film between two crossed polarising filters, shine a light through them, then stretch the film, you get multiple colours where the film is stressed. Brian's idea was to stress the film in a narrow V shape, photograph the result, and overlay that into the area of the lights so that it looked as if the lights were producing rainbows. I tried for a long time to produce the effect, but the colours being so pure, it did not photograph well and the effect never worked. I produced several versions of a cover using the photo, and went to a meeting, I think at EMI, to discuss them. They had several changes to suggest, lights bigger, at different angles, background cleaner, etc, and as a parting shot; it needed to be at the printer's in 48 hours!*

Brian May: *I had a strong feeling, early on, that Freddie was not only our front man but our icon, and ought to be portrayed as such. The little picture of him was something like a figurehead on the prow of those old sailing ships. I thought - this is a great image for Queen ... for the time being, it doesn't matter that there are four of us ... Freddie is the image to put out there. So I stuck the small picture of Freddie on the blown-up picture of the spotlight ... and there was the cover...*Soapbox

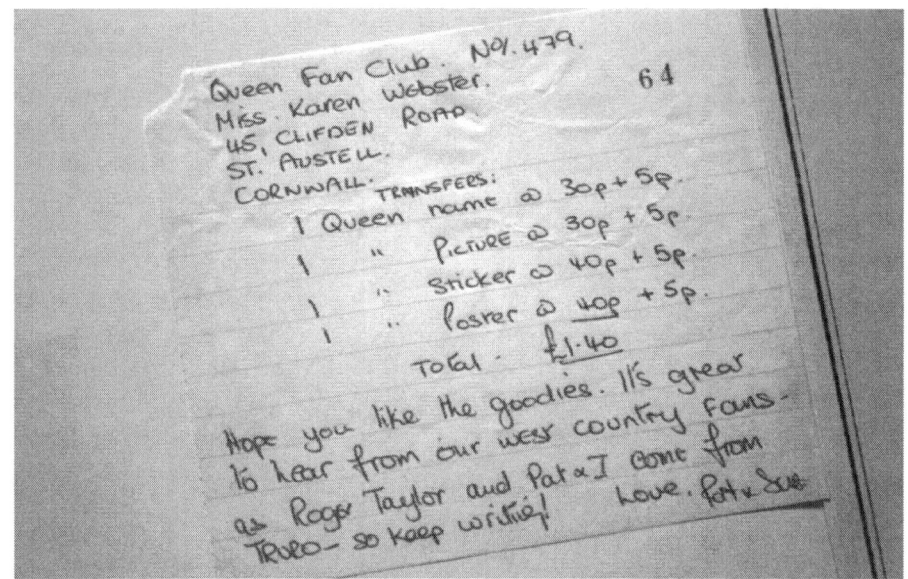
Hand-written receipt written by Sue Johnstone of the Queen Fan Club. Collection Karen Silverlock

Doug: *I went home from the meeting and worked in the darkroom for around thirty hours non-stop. It involved producing several large black and white prints, and making up a composite. This was heavily re-touched. For example you can see that I removed the mic which is jutting into the light. I also re-touched the gloves on both of Freddie's hands, only to discover at a later date that he was only wearing one glove. I then photographed the composite in black and white, then colour-printed the negative, adjusting the filters to give an overall colour cast.*

So the final cover was produced in a very short time, and I think it is not as good as it could have been. My favorite was, and still is, the original Lumière idea. As well as doing the front cover, I also did hundreds of colour prints, which Freddie and Brian used to make the montage that was the back cover. It all involved many hundreds of hours in the darkroom.

A number of the photos on the back of the first album were taken at the fancy dress party in Les Brown's flat in Halford Road. Brian May: *Nobody knows what happened to that original montage. Freddie and I created it, at his flat, double-size, by cutting up and sticking prints made by Doug. It was all glued to a piece of plywood. It was photographed for the back cover, and if we had even this copy transparency, things would be good. Sadly, the copy and the original collage disappeared from the EMI archives some years ago, along with all the rest of our original art work for the first few Queen album covers - it's a bit of a tragedy, really.* Soapbox

Queen's first single, 'Keep Yourself Alive', written by Brian May, was released a couple of weeks prior to the release of the album but it made little impact on the charts, partly because Radio One did not pick it up. The Old Grey Whistle Test, then an influential TV music programme, did so, however, and its presenter 'Whispering' Bob Harris became an early champion of the group.

Queen performing at The Garden, Penzance 1974. Photo Karen Silverlock

In August, after Roger had been awarded his biology degree, Queen returned to Trident's recording studio to work on their second album, Queen II, which was completed before the end of the month. Roger now had time to do some session work, notably with folk singer Al Stewart, and Rick Penrose remembers seeing him in Cornwall. Rick: *Roger still came down to Cornwall. He'd taken up smoking, claiming that his reason was that recording and session work was stressful...*

Brian May was still working on his PhD thesis and even getting work experience as a teacher at a comprehensive school in South London, but there were some early signs that Queen were going to 'make it big': when Elektra released the first album in the US it quickly entered the Billboard top 100.

In October they played their first concert out of the UK, in Germany, and then embarked on a UK tour as support to Mott the Hoople. The tour was seen as a great success.

Rik Evans *Once, when I met Ian Hunter from Mott the Hoople, he said they would watch Queen on stage and we knew they were going to be big - mainly because of the flamboyance of Freddie.*

Wendy Edmonds: *Queen always believed they were going to make it big. I remember the first gig when we saw them supporting Mott the Hoople in one of the colleges in London. And then we also knew then that they were going to make it big. I remember that gig so well because we felt really excited. We had seen them hundreds of times and we had this sense that they were now taking off.*

As a result of the tour the group was receiving more and more fan mail for the group, and by the end of 1973 it was considered necessary to create a fan club. Pat and Sue had already helped the band in this regard. Sue Johnstone: *Pat and I started the Queen Fan Club whilst working on our stalls in the market. It was very informal and we didn't get paid anything at first. There might have been a PO Box that was used initially, because the NME would advertise PO Box numbers. Brian got a lot of mail sent to him. Brian was most keen on the fan club. He liked being in touch with the fans, and liked the personal touch. But they all did and they were all very good with the fans.*

Pat remembers an article in the music press that really opened the floodgates: *Brian May was interviewed by someone at Melody Maker and they said 'you've got quite a big following now' and he said 'yeh*

Pat and Sue Johnstone take care of our fan mail'. The next thing we know we came home from work, went into our block of flats and outside

Karen Silverlock backstage at The Garden in Penzance with Brian May and Freddie Mercury. The t-shirt is one she made herself.

of our door were two big black bags full of fan mail! They were addressed to 'Pat and Sue Johstone, Queen Fan Club, London'. Somehow someone worked out where we lived and we ended up with bagloads of fanmail everyday.

When we first had the bags of fan mail a lot of it was from Japan. And the Japanese fans would send little gifts as well. And there were hundreds and hundreds of them.

Fans in those pre-word processing days, received affectionate letters from the two sisters, and occasionally from band-members as well, particularly Brian. Sue: *The band, mainly Brian, insisted that all letters to fans were hand written, so we spent the hours in the stall between serving customers, writing to Japanese fans etc. When the band started to get too big we became employed by their management and were housed, firstly in the Trident offices in Wardour Street, and then, when they changed management to John Reid Enterprises (Elton's*

management) we had an office within Elton John's Rocket Records offices in South Audley Street. I remember Jack Nelson and John Reid, but didn't see much of the Sheffield brothers. Elton John was always around. Freddie and Elton became very friendly.
The first official Queen fan club newsletter dates from February 1974, and is typed on a single-side of A4, though by 1975 the newsletter has a stapled-magazine format.

Nigel Chappell of Constable Zippos who had played with Smile in St Minver had joined a band that was performing in London on a regular basis: *When I first went up to London Pat and Sue had a flat in Victoria, and I shared it with them for about two years. They had set up the Queen fan club and were still doing it when I started working with Queen's accountants Moore Sloane and Co.*

Pat and Sue Johnstone running the fan club from Queen's management office at Trident Audio Productions. Behind them is a yearplanner marking Queen's commitments during 1975.

Whilst PJ's was going I used to bump into Pat and Sue regularly in Cornwall: they were part of a large group of friends. In fact they also got me work at Kensington Market.

I had started doing Queen's royalties and tour accounts, then I helped out wth the personal accounting for all four members of the band. But Freddie obviously wasn't interested at all, so Mary did all that side for him! We'd phone each other to sort out the bills and talk about the royalty income that Freddie was due.

The Christmas 1974 fan club newsletter included pictures of the band

1974 started with an anti-climax, and with a disappointing first appearance in Australia at an open air festival. Brian and Freddie were both ill with infections and partly as a result the Aussie music press were less than complimentary.

Back in the UK the band were given an unexpected opportunity to appear on Top of the Pops, where they performed Seven Seas of Rhye. The broadcast was on the 21st February, which meant that the release of the single had to be urgently brought forward. The album itself was released in March.

At the beginning of March they started a UK tour; their first national tour as the headline act. For some of the concerts they were supported by Nutz, and whilst on tour Seven Seas of Rhye climbed to Number 10 in the charts.

As their career began to take off, Freddie began to worry that public revelations about his sexuality would affect the group's new-found popularity. Pat: *Freddie invited me to lunch in the garden restaurant that was on top of BIBA and we sat there and we had a little nibble to eat and he said 'Patti, I really need to talk to you, I really need to talk to you. I'm in love with Jack'. I said 'What do you mean? You live with Mary'. He said 'I'm gay and I can't tell anyone because it will destroy everything'. And I just said 'Well as long as it doesn't destroy you that's all that matters'.*

Queen performing at The Garden, Penzance 1974. Photo Karen Silverlock

We sat there drinking cocktails and I didn't know what to say...Come out, don't come out...What should I say? He loved Mary. He never

stopped loving Mary. She was the loveliest sweetest person. She loved Freddie and would have done anything for him - we all would have.

Freddie was complex. He was a person you thought you knew, but he could always surprise you. He could be fearful, and angry, and determined and cold, but he could also be one of the most wonderful people you could meet, despite his own troubled soul. I never knew much about his family background, but he was in the process of reinventing himself and becoming the person he wanted to be.

Queen performing at The Garden, Penzance 1974. Photo Karen Silverlock

The Queen II tour was to be the final time Queen were to play in Cornwall. Karen Silverlock and her friends were amongst the crowd packed into The Garden in Penzance that night. They took lots of photographs of the band who she recalls were within easy touching distance. Karen was amongst the first of the many thousands of Queen fans to join the fanclub, being member 479.

Rik Evans *When they played in the Gardens Freddie didn't play piano as I recall. They were travelling in a Winnebago on that tour at the time parked in the football field car park across from Roger's mother's house on Treyew Road in Truro. I remember we all had a look at this Winnebago as we hadn't seen one before. It looked amazing.*
Richard Halliwell also saw Queen in Penzance: *I remember the Winnebago. It had beds, shower and a kitchen in it. We met them in Penzance where they were staying in the Queen's Hotel and we went back there afterwards. Queen had made serious attempts to get their image sorted out. So there were black and white costumes and special effects.*

As Queen's concerts became more frequent, Roger Taylor's visits to Cornwall became less so, and he was no longer driving the mushroom-coloured Triumph Herald. Richard, following a habit from their days running laps of the rugby field, still refers to Roger by his surname: *Taylor's mother had moved to Treyew Road and you could always tell if he was around in Cornwall because the cars parked there were getting bigger and more expensive. Once he had a white Range Rover, and we went for a long drive down to Porthcurno and all over the place. A bit later I was living in Truro and one night there was a knock at the door and there was Taylor standing there with an amazing sports car, I think a Ferrari. And we went for a drink at the Daniel Arms in Truro.*

Two days after the gig in Penzance Queen played for the first time at The Rainbow Theatre in Finsbury Park, and returned there twice later in the year. Pat and Sue Johnstone saw many of the early Queen concerts. Sue: *I saw them during their days at Imperial and on occasions, later, when John Reid would let us take his Rolls-Royce, and his driver would drive us up to Liverpool, or wherever they were playing. But the one that sticks in the memory is the gig at the Rainbow, which was amazing.*

Alan Mair: *I went to the Rainbow when they headlined in 1974. I'd have gone to the later performance. I saw Pat and Sue there and talked to them for quite a long time. They were also regulars at The Greyhound. Lovely girls.*

Roger was a fabulous drummer, and Brian was brilliant too. But when I knew him at the stall Freddie hadn't yet fully grown into his role. He hadn't yet come into his own. It was as if they were holding his talent in the band, nurturing it in those early years. It would have been easy for them to say 'look this doesn't work'. But it takes a while for things to develop and become rock solid. He already had a nice tone to his voice, and, through practicing and rehearsing, he must have simply become a better singer.

Photo Karen Silverlock

I did eventually tell Freddie what I had thought of the gig at the College of Estate Management and from that point onward he would always ask what I thought. At the Rainbow I was backstage and he immediately came up and asked for my opinion. I said 'it was fantastic'.

Two weeks after the end of the UK Queen II tour, the band set off for their first tour of the States, and supported Mott the Hoople again, this time alongside Aerosmith. These early tours were still done on a shoestring and the band often stayed in budget accommodation. Despite this, on a Holiday Inn postcard franked 8th May 1974 Freddie was able to report, in his own inimitable style, that things were going well.

Dear Pat and Sue,

We're slaughtering them over here at the moment, and the reaction's been very good all round. I've getting sloshed pretty often and pooving and poncing as usual. Hope everything's dandy back home. And less of that whoring and wenching you two -

Love Freddie

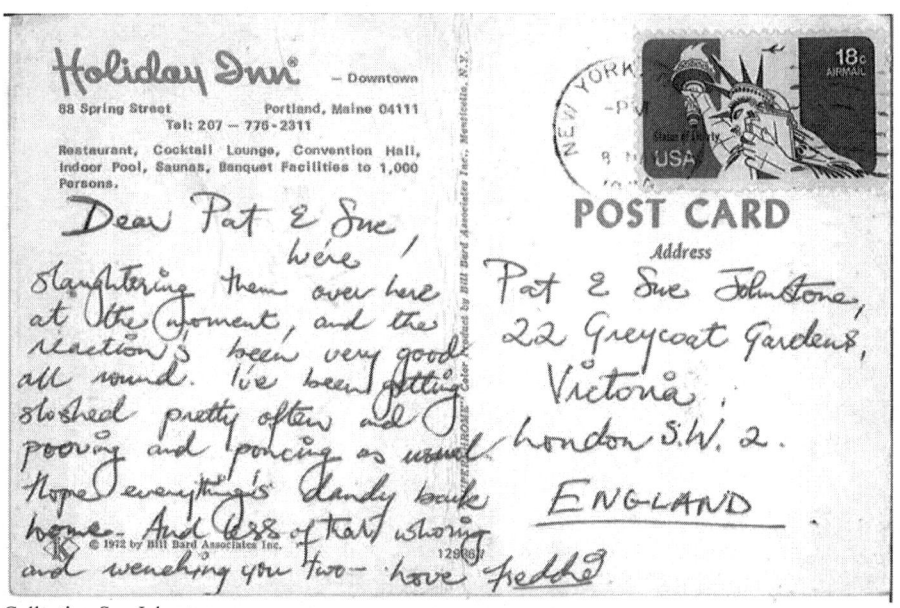

Collection Sue Johnstone

In what was to prove a busy year, Queen returned to start work on their third album, Sheer Heart Attack in July 1974. The double-A single 'Killer Queen/Flick of the Wrist' was released in October. It reached number 2 in the UK charts, did well in many other countries and hit the Billboard top ten in the States. Sheer Heart Attack, the album, was released on November 8th. Before the year was out, Queen toured with support act 'Hustler' in the UK, with subsequent dates across Europe.

As they became more successful, Queen's relationship with Trident, who still controlled their money became more strained, and early in 1975 the band started negotiations to sever their legal ties to the company. Brian May: *After three albums, people thought we were driving around in Rolls Royces already. Actually we were deeply in debt and our accountants explained to us that the management contract was set up so that most of the money would never get through to us. That's when we started to feel resentful. John had a baby by then and he was still living in a bedsit because Trident refused to give him a couple of thousand for a deposit on a house.* ITOW

John Reid, who was already managing Elton John, became their new manager. Pat Johnstone: *We took the fan club with us when they signed with John Reid. Don Arden manager of ELO had also been in the frame, but John Reid won the deal, I think, because Freddie was desperate to come out and Don Arden wouldn't have allowed him to. Although he loved Mary to bits there was this thing that he always knew he had to face.*

At around the same time we narrowly missed being blown up by a bomb. An IRA bomb went off in a pub shortly after we left it. We had a phone call from the police saying that there were alarms going off in John Reid's office, so we went back there and all the chandeliers - he was rather ostentatious - had been smashed to the floor and all the windows were smashed.

Tours of the USA and Japan followed in 1975. Brian: *I suppose my Dad only came to terms with me being a rock musician when he watched us play Madison Square Garden. Until then it was 'That's OK but you'll have to get a proper job later'.* ITOW

The monumental track Bohemian Rhapsody, still regarded as Queen's 'magnum opus' was released on 31st of October. November saw the band make a promotional video for the single, and the release of their fourth album, Night at the Opera. On 25th November, just over a decade after he had first appeared in the City Hall with Johnny Quale and The Reactions, Legendary Drummer of Cornwall Roger Taylor and his band Queen had their first UK number one hit. And Bohemian Rhapsody, in all its pomp and grandeur, would stay top of the charts for a record nine weeks.

Though Roger's mother has continued to live in Truro since she first moved there in the 1950s, she was in Southampton with the band the day it hit the top spot, and she recalled her response at hearing the news: *I was really pleased, and Roger was really excited, but it didn't really sink in. Then on the way home in the car they played the song on the radio, saying it was Britain's number one. I suddenly realised that my*

son was a huge success. He really had made it. It was quite emotional.
TEY

Night at the Opera, Queen's fourth album, also went to number one. Larger sell-out tours of the US, Japan and Australia followed. Queen were not only stars in their own country, they had become stars across the entire world, and, despite the premature death of their talisman Freddie Mercury in 1991, they have continued to be since.